W. D. Ehrhart
in Conversation

ALSO EDITED BY JEAN-JACQUES MALO
AND FROM MCFARLAND

*The Last Time I Dreamed About the War:
Essays on the Life and Writing of W.D. Ehrhart* (2014)

EDITED BY JEAN-JACQUES MALO AND
TONY WILLIAMS

*Vietnam War Films: More Than 600 Feature, Made-for-TV,
Pilot and Short Movies, 1939–1992, from the United States,
Vietnam, France, Belgium, Australia, Hong Kong, South Africa,
Great Britain and Other Countries* (1994; softcover 2012)

ALSO BY W.D. EHRHART

*Dead on a High Hill:
Essays on War, Literature and Living, 2002–2012* (2012)

*The Madness of It All:
Essays on War, Literature and American Life* (2002)

*In the Shadow of Vietnam:
Essays, 1977–1991* (1991; paperback 2011)

Passing Time: Memoir of a Vietnam Veteran Against the War (1989)

Going Back: An Ex-Marine Returns to Vietnam (1987)

Vietnam–Perkasie: A Combat Marine Memoir (1983)

W. D. Ehrhart in Conversation

Vietnam, America and the Written Word

Edited by JEAN-JACQUES MALO

McFarland & Company, Inc., Publishers
Jefferson, North Carolina

LIBRARY OF CONGRESS CATALOGUING-IN-PUBLICATION DATA

Names: Malo, Jean-Jacques, 1958– editor.
Title: W.D. Ehrhart in conversation : Vietnam, America and the written word / edited by Jean-Jacques Malo.
Description: Jefferson, North Carolina : McFarland & Company, Inc., Publishers, 2017. | Includes bibliographical references and index.
Identifiers: LCCN 2017032137 | ISBN 9781476670409 (softcover : alk. paper) ∞
Subjects: LCSH: Ehrhart, W. D. (William Daniel), 1948– —Interviews. | Vietnam War, 1961–1975.
Classification: LCC PS3555.H67 Z46 2017 | DDC 811/.54 [B] —dc23
LC record available at https://lccn.loc.gov/2017032137

BRITISH LIBRARY CATALOGUING DATA ARE AVAILABLE

ISBN (print) 978-1-4766-7040-9
ISBN (ebook) 978-1-4766-3004-5

© 2017 Jean-Jacques Malo and W.D. Ehrhart. All rights reserved

No part of this book may be reproduced or transmitted in any form or by any means, electronic or mechanical, including photocopying or recording, or by any information storage and retrieval system, without permission in writing from the publisher.

Front cover photograph of W.D. Ehrhart in Vietnam (author's collection). The PBS Logo is a registered trademark of the Public Broadcasting Service and used with permission.

Printed in the United States of America

McFarland & Company, Inc., Publishers
  Box 611, Jefferson, North Carolina 28640
    www.mcfarlandpub.com

Table of Contents

Editor's Introduction	1
In the Beginning Was the Deed ADI WIMMER	5
I Couldn't Just Walk Away KRISTIAN GREY CHICKEY	14
However Imperfect the Representation SUBARNO CHATTARJI	16
I Myself Was the Evil YOUSRA HASSAN RASHAD	61
A Bowl of Alphabet Soup TOM CHEN	66
Every Day I'm Always on Patrol ANNALISA BOVA	75
Something Inside of Me AMELIA MORIARTY	81
Lessons Learned and Not Learned LUONG NGUYEN AN DIEN	86
Institutionalized "Sour Grapes" JON DILLINGHAM	90
Long Time to Wait *THANH NIEN NEWS* SPECIAL REPORT	95
Writing as Therapy KATHERINE MCGUIRE	98

Coming Home
    Andrew Herm   102

A Collective Effort
    Nicholas Obradovich   104

Three Poems and Three Questions
    Emily Kunisch   110

The Writer as Straight Shooter
    Jean-Jacques Malo   112

Politics, Polemics and Poetry
    Meggan McGuire   164

We Shouldn't Have Been There
    Adam Gilbert   168

Going Back and Coming Back
    Mia Martin Hobbs   196

Three Unusual Questions
    Miriam Sagan   216

Military History of W.D. Ehrhart   219

An Ehrhart Bibliography   221

Selected Works About Ehrhart   223

Index   225

Editor's Introduction

Though not as well-known as some of his contemporaries, W. D. Ehrhart has to be considered one of the major authors of the Vietnam War. Studs Terkel introduced him as "*the* poet of the Vietnam War."[1] Librarian and scholar David A. Willson called him a "master essayist."[2] *War, Literature & the Arts* editor Donald Anderson termed Ehrhart's memoir *Vietnam–Perkasie* "the best single, unadorned, gut-felt telling of one American's route into and out of America's longest war"[3] while Michael Uhl, writing in *The Nation*, tagged Ehrhart's memoir *Busted* "an American original."[4] Historian H. Bruce Franklin wrote that Ehrhart is "the preeminent figure in Vietnam war literature—treasured for his nonfiction, enormously influential as the foremost anthologist of Vietnam War poetry, and himself unsurpassed as a poet."[5]

Though Ehrhart never meant to be a "Vietnam writer," he has readily conceded, "That experience has haunted my days. It has troubled my nights. It has shaped my identity and colored the way I see the world and everything in it."[6] Nonetheless, ever since Ehrhart started writing poetry when he was a teenager, the topics he has tackled over the years have been far more diverse than has been generally acknowledged, whether it be in his verse or his essays, most of which do not deal with the Vietnam War. In 2012 he wrote me: "The great variety of subjects reflects the great variety of my life. While one might get the impression that I am primarily a Vietnam War writer, in fact I am rather more multi-dimensional. I can't help other people's perceptions, but even a cursory examination of my poetry and essays ought to suggest that the war is only one facet of my life."[7] Indeed, his poetry grapples with love, parents, wife, daughter, friendship, geese in the autumn, the beech tree in his backyard, while his essays range from South Africa, Central America, and early Soviet Russia to tugboats on the Delaware, education, healthcare, and the judicial system.[8]

Ehrhart has appeared in television documentaries,[9] and has been featured on local, regional and national radio shows.[10] In autumn 2017, he will feature in Ken Burns's documentary series on the Vietnam War. For over three decades, Ehrhart has spoken at universities, colleges, high schools, cultural centers and other public venues in 30 of the 50 United States as well as in Britain, the Netherlands, Spain, Germany, Austria, Slovenia, Japan and Vietnam.

Over the years, Ehrhart has also fielded questions—directed at him by post and nowadays by email—from scholars as well as from Ph.D. and Master's candidates, undergraduates, high school and even middle school students from five different continents: America, Europe, Africa, Asia and Australia. Two lengthy interviews with him were published in 1991 and 1996,[11] and one I conducted myself was published in 2014.[12] Surprisingly, to me at least, one finds no other interviews with Ehrhart in any significant publications. No comprehensive collection of his interviews has thus far been compiled.

The first time I met Ehrhart, I was taking part in the Popular Culture Association/American Culture Association Conference in Toronto in March 1990, at which he was a guest presenter. There I got my first Ehrhart book, *To Those Who Have Gone Home Tired*, graciously signed by Ehrhart, who wrote, "To Jean-Jacques Malo—at the beginning of a long friendship." This has proven true.

In 2012 and 2013, while I was working on *The Last Time I Dreamed About the War: Essays on the Life and Writing of W. D. Ehrhart*, I interviewed him by email. We ended up with a 34,000-word interview, but for reasons of length I could include only the portion dealing with poetry in that book. I also discovered that other scholars, Subarno Chattarji from India and Adam Gilbert from England, had interviewed Ehrhart at length without publishing the interviews. Finally, I learned that students at all levels and from five continents have been contacting Ehrhart for years with questions about his writing, American culture, and the Vietnam War. As recently as September 2016, poet Miriam Sagan featured Ehrhart on her website.

Hence I was convinced that this material, accumulated over twenty-five years, should be made available. With Ehrhart's help, I ended up with approximately 145,000 words—including the published pieces. I eventually convinced Ehrhart and the publisher that a comprehensive collection of Ehrhart interviews had to be published.

As I said, I have been interested in Ehrhart's writing since I first heard him talk in Toronto in 1990, but I had forgotten that I had first thought to interview him long before 2012. As I was addressing the last details in the manuscript for this book, I happened upon a 90-minute audio cassette on which I had handwritten: "Interview with W. D. Ehrhart, La Salle U, Philadelphia, PA. April 17th, 1991." A treasure! Unfortunately, only side A is audible; side B has suffered so much from time that not a word is comprehensible. It is too late to include this piece, but twenty-six years later I have come full circle.

The intent of this book is to show how widely Ehrhart is read, what sort of relationships the writer establishes with his readers, what questions actually interest the latter, what the evolution of his thinking has been over three decades, and whether his positions, ideas, opinions, and perceptions have changed over time.

Of course, I had to make choices in order to have a manageable-sized volume. Therefore, I decided not to include the three long interviews already published in English (Boughman; Anderson & Bowie; Malo) because they are already available in print. I found two interviews published in languages other than English: one in German (see Adi Wimmer) and one in Italian by Professor Stefano Rosso. I elected to drop the latter for copyright reasons and space limitations, as well as because Rosso's interview included both Ehrhart and John S. Baky, curator of the Imaginative Representations of the Vietnam War Collection at La Salle University in Philadelphia.[13] Two interviews that originally appeared in high school journals are included here because they are not readily available, as is true of the interview that appeared in Vietnam's *Thanh Nien News*. The rest of this material has never appeared in print, and one would have to be able to access the work of students throughout the USA, Italy, Egypt, and Australia even to find snippets of these interviews incorporated into papers, theses, and dissertations.

English historian Adam Gilbert posed a special problem because he interviewed Ehrhart twice: in March 2010 for his doctoral dissertation, "Morality, Soldier-Poetry, and the American War in Vietnam"; then in October 2015 for a book he was researching. Though some topics come up in both 2010 and 2015, the two discussions have different focuses. Length again precluded using both interviews; hence Gilbert and I decided jointly to keep the latter and more politically oriented interview, particularly because the mechanics of writing are dealt with in other pieces.

Out of my very long 2012 summer interview, about a fourth was published in *The Last Time I Dreamed About the War*; the remainder of the interview is included in this collection.

Once the selections had been made, I had to decide how to organize the volume, but ultimately it just made sense to choose chronological order. This will enable the reader to compare the interests of interviewers over three decades, see how they vary with the interviewer's status (e.g., high school students versus scholars), and ascertain the extent to which Ehrhart's responses and opinions have evolved since the early 1990s.

NOTES

1. Interview with Gerry Nicosia, WBZE-FM, June 25, 2001.
2. David A. Willson, "W. D. Ehrhart, Essayist," in Jean-Jacques Malo, ed., *The Last Time I Dreamed About the War: Essays on the Life and Writing of W. D. Ehrhart* (Jefferson, NC: McFarland, 2014), 47.

3. Donald Anderson and Thomas G. Bowie, Jr., interviewers, "A Conversation with W. D. Ehrhart," *War, Literature & the Arts: An International Journal of the Humanities*, 8:2 (Fall/Winter 1996), 51.
   4. Michael Uhl, "On the Lam from Vietnam," *The Nation*, September 18, 1995.
   5. H. Bruce Franklin, Foreword to *Busted: A Vietnam Veteran in Nixon's America* (Amherst: University of Massachusetts Press, 1995), xi.
   6. W. D. Ehrhart, *The Madness of It All: Essays on War, Literature and American Life* (Jefferson, NC: McFarland, 2002), 1.
   7. Ehrhart, email to Malo, December 3, 2012.
   8. W. D. Ehrhart, *In the Shadow of Vietnam: Essays, 1977–1991* (Jefferson, NC: McFarland, 1991); Ehrhart, *The Madness of It All: Essays on War, Literature and American Life* (Jefferson, NC: McFarland, 2002); W. D. Ehrhart, *Dead on a High Hill: Essays on War, Literature and Living, 2002–2012* (Jefferson, NC: McFarland, 2012).
   9. *Vietnam, A Television History* (13 episodes, 1983; series director: Bruce Palling) and *Making Sense of the Sixties* (6 episodes, 1991; director: David Hoffman).
   10. For example, on "Radio Times," host Marty Moss-Coane, NPR-affiliate WHYY-FM (in the Philadelphia area), August 6, 2012. Ehrhart has also been featured on national radio, e.g., on NPR's "All Things Considered" and "Morning Edition."
   11. Ronald Boughman, ed. *The Dictionary of Literary Biography Documentary Series*, vol. 9 (Farmington Hills, MI: Cengage Gale Research, 1991), 63–82. Donald Anderson and Thomas G. Bowie, Jr., interviewers, "A Conversation with W.D. Ehrhart," *War, Literature & the Arts: An International Journal of the Humanities*, 8:2 (Fall/Winter 1996), 149–157.
   12. Jean-Jacques Malo, "The Art of Writing Poetry: An Interview with W. D. Ehrhart," in Jean-Jacques Malo, ed., *The Last Time I Dreamed About the War: Essays on the Life and Writing of W. D. Ehrhart* (Jefferson, NC: McFarland, 2014), 139–153.
   13. Ehrhart's entire literary archive is now housed at La Salle's Connelly Library. Both he and the editor want to express gratitude to John S. Baky, the curator of the Imaginative Representations of the Vietnam War Collection at La Salle University in Philadelphia. His active support and help were essential in the editor's research and in the creation of this opus. This Vietnam War Collection is the most important research center in the field. Ehrhart's entire literary life resides in that collection with almost every variant and format represented, with over 1,000 items by and about Ehrhart. This is the place where any researcher should work on Ehrhart, as well as on all the diverse forms of the imaginative representations of the Vietnam War.

In the Beginning Was the Deed
ADI WIMMER

AW. Bill Ehrhart, you were born in 1948 to a protestant minister, you grew up in a small town near Philadelphia and you published your first poems and short stories while still in high school. Graduating, you volunteered to join the Marines to fight in Vietnam where, during your tour in 1967–68, you were wounded. In 1971 you joined Vietnam Veterans Against the War. Since 1972 we have had various publications of your poetry and prose. Currently (1989/90) you are a visiting professor at the University of Massachusetts in Boston in matters pertaining to the Vietnam War. A short while ago I checked the *Bulletin of Concerned Asian Scholars* issue 21, where I found ten selected seminar programs of U.S. universities dealing with the consequences of the Vietnam War within the United States instructed in the fall semester of 1990, and in virtually *all* of these your poems, your collections *Carrying the Darkness* and *To Those Who Have Gone Home Tired*, are listed as required reading. One of these seminar announcements even mentions a guest appearance by poet William D. Ehrhart. All of this leads me to conclude that you play a major role in the current discourse on Vietnam. For me you are the most active and visible poet of that era.

    WDE. I am not sure that in your assessment even such an innocuous term as "Vietnam War Poet" is correct. A large part of my early works and nearly all of what you might call "juvenilia" is Vietnam War related. And so a fairly voluminous share of my work fits that category. But meanwhile I have—at least this is my view—published a body of texts that are not Vietnam-related. It is my hope that in the foreseeable future, when all this dust has settled down, I will be recognized as a poet who is capable of writing stuff other than the war poems for which I seem to be known. At present I must accept that it is better to be recognized as a genre-specific writer than not to be recognized at all. But I sincerely hope the straitjacket of "Vietnam War Poet" will not dog me until the end of my days!

AW. You are not the first writer who arrived at a totally new world view as a result of his war experience and who is capable of describing the process in artistically adequate ways. Is your metaphor of the "strait-jacket" therefore appropriate? As well as your reference to the dust that needs to settle down. My reading of your poems has always given me the impression that you are one of the foremost speakers to prevent a settling of the dust. If we are interested in an appropriate taking-account of one of the most traumatic eras of U.S. history in the 20th Century, is it even desirable that the dust settles?

WDE. Okay, the metaphor is not a particularly good one because obviously we all want the Vietnam War not to dissolve into oblivion, but we also want to see clearly. I have devoted many years of my work as a poet to this issue and so I find it quite natural to speak, in furtherance of my role, before high school or college students. Has the discourse on Vietnam abated? When you think of the movies of 1990, movies by Oliver Stone or Brian DePalma, it would appear not. The American culture machinery, Hollywood in particular, still shows a great interest in this war, albeit frequently in a trivialized form. I am of two minds on this: on the one hand I am still pretty angry at how rare and puny the attempts at a serious engagement with the war have been and how little official regret has been voiced. Not a single politician and not a single general has ever apologized for Vietnam to us; even less so to the Vietnamese. Not a single one has suffered any negative consequences for his wrong assessments. On the other hand I also wish to be taken seriously as a "normal" poet and not as somebody who can only speak about Vietnam.

AW. But this is how it started, did it not? In your autobiographical essays you dedicate a lot of space to your idealistic youth, for instance your reverence for JFK. Such idealism led directly to Vietnam. To use a Faustian term, in your case at the beginning was the deed and not the word. How your writer's awareness evolved is given scant attention.

WDE. Straightaway I must point out that my political and with it my artistic awareness were slow in growing. I also arrived relatively late at an independent attitude to the war. When I shipped out to Vietnam, I had a deep attachment to my country and a kind of blind faith in my government. That did not dissolve by itself in Vietnam. What was added was abysmal confusion as a result of what I saw and experienced. These experiences did not fit the matrix acquired in my youth. One of the reasons why I went to Vietnam was that I wished to fulfill my poetic ambitions there. My great ideal was Wilfred Owen; at the time I was not yet capable of seeing the contrast between his writing and my patriotism. I wrote regularly during my last three years at high school but quickly stopped writing after my arrival in Vietnam. I was simply unable to keep on with the type of prose and poetry that I had so far brought to paper. And afterwards, I only wanted to forget Vietnam and that as fast as possible. When I got home I was 19 and was helpless in the face of the things around me. I only knew that I had been part of something *evil* and that it hurt. Everything hurt, I did not know why and I wanted to forget it all, forget it completely. I simply did not want to deal with it anymore. Why this did not work had two reasons, one interior in nature and one external. For years I had nightmares. For years I dreaded nighttime and sleeping alone. All those dead. Well, all of that would not simply let go of me. And the external reason was that during that era, around 1970, it was impossible, *totally impossible* to live anywhere in the USA and to ignore the Vietnam War. Even in truly remote regions you were constantly brought face to face with it. C.D.B. Bryan's book, *Friendly Fire*, aptly demonstrates that. And when I finally realized that Vietnam would not dissolve into thin air I did two things. Firstly, I began to work my way through mountains of historical literature. This I described in my second autobiographical book *Passing Time*. It opened my eyes to many a dark chapter in America's history. And then I began to deal with my war experience in a literary fashion. For a while I wrote poems that would not stand up to any critical scrutiny. In my second year in college, however, I began to write poems that had at least some literary merit. The urge to write had a lot to do with my college existence: There I was in a liberal-leftist institution and I was the only Vietnam War veteran. Nobody understood me, nobody had the slightest idea of what I had been through. I tried to make myself understood to people on a rational level. On the subconscious level I used the written word as a means of self-recognition.

AW. And when did you first present the results of your self-finding process to the public?

WDE. I sent my first poems to an organization named Vietnam Veterans Against the War in the spring of 1971, for their anthology *Winning Hearts and Minds*. A professor of mine saw an ad in the *New York Times* asking for poetry submissions from Vietnam War vets. The editors accepted eight poems, which was a huge boost to my morale. The volume got a lot of publicity and excellent reviews.

For the next three years I wrote often about the war. After graduation I still had a raft of problems: I was still angry with my country (and that is putting it mildly) and so I got myself a job as a seaman on an oil tanker. Even today I have a deep connection with the sea: there is a whole volume of poems dedicated to the Outer Banks, a string of islands off the coast of North Carolina. When I lost that job, I went back to writing, sending my poems to various small magazines. The editor of *Samisdat* magazine, Merritt

Clifton, was one of the first who recognized and appreciated quality in my works. For a number of years *Samisdat* was the major publication outlet for my poetry.

AW. Might one say that you wanted to create a distance between yourself and your fatherland by taking to the seas? Herman Melville comes to mind who wrote that water and meditation are wedded forever. I daresay your experience as a seaman was a time for ruminations on your identity. How did this process involve getting to know other poetic identities?

WDE. One has a lot of time on a ship for thinking and reading, yes— your surmise is correct. In high school I had a rather solid training in English and American literature, but the poets that excited me the most were Walt Whitman, Stephen Crane and to a certain extent also Wilfred Owen. I found myself attracted to Owen because I had a lot of quasi-romantic feeling for the military. Later I was influenced by Yeats and when I was in my mid-20s two American poets, W.S. Merwin and Richard Hugo had a pronounced influence. I am aware this is a rather conservative selection—I was never much impressed by the Black Mountain School of Poetry for example or by the San Francisco poets, with the possible exception of some of Allen Ginsberg. The San Francisco poets often seem to be vomiting onto a page and then they do not even bother to structure their effluents or to give the slightest thought to what they said, and that I find a tad frustrating. I discovered poets such as Robert Bly or Denise Levertov later in my life, after I had been active in the anti-war movement for some years, and I admire some of their poetry as much as I do their political engagement.

AW. Both these poets are in the anthology you edited, *Carrying the Darkness*. Did you by any chance try to create an alliance between the "old" and "new" anti-war writers? It must have been as disappointing to you as it was to me that the poetical discourse on Vietnam ended as abruptly after America's troop withdrawal in January 1973 as the public protest against a war that continued to rage on for another two years.

WDE. Yes and no. I remember that *Poetry* magazine issued a special number in early 1972 with a thematic focus on "Vietnam." I had sent them some works but they did not get accepted. When the special issue appeared I got myself a copy and found out that they had not included a single poem by a Vietnam vet! And that did it for me. To some extent I still have that slightly huffy attitude, namely that only Vietnam vets are really entitled to write about Vietnam. You must not forget that until the publication of *Winning Hearts and Minds* nobody paid the slightest bit of attention to Vietnam Veterans' writing. And my attitude then was: who the hell cares what Denise Levertov has to say about that war? What would she know about it? Today I have a more tolerant attitude, today I know that the war affected a great many more people than the combatants, in very real ways.

AW. Immediately after the war ended poet Alberta T. Turner edited and published an anthology titled *Fifty Contemporary Poets: The Creative Process*. Fifty of the best-known U.S. poets each presented one poem which was supposed to engage with America's most urgent social or political issue. And not one of these fifty poems dealt with Vietnam, not even marginally, which seems to demonstrate a collective American wish to forget and bury that troublesome era. So the social context was not exactly encouraging for a project that you and Jan Barry tackled in 1976: to publish a sequel to *Winning Hearts and Minds*. How did your volume *Demilitarized Zones* come to life and what editorial line did you take?

WDE. Barry was one of the three editors of *Winning Hearts and Minds* and the original plan was to publish two follow-up volumes. There was a collection of short stories in 1974 and then the plan was to have another volume of poetry titled *Postmortem*. But sadly First Casualty Press fell apart before the third volume was ready. I met with Jan Barry in 1974 and we both bemoaned the loss of that third volume. In any case, life *in* Vietnam had been a lot easier than life *after* Vietnam. Most of the poems in *DMZ* dealt with Vietnam veterans' lives after their return, a life of much hardship and social marginalization. There was something like a low-intensity war against us— the title of the volume is ambivalent and ironical.

And so we created a small publishing company called East River Anthology and began to gather poems and to raise money for our project. We wrote hundreds of begging letters to friends and sympathizers, we tried to tap any imaginable source of money and we did in fact raise enough to print 5,000 copies of a 168 page volume of poetry. The volume did reasonably well, not as well as *WHAM*, which sold 10,000 copies in only eight weeks through nothing but word of mouth, but we sold many of those 5,000 copies. And this in the summer of 1976, at the height of the darkest collective amnesia.

AW. I recall a review of a book titled *Viet Journal* by James Jones in the *New York Times* that started with the sentence "quick—before your eyes glaze over with yet another report about Vietnam." That was indeed the mood of the times. When, years later, the first academic critics dealt with Veteran Literature, their verdict was often negative. Veteran literature, thus Philip Beidler or Jeffrey Walsh said, had some merit as historical or didactic material, but was lacking in artistic quality.

WDE. I find it hard to keep those two halves apart. To view our texts as "pure" literature seems impossible to me since they are eminently important not only in an emotional, but also in a political sense. We are talking about a political complex, there were certain historical events and certain political decisions and I am much more interested in the reality of this experience. In what it meant then *and what it continues to mean today* rather than in an Olympian debate about literature and art. Besides, there is an aesthetic of resistance, an aesthetic of dissent and rebelliousness, an aesthetic of knowing certain things that are meant to be kept under wraps. One example. *The Deer Hunter* is most certainly an impressive movie but it contains a significant number of distortions and outright lies, so it may be art, but it's dishonest. I don't know. Maybe I am not a good evaluator of Vietnam War Art—I am too close to certain matters.

AW. My reading of your poems has led me to categorize them into four groups; let's see whether you agree with me. There is a kind of descriptive experiential poetry dealing with a Marine's life in Vietnam. A second group features fragments of that soldier's life in the USA after rotating back, but added to these are reflections on that life. A third group addresses past or present historic events of the nation. And the fourth group is probably closest to what academic criticism likes best: confessional poems of a man in middle age, poems about family life and relations, fatherhood, death; themes emptied of the "vulgarity" of politics.

WDE. That's about right. But I have to add one thing coming from my perspective: all these poems are part of my own story and that story is my life. Sometimes my life is political and sometimes it is not. Take my poem "Responsibility." Its first stanza is about my waking up after a night of love, but from there the poem turns to Central America and the whole dictatorial system of the region. I think that poem is a successful example of how private and public awareness can blend into one another. Which is probably a consequence of my experiences in Vietnam: they taught me to see links that other people do not see.

AW. Allow me to present a hypothesis based on your last sentence. You seem to fit best into a tradition of socially committed, realistic *prose* rather than poetry, prose that reached its apex in the early 20th Century. In poetry, it would seem to me that Carl Sandburg pursued the same goals. It is probably no coincidence that Sandburg as a representative of socially committed literature is like a star setting in the night sky. Like Sandburg, you tend to satirize political abuses and the arrogance of power, you warn against nuclear or ecological catastrophes as a result of aggressive policies. When your poems deal with "real-life" individuals (such as "Matters of the Heart" or "Last of the Hard-hearted Ladies"), these protagonists hail back to the great depression that divided the nation. More recent texts have come out of your travels to Vietnam (1985) and Nicaragua (1986); they sketch the lives of people suffering under the consequences of Reaganite politics. These poems do not shy away from taking a moral stance. They do not escape into a greyish area of not taking part, of being indifferent.

WDE. I have great respect for Sinclair Lewis or Theodore Dreiser, but as far as the possibilities of prose are concerned they do differ substantially from those of poetry. I do share, however, their great distrust of political and economic scheming. In this day and age it is not only embarrassing to be an American citizen, it is also risky. We are once again about to send 100,000 men into the Arabian desert in order to parade our global power.

The comparison with Sandburg is flattering. I myself remember how in a college course surveying the field of American poetry, the instructor, a formalist brilliantly acquainted with all the nuances of New Criticism, found it hard to deal with Sandburg's crystal-clear analyses. Perhaps I am also too direct in my diction. I have a readership of my poetry that is very positive towards my efforts, and then I am sure there are folks that view me as some devious communist. What matters however is that the first group ostensibly thinks rather well of me and supports me. In this country the likes of me often have a feeling of helplessness and isolation and when somebody appears with similar interests and concerns we are hugely grateful. And if one of those concerns actually gets into the public arena we are very happy.

AW. Your poem "To Those Who Have Gone Home Tired" is like a "pavane" of explosive issues that are evoked through a simple name like My Lai or Hiroshima or Pine Ridge, through interconnected metaphors like "After the last whale is emptied from the sea / and the last leopard emptied from its skin / and the last drop of blood refined by Exxon." There lies a Whitmanesque prophecy in such metaphors of as yet unimaginable disasters and a fear that no one will understand the connections between them all. Is it a given for you that these connections indeed exist?

WDE. Sure, one has to be careful with conspiracy theories: those baddies out there are the cause of all that is evil in the world. But there are a few general behavioral structures, especially regarding the interplay of power and political systems. I will not maintain that either capitalism or communism is the origin of all that is evil, but there are similarities in the ways they appear in our world. The way we "had to destroy the town in order to save it," or the way we dump an oil refinery smack-bang into the middle of a wetland even if this means the extinction of a bird species—those two types of insensitivity have something to do with one another and we find them in both power blocs. They emanate from an ignorance of our responsibility for more than just our own lives, or put another way, more than just a narrow circle of "we." The world is often structured into "we" and "the others," I think it was Bruno Bettelheim who extensively wrote on that subject. The ways how "we" deal with "the other" are terrifyingly similar, whether it is the U.S. in Vietnam or oil managers ignoring the bald eagle or Japanese whalers slaughtering whales. In the 1960s people began to establish the links and similarities. The anti-war movement interlinked all those issues; it sensitized many people for many concerns. But when the protest movement ended—and it ended a long time before the war itself came to an end—people stopped caring.

AW. You are right: I have noticed a general loss of sensitivity in the 1980s, a general loss of solidarity. People withdrew into their private lives. Did you notice it too? In a poem that you wrote in 1988 you write: "It's never as simple as this, of course. / Most of the time, hard questions // gnaw at the brain like rats, / and it's hard to imagine a life // that isn't forever perplexing." Did you mean to attack those amongst us, maybe even artists, who have withdrawn into the safe corners of a private aesthetic?

WDE. Yes, indeed. The problem with my own poetics (which I hope are mainly concerned with genuine and serious problems) is selection and weighting. For example, I do not know how to place a value on certain aesthetic concerns. I do not know how to place a value on the whooping crane. I only know that it is threatened with extinction and once it is gone it is gone for ever and ever and that would be appallingly sad. I also know that over many millennia a kind of natural balance evolved in our world which we now upset in nasty, evil ways. I fear that this will all boomerang on us one day, creating gargantuan problems. So often we act in pursuit of short-term goals neglecting our long-term interests, for instance when we back all those chickenshit dictators simply because they are *our* dictators. The example of Iran is instructive: we have lost all our currency in that country. See, my concerns are not all of a moral kind, they are sometimes quite pragmatic. As an American I am terribly irritated by the chronic short-sightedness of my government.

AW. Which brings me to the Reagan years. Your poetic diction of that era is imbued with a cultural pessimism bordering on an apocalyptic mood. In "Letter to the Survivors" a nuclear holocaust seems inevitable. In "Empire" the social context is an Orwellian dystopia. In "Briana" you thematize something that seems typical for contemporary American society: somebody is murdered for no rhyme and reason leaving a huge gaping loss. But then there are nuggets of hope in the midst of poetic gloom, poems like "The Vision" with its pugnacious optimism, or "The Reason Why" in which you afford yourself the luxury of what I'd call tongue-in-cheek doggerel.

WDE. When I look at the world around me, the prognoses are rather bleak. Okay, we had a thawing between the two super-powers, but the present situation in the Gulf shows there is no reason for facile optimism. It is very naïve, for example, to think that nuclear weapons can be stored and *not* used indefinitely. Each and every weapon that was ever invented in the history of mankind was also used, in wars. And so one ought to despair, really. But what to do with despair? And this is not an abstract issue: For about ten years of my life I existed in a white-hot state of anger paired with despair. It was a wholly unproductive situation. It's like this: we all have to cope with reality, but at the same time we keep our vision of things and how they ought to be. There is a long tradition of despair in American poetry but I have no wish to end like Hart Crane or Anne Sexton or Robert Lowell.

AW. In Philadelphia your hometown you are accepted and cherished as a poet and seer, and the same holds true about a growing circle of scholars interested in Vietnam War literature. How about the wider academic world of the United States?

WDE. It's certainly true that Vietnam War scholars have paid attention to my work, and that is gratifying, but I would not exactly say that Philadelphia accepts and cherishes me as a poet and seer. And as for the larger academic world, I am largely ignored by it, and if I am going to be honest, that hurts. Our literary scholars are very conservative and, what would be the right word? Timid? Safe? A poetics of social engagement raises eyebrows. You should not forget that in the last decade American universities had to accept massive cuts in state subsidies which were matched by massive (and lucrative) research requests coming from the military sector. Well, you bend and adjust. Another aspect is that literary scholars and professors and such seem to frame their thoughts in concepts like post-modernism and deconstructionism. Geez, I don't even know what those terms mean. I simply have things to say, and I'm trying to say them as clearly and compellingly as possible.

AW. Dare I ask you a bold question? You have published a dozen volumes of poetry, three autobiographical novels and you have edited three more poetry volumes. Your poetry has featured in some 200 journals, a figure which I would never believe had I not researched it myself. Moreover, you have been successful as an essayist and journalist. Are you by any chance an affluent person?

WDE. No. Oh my God, no. In the last ten years I've eked out a living as a sometime teacher and itinerant poet/lecturer/speaker. In the spring term of 1990 I was Visiting Professor at the University of Massachusetts in Boston teaching Vietnam War writing and doing research for the William Joiner Center for the Study of War and Social Consequences. And now I'm back to part-time high school teaching. For years my wife has sustained me with her work as a computer programmer; she has faith in my poetry.

Adi Wimmer was a professor at the University of Klagenfurt, Austria, at the time of this interview, which appeared in German in Weimarer Beiträge *37 (1991) 3, 412–22.*

I Couldn't Just Walk Away

Kristian Grey Chickey

KGC. Can you give a brief overview of *Vietnam–Perkasie*?

WDE. It's an account of the thirteen months I spent in Vietnam and about five weeks or so after I get back from Vietnam with one chapter about growing up in Perkasie. I tried to be as accurate as I could in terms of the language. I wanted to put the story in the voice of the eighteen-year-old that this is happening to. I was in my early thirties when I wrote the book, but I wanted to have a reader pick that book up and see that experience through the eyes that I saw it through then.

KGC. The narrative of *Vietnam–Perkasie* ends abruptly. What happened after you got back?

WDE. Well, what happened after is in a book called *Passing Time*. It's interesting really because *Passing Time* is the book I meant to write all along. I didn't really want to write a book about the war. I felt I had already written enough about that in my poetry. What I really wanted to deal with was the sense-making process that I went through after I came back.

When I was in Vietnam, what was going on around me wasn't what people had told me was happening. I didn't know how to make sense of it. For instance, I thought that God created South Vietnam. That it had always been there. Nobody ever taught me that South Vietnam had been created in 1954 by a conference of European powers, in Geneva, Switzerland; that the division between the two Vietnams—the 17th parallel—was not supposed to be a political boundary. (In fact, there were supposed to be elections held in 1956 to unify the country.) The Americans and their Saigon clients refused to hold those elections because they knew that if they had their elections, Ho Chi Minh would win. A communist North Vietnamese would win the elections—free and fair elections. So, they didn't have the elections.

I didn't know any of that stuff when I went into Vietnam, and you can't make sense of what is happening if you don't know the context, if you don't know the history. After I got back, I really wanted to know, to understand, what had happened to me, so I began to learn a great deal. I began to read. *Passing Time* deals with the five years after I came back from Vietnam, and how I made sense of this stuff. And the effect it had on me was enormous. I could tell you the nuts and bolts of what happened, but I'd have a hard time really explaining. I was back in the states for only a couple of months before I left again because America was crazy. I always thought if I was alive on March 5th, 1968, my rotation date, I could go home and the war would be someone else's problem. However, I discovered I brought the war home with me, and it continued to gnaw at me. Within a month after my getting back, Martin Luther King, Jr., was murdered, and a couple of months after that Bobby Kennedy was murdered, and a couple of months after that at the Democratic National Convention, the Chicago Police went on a three-day riot. I thought, boy, and I thought the war was in Vietnam!

So I left the U.S. again, spending my last year in the Marines in Okinawa, Japan, and the Philippines, and I came back in the spring of '69. I got out of the Marines, immediately left the country again, and went to England. I ended up working the whole summer on an Irish coastal freighter, and finally started college in June of '69.

I tried to get through my first year of college pretending that nothing was happening. I drank very heavily; engaged in all kinds of self-destructive behavior. Then in the spring of 1970, my first year in college, the Ohio National Guard murdered four students at Kent State, Ohio, and injured nine others. At that point I began to come to terms with the fact that the war was not over; I couldn't just walk away from it. It was not going to let me do that, and I began to connect that this outstanding self-destructive behavior I was engaged in was directly related to what happened to me in Vietnam.

That was the time I began to read books, and I got involved in the Anti-War Movement. The war just went on and on and on and nothing I did mattered. By the time I got out of college in the spring of 1973, I thought I hated America and I didn't want to be here anymore. I didn't want to kill myself and I didn't speak a foreign language, so I went to sea. I got this job on this tanker and floated away. *Passing Time* ends with me still out on this oil tanker in the spring of 1974.

Kristian Grey Chickey was a student at Freedom High School, Bethlehem, Pennsylvania. This interview appeared in the school's literary magazine, Pen & Ink, *No. 27, 1993–94, p. 44–45.*

However Imperfect the Representation

Subarno Chattarji

For Jon Stallworthy

SC. I'd like to begin with the idea of the "personal" in poems such as "A Confirmation." The idea of friendship and affirmation is moving. Did you see the personal as some kind of an antidote to the lies that the war provided you with? Also, the fact of nature, out in the woods.

WDE. I think it's fair to draw those kinds of conclusions, but certainly when I was writing the poem, I was not in any way consciously thinking about any of that stuff. In a way, what this all comes down to is, it's my job to write the poem, it's your job to make sense of it, to make those kinds of connections and associations. So, I can't say that I was consciously setting out to make the friendship between Gerry Gaffney and me the antidote to the bankruptcy of the people who sent my generation to Vietnam or however you want to say that but when you talked about this yesterday, when you pointed it out to me, I think, yeah, it makes sense. And of course, the natural surroundings that get described in some detail in that poem certainly are an antidote to the way in which we in Vietnam destroyed nature. Part of the consequence of the war was the terrible havoc on the natural world, everything from deliberate defoliation to just when a Marine company goes out into the bush and digs in for the night. By the time you leave, you've got holes everywhere. But the poem is a real experience which happened to me. I found Gerry Gaffney four years after we had left Vietnam and spent several days with him. We happened to go camping in this beautiful place in western Oregon. All I am doing is describing what's there, both in terms of the friendship and the surroundings.

SC. With reference to the Klamath Indians, I found it interesting because some of your writing links Vietnam to the history of America.

WDE. Yes, that's quite deliberate. I was aware that there was a large reservation just south of where we were. The poem makes a deliberate association between what the white Americans did to the indigenous population and what the white Americans did to the Vietnamese. That connection is, I hope, not too heavy-handed.

SC. It occurred to me immediately and I liked that. And the nature bit occurred to me because part of Vietnam was not only the fact of defoliation but also the emphasis on technology, the pride in technology, the fact that it was a technologized war, so nature again as a kind of an alternative because in some poems, not so much yours but some of John Balaban's poems there is a pastoralization of Vietnam.

WDE. Oh, he's a wonderful master of the natural world. He remembers things, he remembers the names of flowers, plants, trees in all of his poetry, not just those about Vietnam. Part of the thing that I admire about him and I have tried unsuccessfully to emulate is his beautiful cataloguing of the natural world. I can't do that. I know what a Douglas fir looks like, and a maple tree, but his knowledge of the names of the natural world startles and delights me. For me, you know again I think that's probably the kind of association that you can safely make that I wasn't making when I was writing. In spite of my ignorance of the nomenclature of the natural world, I do love outdoors. I lived in this little town in Pennsylvania. We were outdoors all weather, all year round, and it shows up in my poetry, not just in the Vietnam stuff, and I think what you pick up in my poetry is simply that affinity for, love for the natural world. That idea of the war as technological phenomenon, William Gibson writes about that in *The Perfect War: Technowar in Vietnam*. That was all true but down where I was, you know, the level I was operating at, we had rifles and grenades, we slept on the ground and we were lucky if we had a poncho tent to throw over our heads when it rained; I wasn't fighting a technological war down where I was. We had our support and stuff like that but for basic foot soldiers, one was not particularly conscious of fighting a technological war and therefore, I don't view the natural world as a foil to counterbalance that.

SC. Quite a few of your poems are taken up with the idea of the veteran-poet as teacher and prophet, particularly the poem "The Teacher." How much does it mean to you? Do you see it as a way of ensuring (perhaps not the right word) that another Vietnam doesn't happen?

WDE. That was my thought. If you had met me fifteen years ago, maybe even ten years ago, I would have told you something very different than what

I'm going to tell you now. When I finally began to make sense of what had happened to me in Vietnam, in the spring of 1970 and over the next couple of years, I came to believe that the only way I could endow what had happened to me and my country with any positive meaning at all was to use it as an experience to learn not to do that again. I joined the Marines as if I was on this crusade: I was going to save the Vietnamese from communism. Then when I finally decided that the war was wrongheaded, my next crusade was that now I'm going to make sure America never does this again. I believed with great passion that I could make a difference, that my writing could really change the way this country does business with the world, and you see that reflected in my writing. I have had in my 40s to come to terms with the fact that that's not likely to happen, that my writing is not going to change anything in any significant way. It can touch individual lives, perhaps, but the fact is governments will continue to do business with the world pretty much the way governments always have and children will grow up and join the army the way they always have and the generation of young people now who are in the U.S. military weren't even born when the Vietnam war ended, it's just history that old guys like me talk about. I look at those poems now with some embarrassment. But on the other hand, I don't take back anything I said. I think what really tore the heart out of me was the Gulf War, to see how readily my fellow citizens answered the clarion call of George [H. W.] Bush rambling on about evil Saddam Hussein. I expect politicians to talk like that. What I found profoundly sad was how readily my fellow citizens were going to believe the guy and send their kids off to die, and at that point I finally had to really come to terms with the fact that the world goes on the way it always has and there's not a lot I can do about it. So I'm in the process of trying to sort all that out, to figure out: why do I want to continue writing? That's a different answer than I would have given you fifteen years ago.

I don't know if you have seen this book yet, *Reading the Wind* by Tim Lomperis, which is a book about a conference that was held at the Asia Society in New York in 1985, where I am quoted in there as saying, "I don't give a goddamn about art! My writing is a tool of education!" I was a chump. But I still believe all that, I'm just having to recognize that I'm not a very respected educator, it's not going to have the kind of impact I would like it to have, but I still think I was right to want to educate people in that way. And I think the world is worse off that I have not succeeded very well. I doubt that I would ever be able to write another poem like "The Teacher." But I don't take those poems back, I'm not trying to repudiate them. I still believe those things. Does that make sense?

SC. Yeah. A poem like "A Relative Thing." Probably one of the most direct poems…

WDE. But also, one of the most ironic poems that I have ever written. When I wrote that poem the only Vietnam veterans I knew were people who were in Vietnam Veterans Against the War, so when I talk about "we are your sons, America" and we will still be here, I am thinking of them. But what's happened over the course of twenty-five years is that all these other veterans out there who think that we should have nuked Vietnam have appropriated the poem. You know the presence of Vietnam veterans in American society has become really paramount now but in a very right-wing, Americanized kind of way that I never anticipated when I wrote that poem. I had anti-war veterans in mind when I'm talking about we will still be here when you wake up, and instead what you have is many of these guys who have these parades like the Welcome Home parade in 1985 for people who had a much more traditional attitude about all this. I don't read it much anymore in public because the world changed in ways I had not been able to anticipate in 1972 when I wrote it.

SC. Is the problematic relation of protest and poetry because of what has happened to Vietnam protest literature, the appropriation of protest by, if not the state, by the right wing? Does the academic pursuit of Vietnam literature contribute to the appropriation, the emasculation of…

WDE. I don't know. I am often uncomfortable with the scholarship that I read about both the war and the literature of the war in particular. I have actually gotten myself into trouble on several occasions, trying to remind scholars at conferences that we are not talking about some abstract thing, we are talking about millions of lives that were destroyed, we are talking about bodies coming apart forcibly and you have to remember this, that this stuff was real, killing was on a grand scale and I sometimes get the sense that occasionally at academic conferences, people tend to forget what they are actually talking about. I now realize that I have some serious deficiency in my diplomatic skills when I do certain things, I occasionally upset people but there you go. There's something you ought to read, a book by Robert Slabey called the *United States and Vietnam: From War to Peace*. There's an essay of mine in there called "The War and the Academy" that talks about this. However uncomfortable I am with the Vietnam War as academic quest, sooner or later that's all it's gonna be. The first-person witnesses like me are not going to last so long. We are all going to be dead. Everybody who ever fought the Vietnam War or fought against it, we are all gonna be dead.

And then what do you do? Then it will disappear out of public discourse. If anybody is going to keep any of this alive and if there is any promise of doing so with any degree of accuracy, it will be people like you. It will be the scholars and the historians and the academics, and what I have to hope is that some of them will see that whole experience the way that I do and will represent my ideas reasonably and fairly. I no longer expect that my ideas will become the mainstream projection of the Vietnam War. I know that's not gonna happen. It's sad but I think what is being preserved as the mainstream, our cultural memory of the Vietnam War is wrong, dangerously wrong. I can't do anything about that but I hope to have my perspective and my point of view preserved and that someone like you will do that. So even though I am uncomfortable with the Vietnam War as academic quest, I have to accept that it's either that or nothing in the long run. And some people will do it well and some people will do it poorly. There are people who are as intelligent as me, who went through similar experiences as me, who believe things as passionately as I do and what they believe is not what I believe. And I absolutely think they are wrong. But of course, they think I am wrong.

As far as the protest stuff, one of the problems with war poetry or most political poetry is that circumstances change and things become, at the very least, dated. One of my poems that I really love is "Responsibility." It deals with Central America, but I can't read that poem to most audiences anymore. They won't know what I'm talking about. Already in a space of eight years, a college aged audience, those kids were in elementary school when Reagan was waging war against Central America. They don't know what I'm talking about. The whole context of the poem has become irrelevant to contemporary eyes within the passage of eight or nine years. That kind of writing doesn't have any staying power. It needs a context in a way that when you pick up one of Shakespeare's sonnets or one of Keats' odes, you don't have to have a historical context. I'd like to think that some of the poetry that I'm writing does not require a historical context. I think that's true but certainly a lot of the stuff that I write and a lot of what has been written about the war is very dated and then you get these weird things happening like with "A Relative Thing" where, not only is it dated but it almost means something very different from what I intended it to mean twenty-five years ago because the audience now may think that the Vietnam War was justified.

SC. This problem of—is poetry useful and can poetry achieve something—is something that bothers me. "I'm not an artist, I'm an educator and if it doesn't teach people something, I'm a failure." Do you see yourself as an artist who has educated? Poetry cannot, may not, overthrow a political regime as such, but you say yourself in some of your essays that you must continue, that you cannot give up. It's in one of your poems, I think "Matters of the Heart."

WDE. For so long I've believed so passionately in writing as a means of changing things and I am simply having to come to terms with the fact that if it changes anything it does so in very tiny, tiny increments and meanwhile I have thrown away anything resembling a career. I am 48 years old and I don't have a real job and I'm not likely to have one. I can't get a job teaching in a university, I don't have the paper credentials and other things like that, but I'm out there, fighting the big fight and then I find myself almost left with no security of any kind with an income that is embarrassingly small. My wife basically supports us. It's hard to remember that what I have done and what I am doing is worthwhile. You get tired after doing this for so many years and getting finally almost nothing in the way of reward or acknowledgment that somehow you are doing a good thing. I don't know how to deal with that exactly. I believe that if I cannot succeed in educating people then whatever I have done, I am a failure. Where does that leave me? I've obviously not educated very many people. My last book sold a few hundred copies. How many people got educated with that book? I have been wrestling very hard with this sense of failure. I look back at what the hell have I done with my life. I mean, look at so many of my peers, they are university professors, they've all got careers. Meanwhile, I've got a resume that looks like a minefield a drunk staggered through.[1]

But the disaster that befell me as a consequence of my joining the Marines and going to Vietnam, and really I think my generation, a large portion of it, pales in comparison to the people of Indochina; what happened to us was nothing compared to what happened to these people. You know, I still want that to have some meaning and the only meaning it seems to me it can have is that somehow someone can learn something useful out of that experience. I think what the American people have learned and what the military and politicians have learned are the wrong lessons. "Next time, let's fight the war. Next time, let's not have the media present." Those are the wrong lessons, those are not the ones I think people should learn. That's kind of a wrong way to answer your question but there it is.

SC. I think the artist-educator dichotomy is probably a little too harsh.
WDE. Yes, maybe.

SC. Isn't it weird that I come from a completely different place and it makes me angry, it touches me. That's certainly one person, it doesn't change U.S. government policy, but I'm sure there are people here who read and are influenced.
WDE. I tend to underestimate the impact of my writing. As I said, I have always been this kind of extreme person. In the great fable of the tortoise and the hare, I have trouble taking the tortoise approach to life and so what I see is the way the world ought to be, if I can't make it be that, then I've failed, which is an outstandingly egotistical way to look at things. In fact, and obviously, I have no idea who's reading my stuff. I have a dear friend who's a professor in Austria in the University of Klagenfurt whom I met because

he found *To Those Who Have Gone Home Tired* and then called me.[2] I'm probably having more of an impact than I realize. I'm rambling but I'd like to think that I have become some reasonable kind of artist. I tend to shy away from talking about art as art because it makes me uncomfortable. At least half a dozen people have quoted me saying, "I don't give a damn about art" and berated me with it, but you have to understand that it came amidst a long panel discussion and I finally said that in great frustration and of course all the rest of that discussion is not recorded in that Lomperis book. It's an accurate statement but it's only a small piece of what I think.

SC. Yeah, I was a bit taken aback with people berating you. I thought it's not as simple a dichotomy as that. You write elsewhere "Nothing I do will make any difference but to do nothing requires a kind of amnesia that I have yet to discover." Isn't that contradictory?

WDE. The piece from which Kali Tal quotes, "Stealing Hubcaps," I wrote in 1988 and by then I am beginning to understand that I'm not going to change the world.[3] My writing is not going to have the kind of impact I wanted it to have. In the essay, I'm wrestling with how to resolve this contradiction: it's not gonna change, nothing I do is gonna make any difference, but how do I just walk away from it and know what I know? And I can't make myself not know. I guess I don't know how to resolve that contradiction. Some days I decide I don't want to talk about this stuff anymore and other days, I think how do you give up? It is one of those things which is not resolvable. It's simply there, for me at least. I think that a great many people have resolved that contradiction by walking away from it all. I envy them. Most days I just wish I could do that.

SC. You have to speak and that's what makes your poetry different, moving and more engaging.

WDE. Well, I'm finding that for now at least I'm not writing a lot because I don't know what else to say. Actually, if you start looking, as you have, there are other people who are better writers than me I'm sure, but mostly no one in my generation has produced the kind of writing that I've produced. There's a stack of books that I have written in the last five years. What else do I have to say? I don't know. Maybe, five years from now, or two years from now, I'll decide there are other things to write. For now, I've written very little of what you could consider political poetry in the last few years. I'm doing much more of the personal stuff, family stuff, things like that. And that may change; writing comes and goes in cycles like that. I'm actually going to West Point next month [March 1997] to talk to cadets there. I don't know why but they have my books of poetry. I'm not sure what the guy wants.[4] It's not that I sing a different song to these cadets or anybody else. I'll go talk to them. I'm still convinced that what I've learned and the consciousness you understand by the end of *Passing Time*, I haven't been given any reason to change my opinion about any of it in the last twenty-five years. I'm certainly less messianic about the whole thing, but I still believe it.

SC. In earlier poems like "Briana" you write poignantly of a friend's daughter as one who "Light[s] the awful silence with your laughter." It isn't that you write only of politics or war. There are many other poems dedicated to Leela, your daughter.

WDE. I've always done that, if you look at even the Vietnam War poems written between early 1970 and early 1973, I was an undergraduate student, even then I was writing other kinds of poems. None of those poems are all that good. I think the only reason the Vietnam poems survived is that they are about Vietnam, but all these early poems, you can see I'm still learning how to be a writer, I was still very young, but I was writing about other things, not just the war. War has never been the only concern in my life. Personal friendship, for instance, has always meant a great deal to me, and I think that comes out in my writing.

SC. Robert Bly (channeling W.B. Yeats) writes of political poetry not as propaganda but that it "moves to deepen awareness." Did you think the intertwining of the personal and your experiences which are both personal and political, contributes to the deepening of the awareness?

WDE. I don't know, I hope so. There are three different kinds of poems, some of them overtly political and deal only with that, some of them overtly personal and only deal with that, think of poems like "A Scientific Treatise for My Wife" or "The Beech Tree." Then there are poems where I take the personal and the political and put them together, and I like it when that happens, "Responsibility" is like that, "Song for Leela, Bobby, and Me" does that; it's dealing with overtly political ideas, but also it's a love song to Bobby Ross. I'm constantly going back and forth between the personal and the political.

SC. One of the things that I'm trying to work out is some kind of an aesthetic of political poetry, that political poetry isn't some kind of separate genre of poetry.

WDE. I'm trying to remember who it was. Orwell? Or George Santayana? One of those famous guys, who said that all writing is political, even the choice to write about trees and flowers is a political choice.

SC. The personal is political.

WDE. The one thing that Lorrie Smith says in her essay in *War, Literature & the Arts* that most pleases me is her recognition that in all my poetry, all my life, basically it's all personal. I'm glad I got to say that because that's important to me. What I write about in essence is my own life. I'm not very imaginative. I'm writing about what happened to me and my friends and things like that. My vision of the personal is probably broader than it is with many people and I think that's a direct result of my experiences in and after Vietnam. I took the whole Nixon Watergate fiasco as a personal affront; that wasn't something political, that was personal. So I think that, with my writing, it's all personal. What goes on, what went on for almost ten years in Central America, I took very personally. Unlike a lot of people, I have been at the other end of the U.S. tax dollars, where the artillery shells explode and people step on mines and I know what happens. I was keenly aware of the consequences of U.S. tax money in Central America, the fact that U.S. tax dollars were spent at a million and a half dollars a day in El Salvador. They are doing that in my name. If that isn't personal, I don't know what is. So as you try to figure out how you come up with an aesthetic of political poetry, for me, for my writing, it's all personal. I don't consciously set out to write a personal poem, or this will be a political poem. I get anything written, I'm happy, it's almost impossible for me to sit down and say I'm going to write poems about such and such, so the kind of distinctions that one can make with my writing are the kinds that one can make only after the fact. I don't make them when I'm writing. I'm just happy to be pushing the pen across the page. I've gone through periods when I'm not writing, and it's very difficult sometimes. In 1995, I wrote four poems, that's an average of one every three months, in 1996 up until mid–October, the first nine and a half months of last year, I wrote one poem. That's really scary; especially when you've given up anything resembling a life in order to write poetry and then you can't write poetry. So when I get something written, anything written, I'm happy about it. In essence, I have had to teach myself how to write poetry again because the circumstances of my life have changed in such a way that what used to work doesn't work anymore. I have had to figure out other things, other ways that will facilitate my writing. Detroit helped me do that actually.[5] Detroit taught me a few things, not deliberately, but the way things worked out. What I realized was that I have to get out of my house. For now at least, I can't write poetry at home because home is my workspace and everything that's going on happens there. So, I always am distracted, I work hard to get that mental space, I used to get that mental space at night. All of my poetry, at least the initial composition, I used to do at night, all my writing life, late at night, midnight, 1, 2 in the morning.

Then my wife and I had a child. That changed things. And a few years later I quit smoking cigarettes. My whole sleep pattern changed. Now, it's very hard for me to stay up in the middle of the night. It took me almost four years to understand the direct connection between smoking and writing. The nicotine allowed me to stay up at night, and in the middle of the night, the telephone is not gonna ring, I can't go grocery shopping, the world is kept at bay simply by the hour, the rest of the world is asleep by now. In Detroit, I was not up in the middle of the night, but I was out there away from my family, away from my work space, no one called me on the telephone. The world was held at bay in a different way, but I realized I can't do this every night, but maybe one day a week, one day every other week. I'm trying to make it one day a week. It's been working reasonably well. I've done this five times and come away with four poems, and they really aren't very good poems, but you've got to write a lot of lousy poems to get a few good ones.

SC. Do you rework your poems a lot?

WDE. I don't as much as I should. I have a bad habit of getting things more or less ok, and then I sometimes slack off unless somebody forces me to re-work something. Of course, I hope I'm a better writer than I was fifteen years ago. I can get to the point faster than I used to. I also can tell sooner when a poem isn't going to work and abandon it. Fifteen, twenty years ago, I would keep working and working on it, trying to save it, but now I won't do that. If it doesn't feel right, I just let it go. I do a lot of revising just in the process of the initial composition. My wife has become my first critic, and in many cases my only critic. She's quite good at it. When we first got married seventeen, eighteen years ago, she used to feel like, what do I know about poetry, what can I tell you? But I was able to encourage her to realize that she's a competent reader, she doesn't need a different gear to read poetry, she has opinions that are valid and valuable. So what do you think? Tell me what you think. And she became a very good critic.

But I've let some really egregious stupidities get into print. If you find the first edition of *To Those Who Have Gone Home Tired*, in there is a poem called "The Invasion of Grenada," the last two lines of which are, "But no one / ever asked me what I wanted." I had written the poem days before I sent the manuscript and the book comes back about five months later, literally my first book that has a nice glossy cover, perfect-binding, and I was just, oh man, it was a wonderful day, and I was slowly reading each poem and I get to that poem, I read it and Oh God! Who did that? This poem isn't about me, but the last two lines make it seem like why don't they ask me? That's not important; what's important is what we have still to learn as a nation. I managed to get it corrected in the second printing. I had those last two lines taken out.

Another example: "A Confirmation," which I otherwise love, the ending of the poem isn't very good, the last line in particular is very weak. There's no hard consonant in it, it doesn't come out of your mouth with a kind of finality to it. That poem was hard work. I spent days on that, a very concentrated writing time and I got it almost there and basically figured, I'm tired, that's good enough. But it's not. What could've been a terrific poem was only a good poem because I was just too lazy to work at it hard enough, to go back, though I knew I didn't really like the ending.

SC. The last two lines of "The Invasion of Grenada," now that you've explained it…

WDE. Any reference that you make to that poem, it is the revised version that counts and in fact, I ended up having a terrible experience with that. Bruce Franklin has a book called *The Vietnam War in American Stories, Songs, and Poems* published last year, and he asked if he could use this poem and I said sure. It never occurred to me to ask which version of it he had because the first edition was in and out of print within a year or two, maybe about a thousand copies. That first version I hadn't seen in many years and it didn't even occur to me that Bruce might be looking at the first edition of the book, so his book comes out and there it is: those stupid last two lines. The thing is, once you put a bad version into the public domain, it keeps coming back to haunt you.

SC. What is your view about the Vietnam War Memorial? I ask this question also because it's connected with the earlier one about the way in which the state appropriates protest and even memories.

WDE. My great fear from the time that anyone ever even talked about building a memorial to the Vietnam War was that it would become a political symbol no matter what anyone was trying to do, that it would be appropriated by the state and by the powers that control the state. And god damn, that's exactly what happened to that thing. It is this paean to duty, honor and sacrifice and there is no acknowledgment of all the fifty-eight thousand people who died because of nothing but the egos of men like Robert McNamara and Henry Kissinger. It's just a traditional symbol, however untraditional we may see the design, its function is very traditional. It reinforces the notion of duty, honor.

A professor of communications at Trinity University in Texas, Harry W. Haines, another Vietnam War veteran, has written a lot about the way in which the war is remembered and I first encountered him because a mutual friend sent me an article he wrote about the Vietnam Veterans Memorial in 1986. The research was clearly done in '85. Less than three years after this thing was built, Harry was able to argue quite convincingly that it had already been appropriated by the forces of traditional conservative nationalism. I don't much like it, I don't like war memorials very much. I think if they want to build a memorial about the Vietnam War, what they ought to do is take that famous picture of the body lying in the gutter with that young woman kneeling behind it, take that photograph, cast it larger than life 3-D, that would be the memorial I would like to have. One of the things that really bothered me about the Vietnam veteran memorial is that it's as though the Vietnam War was this thing that happened to a bunch of American teenagers, the Vietnamese aren't even there, the Cambodians, the Laotians. It's all about us, it doesn't acknowledge in any way what actually happened there and why it happened. But of course it's not meant to reflect the reality of the Vietnam War.

SC. I can't understand why America, as a nation, well, all nations have their contradictions, but why does America find it so difficult to acknowledge its history and the problem of that history?

WDE. I don't think we are much different from any other nation and so I think that the final answer to your question here is that it's human nature. The British weren't any more forthcoming about acknowledging their history, plus we are a country that doesn't have a history. How long have we been here?

SC. One of the ironies of the Vietnam War is that the U.S. is fighting for democracy and freedom while some of the soldiers there don't have freedom back here.

WDE. But of course, we weren't fighting for freedom and democracy, that's just the rhetoric. You can't get up there and say we are fighting for the power of American corporations abroad. What politician dares to say that? But what was the Gulf War fought for? Big oil companies, but you can't say that. Nevertheless, we as a nation have done nothing unusual and so to ask this question, why can't Americans come to terms with their history, implies that America is doing something different. We just have a different rhetoric to explain what we are doing. In fact there was a time in the last century when imperialism was a good thing. The British would say, we are doing this for Empire and think this is a wonderful thing. We are not doing it for empire, we are doing it for these corporations. Finally all of this stuff is economic and it has to do with who gets the pie. So I can't really explain why Americans do this. I think it's really a matter of human nature. I think those with power don't like to have to admit the immorality of what they do and what they have, and those without power don't like to have to acknowledge that they have no power.

Millions of Americans take great pride in being citizens of the most powerful nation on earth. I think it's the same phenomena with sports teams; people in Philadelphia get all excited when their football team is playing well, as if there were some connection between professional football players who get paid multi-millions of dollars and the fact that you happen to live in

Philadelphia. But it's more dangerous when you're talking in terms of nationalism, patriotism (or what passes for patriotism). I may be a trash collector or a college professor or whatever, but I'm a citizen of the most powerful nation on earth, the freest nation on earth, the best nation that God ever invented, and that somehow makes me feel important. Well, if you start looking at the best nation that God ever invented, you realize that it didn't include Blacks and it didn't include Asians and it didn't include Native Americans, or women, or poor white men. It starts to look fuzzy when you look closely at the details, but most people don't look at the details. I think this is true of any culture; the way that most people view contradiction is to simply take one part of that contradiction and dispatch the rest. What if people end up like me? Who wants to live like me? Get up in the morning and I'm angry. I go to bed angry. And I'll be angry for the rest of my life because things aren't going to change. I would actually like to be able to let it all go. I can't, but many people can, and I've actually reached a point in my life where I'm not so judgmental about them as I used to be. It is hard work, and when you finally recognize those contradictions, you also realize there's not a lot you can do about it anyway. But we as a nation we live daily the consequences of our societal and cultural contradictions: race relations in America are still a big issue. Black people in this country still for the most part occupy the lowest rungs of the economic ladder. It's just that most white Americans think that enough has been done for Blacks already. Heck, slavery ended 150 years ago, didn't it? Most Americans see these American colonies, we did all these wonderful things, we fought the British for our freedom and we set up these wonderful representative governments with democracy, and then there was this ugly thing called slavery, but eventually that got resolved by the Civil War. Most Americans have no idea that the United States of America would not exist without slave labor, it was built on slave labor, the entire structure of America depended upon it, not just the slave-owning south. Most Blacks are aware of it, but "they don't count," they are for the most part marginalized. Then there are Native Americans, who are even worse off as a group than African Americans. It's also true, as you pointed out, that most Americans don't learn about these things in high school or anywhere else. All through American history, from the revolutionary period on, there has always been a significant dissenting stream of thought, and it's a history that is largely ignored. One has to dig hard to run into that part of American history, but in every age there have been people like me. Have you ever heard of Lydia Maria Child?

SC. No.

WDE. I had never heard of her either until recently. This woman, through the 19th century, was an outspoken critic of slavery and also part of the women's suffrage movement, a significant voice whose writing is important, yet she's been completely marginalized, erased from mainstream history.

But there are people like that. Everybody's heard of Tom Paine, but Americans don't know Tom Paine ended up as a vocal critic of the 1787 Constitutional Convention and of the U.S. Constitution itself. He felt the central government created by the new constitution was too powerful, a return to the abuses of the English monarchy and parliament. In the 1790s in fact he left America in disgust because Paine felt that the moneyed classes had taken control of the American Revolution, but we don't learn about that in school. What we learn about is the Tom Paine who wrote *Common Sense*, who fired up the Revolution, not the Tom Paine who vocally criticized the white wealthy elite.

SC. It's worrying that unquestioning patriotism is a global phenomenon and governments do lie. In what ways did this consciousness contribute to your going to Vietnam?

WDE. What happened to me in Vietnam was so deeply disturbing because it never occurred to me, nothing I had ever been taught had prepared me for the fact that my government might be wrong, not only wrong but immoral. That my government might be, as I say in an essay much later on, a force for evil in the world. Whatever the intentions—and these might be debated—the United States of America has wrought terrible evil in the world by the way in which we have dealt with other nations. I got my first hints about it in Vietnam, I thought I was off to do good and what I was a part of was nothing of the sort. Americans had no business in Vietnam. We went half way round the world to destroy a country and a culture that had never done us any harm and never would do us any harm. And it never occurred to me until I was in the midst of it that the United States of America could be capable of doing wrong, that politicians lied to me, that my high school teachers, I don't think they lied, I think they believed what they told me. So yeah, I don't know what I would have done in 1966 if I had been given an accurate understanding of American history. What I know is that I was never given that opportunity. I was given a sanitized version of who we are as a people and as a nation and based on that I made a decision that had disastrous consequences. I don't know if I've ever said this in writing but it's as though someone gave me a deck of cards and told me to play solitaire, to keep playing until I win. So I'm playing, playing, playing and only after I play but I never win, do I finally sit down and count the cards and realize that I'm playing with 28 cards in my deck, there aren't 52 cards in my deck, but the people who gave me the deck said "you have the full deck." That's what was done to me and all the rest of us who were sent to Vietnam.

SC. Is part of the problem of Vietnam (specifically your involvement and subsequent anger and disillusionment) related to what Tim O'Brien in an interview calls "moral schizophrenia"? He says he knew that the war was wrong, that there were problems, but that the way he was brought up, where he came from, emotional duty and honor led him to Vietnam. It wasn't similar with you?

WDE. No, he was in some ways, in a much more awkward position initially at least. He came to the war older than me. He is two years older than me. When he graduated from college in '68, he was twenty, twenty-one years old, and he was faced with now what do I do? I was seventeen in 1966 and there was no moral schizophrenia, I believed that I was right, that my government was right, that my government wouldn't ask me to fight in Vietnam if it wasn't on the right side. I thought we are always on the right side. My problem developed only after I got to Vietnam and I began to observe what was going on around me and it's not making any sense within the framework of the understanding I had been given and that's finally what *Passing Time* details. Tim already had concluded that the war was wrong, but if the war is wrong, what do I do? I think the war is wrong, I have this draft notice, what do I do now? I was in a different position. I was younger, and I volunteered, I was too young to be drafted. I quite voluntarily put myself in the position I was in.

SC. One of the interesting things that I found in *Passing Time* is that you seem to veer between commitment to American ideals ("I do not doubt for a moment the sincerity of our commitment to Vietnam") and trenchant criticism and awareness ("Truth, justice, and the American way means fat dividend checks, lucrative government contracts, private schools for the kids, and fuck anybody and everybody."). Is this part of the process of coming to terms with what Vietnam, meant in political, moral terms?

WDE. Yes, you have to look at the chronology of that book to see where I am at any given point. The point at which I'm talking about America's sincerity is the spring in 1970, when I'm just beginning to have to acknowledge that the war is wrong but I haven't learned enough to come to terms with the fact that my government can do this evil thing for the worst and most arrogant reasons. I'm still trying to come to terms with this stuff. By the time I'm talking with Roger, it's late winter, early spring of '73–'74, I'm on the tanker by that point, so that's a lot of time I've spent and I've learned a whole lot. One of the things that really, really changed my thinking was reading the *Pentagon Papers*, which I didn't encounter until June 1971. If you read the *Pentagon Papers*, then it's not possible to believe any more that motivations were pure. It says right in there that 70 percent of our fighting in Vietnam was just to save face, to save us from looking like fools. All these notions of freedom and democracy, just empty words. The *Pentagon Papers*, if you've never read it, it's worth at least reading the condensed paperback This is not something written by some whacko leftist; you can bet no American government will ever produce a document like that again, they'll never make that mistake again, you only get this one-time glimpse into the way government really works. It's clear that the war managers don't care about the Vietnamese, they don't care about freedom, none of that matters. But what really amazes me, is that the information is there in the public domain, yet the American people still don't accept it. I can get up and say this stuff and people think I'm a Commie, a lousy, lying no-good traitor when all I'm doing is stating the facts; this is not stuff I've invented. Anyway, *Passing Time* jumps around chronologically, so you've got to pay attention to what I'm saying at any given point in the actual chronology of elapsed time because my thinking is evolving over time.

SC. Vietnam has been made to seem a noble cause and I'd just like to revisit that about ten years later.

WDE. Well, you've got to figure that I'm actually writing the book in 1984 but I think I am being accurate. I knew that was going to happen, you could see that coming. You know, powerful people who have been humiliated are not about to say, well, we were wrong; just studying history one learns that power is always conservative.

SC. What do you think of McNamara's memoir *In Retrospect*?

WDE. I think it's bullshit. I think the guy still doesn't get it. I think once again what you have is a powerful rich white guy, who's rich getting richer on other people's misery. I'd at least believe his sincerity if he gave all the profits from his book to charity, but he's not doing that, he's keeping it all. He's a horse's ass, he was a horse's ass before he wrote that book and he's still a horse's ass. He doesn't have a clue what went wrong, doesn't have any idea. It amazes me that people listen to a man who didn't know what he was talking about thirty years ago and still doesn't know what he's talking about.

SC. One other thing, this whole feeling, in *Passing Time*, is it some kind of a metaphor for freedom, an alternative to going west?

WDE. Well, it's your job to find the metaphors. In fact, that's what I did, when I got out of college I went to work on this tanker. At that point, I no longer wanted to be in the United States. I was sick of Nixon and Kissinger and the Vietnam War and the whole nine yards. But my options were fairly circumscribed. I've got no skill to speak of, a BA in literature and an honorable discharge from the Marine Corps weren't gonna get me a job in Australia. So I figured, I'm gonna go to sea. I had worked on that Irish ship four years before and I just felt it was for me, an escape, a getting away. In the same way that during the time I was in college, I kept driving. Whenever I needed to get away, I'd get into my car and just go. Basically I'd gotten to the end of my road, so I got on the ship. Now what happened, a few days after *Passing Time* ends, the ship was raided by the coast guard and I was busted for possession of marijuana and tossed off the ship, which is where the title *Busted* comes from. Otherwise I might have stayed there for the rest of my life. You can't say I was happy but I was content. I was learning all sorts of stuff about engines, I was preparing to move up from wiper to the next level, fireman/oiler. I just needed a couple more months, a certain amount of time before I could take the exams. I might have stayed there a long time.

SC. You say at the beginning that you are welcome to read *Passing Time* as a novel.

WDE. *Vietnam–Perkasie* would have been called a novel if McFarland published fiction only, but McFarland didn't publish fiction, and essentially, all three of the memoirs are nonfiction. But I'm making all kinds of choices about what to include and what not to include, and how to say things. I think the whole chronology of *Passing Time* is pretty nifty. There are three different timelines that run through it and they all come together at the end. I never did any kind of pre-planning for that. I'd get up each day and think what do I do next. For instance I spent a lot of time on that relationship with the woman I call Pam, but from the time when I struck her, hit her, it took another four months for that relationship to grind to an end. but those details didn't matter. What really mattered at that point is how did the relationship end? What I realized while I was jogging one morning is, oh, I really can explain what happened in one paragraph. So I moved back to the tanker and explained to Roger in a few sentences that whole last four months. Did I ever actually have that conversation with Roger? It didn't matter. I can convey certain factual information to the reader using that conversation. All the way through that book, I'm doing things like that. I used to talk about this stuff all the time, long political conversations. I've had people criticize that book because they just read it as political propaganda. But I used to talk like that; as I said, the politics has always been personal for me. It doesn't make good art; it certainly doesn't make relaxing reading for most readers. That's maybe why my books don't do very well, but those conversations, those monologues, I used to do that. Roger heard a lot of them. So I think it's reasonable to talk about the sea as a metaphor so long as you keep in mind that I actually went to sea. It wasn't a metaphor, I really was escaping, I was going away into the sunset.

SC. I want to get back to some of the poems. I find "Guerrilla War" very disturbing, it's probably the way you saw the Vietnamese, they all look alike, civilians and soldiers cannot be distinguished and then you write that "After a while, / you quit trying." I was just wondering, did you try to figure out why young boys and girls and women were fighting?

WDE. Oh, there's no way you can wrestle with questions like that when you are in the midst of the war, you're eighteen years old. There was no way to deal with that. The poem should be very disturbing. It's meant to be very disturbing. The fact is there was no way to distinguish who's our enemy and who's not. Especially because a big part of the warfare that we were dealing with was mines and booby traps and we suspected (and were mostly right) that a great many of those innocent civilians were helping the VC; sweet little girls pedaling along on their bicycles were checking out how many Americans were at this location, they were spying. I met a woman in 1985 when I was in Vietnam—she was twenty-eight when I met her, and from the age of eight to the age of eighteen she had lived in the tunnels of Cu Chi. They would send her out to gather intelligence since she was this little adolescent girl. Americans didn't pay any attention to her, but she's collecting information, bringing it back, telling her people. So that poem is true. At the time, if we thought about it at all, the way we explained it to ourselves: this is just how evil and inhuman Communists are that they even twist the minds of little children. But of course, that didn't hold up very well. Every now and then, you'd get a fleeting sense of why people hated you, but you push it away. You get these insights, but what could you do with them? You're eighteen years old, you've got another six months, eight months, ten months to do in Vietnam, you know that if you go to your battalion commander and say, "Colonel, I quit," you're going to get sent to prison for twenty years. So what you do is put on the horse blinders, you just keep going and hope that you get out alive and then you won't have to deal with it anymore. From the moment you got to Vietnam, you knew when you could leave again if you're still alive, and that became the reason for being. My reason for being there was to stay alive until March 5th, 1968, when I could go home. The question of why is too disturbing, the answer is a paradox, you tried your best not to think about it, but yes, that poem is pretty disturbing, it's meant to be.

SC. To what extent was the killing of civilians the result of not only cultural difference but ignorance?

WDE. Ignorance is what it came out of. I'm not so sure if cultural difference is as important as ignorance. A lot has been made of the way in which Americans dealt with Asians, and the Second World War is certainly an example of American racism toward the Japanese, but there was a lot of ugly stuff that went on in Europe that does not get talked about very much. I'm not sure that had we been fighting a European enemy, it would have been possible to distinguish between friend and foe. Soldiers always de-humanize the enemy. In the First World War, we called the Germans "Huns" and "Bosch." We demonize the Other, whoever they are. I'm not entirely convinced that what we did in Vietnam was done because they were Asians and we therefore held them in greater contempt than we would have Europeans. What I know is the situation I found, in which we really couldn't tell who was on their side and who wasn't, every single person we encountered could kill you and every now and then, one of them did, this wasn't stuff we invented, wasn't things we made up. There was a reality there, and the safest thing to do was to ask questions later. It's hard to ask a bunch of 18, 19-year-old kids to do any differently and that's why ultimately we never could have won that war unless we killed every last Vietnamese in Vietnam, and what sort of victory would that have been, even if it had been possible? Ignorance, maybe, cultural stuff, maybe, but the fact was you couldn't tell who was for you and who was against you. And whatever else was going on, that was true. I really think that, while massacres similar to My Lai occurred more often than we've acknowledged, most American soldiers really were trying to do the best they could in really bad circumstances. And part of the bad circumstances was that the guys on the other side didn't wear any uniforms, they quite deliberately and skillfully blurred the line between civilian and combatant. The Viet Cong did this with great skill. They were quite deliberate in going into a village, taking a couple of shots at the Americans, and then there would be an airstrike with all these civilians killed and maimed, and then the VC would come back and oh, look what the Americans did. If you're trying to win a war, it's pretty smart. It is very effective.

SC. One problem that I have with some of the Stateside anti-war poetry is the way in which it takes absolute positions, the North Vietnamese and Vietnam become epitomes of good and Americans as absolute evil.

WDE. I think it's very normal if you believe, as most Americans are raised to believe, in a binary world, the white half, black half theory. We're the guys on the white horse in the white hat, we're the good guys and the other guys are the bad guys. If you see the world in this kind of black-white dichotomy, and you suddenly come to believe that you're the guy in the black hat on the black horse, then the other guys must be the good guys. If that's the way you've been taught to see the world and that's the way most Americans are raised to see the world. So people who opposed the war, by this process of transference, ascribed to the VC and the North Vietnamese a kind of purity and goodness that was as much mythology as was the goodness and purity of the United States. But it results from the extreme disillusionment that comes when you've spent seventeen or eighteen years being taught quite explicitly that your country represents this, this, and this, and then you realize that no, your country does not represent that, it represents exactly the opposite of that, and then you tend to identify with the enemy. Those poems are being written in that context.

You also have to consider the difference between veterans and non-veterans. I think that the Ginsbergs and Levertovs had their hearts in the right places, but most of what they write is not good poetry. I think that the civilian anti-war movement was staggeringly naïve about the nature of the Vietnamese, but if you realize that you are the bad guys, then it's very natural to decide that they must be the good guys. It's also worth saying that it is not possible to make the atrocities equal; the evil of the war was not equally distributed between North Vietnam/ Viet Cong and the United States of America. We came halfway around the world to wreck their country; the North Vietnamese did not come half way around the world and attack us, and the country that we called for twenty-seven years South Vietnam would never have existed had the people of Vietnam been given a free choice in 1954 of who they wanted, or in 1946 or '45. Whatever the sins of Vietnam were, whatever the sins of the North Vietnamese were, they pale in comparison to the United States intervening in a situation where we had no business in the first place. Look at the number of bodies and the amount of destruction that American pursuit of that war caused the Vietnamese.

Yes, the VC did murder village chiefs, but where did the village chiefs come from? They were appointed by Saigon. In all Vietnamese history, village chiefs were always chosen by their own villagers; you might not exactly call it a democracy but they were chosen within the village. There's an old Vietnamese saying that the power of the emperor stops at the village gate, and that was true, the emperor could say how much the village owed in taxes but it was the villagers themselves who decided how that tax burden was going to be distributed within the village. And Diem[6] overturned the whole traditional village structure and began appointing officials from Saigon, and most people hated these Saigon-appointed village chiefs. The Communists killed the chief and maybe his wife too, just to make a point; it was terrible, horrible stuff to do, but there was real purpose to it. It's a whole lot different from having somebody snipe at you, so you call in an airstrike and kill twenty-five people who just happen to live in that village. Our destruction, our atrocities were random, whereas for the most part, the Communists used violence to their political purposes: they knew who they were killing and why they were doing it, not that I'm trying to say that it is ok, but the scale of atrocity is not equivalent.

SC. Did you feel a sort of sense of alienation when you came back home, have you felt this and does the veteran community help to alleviate this alienation?

WDE. Alienated, yes, and the veteran community was no help because there wasn't and isn't a "veteran community." We're as diverse a group as the population at large. I don't feel much of a sense of community with people who think we should have nuked Hanoi and fried Jane Fonda in cooking oil. Veterans who think like that, God bless them, they did their time in Hell, but they don't make me feel any more comfortable about my situation; they make me feel really nervous. And the guys who are actually convinced that there are Americans being held against their will in cages in Laos, I have nothing in common with these guys except the sad fact that we all served in Vietnam. There are veterans that I'm comfortable with and that I talk to. The older I get, the more of my trusted friends are Vietnam veterans, but they are veterans who for the most part have made the same kind of sense of that experience as I've made, and that's where the feeling of community comes in, that we share ideas, not the experience itself, but the sense we made of it.

One of the great sadnesses of my life is that I am an outsider in my own country, I cannot ever feel fully a part of this society. And that's too bad, I wish I could feel good about the country I live in, but I can't. In my poem, "Letter," I write of coming back to a people I can never feel at ease with anymore. I think that's true of any minority, and I'm a member of a minority in my political ideas and my understanding of history. I'm an outsider. Sometimes I wish I wouldn't have to be, but as I said, I can't forget what I know. I can't change what I've learned, but there is no community to which I belong except this very scattered community of poets. Yet even these poets are not a community. The older I get, the more I see that various people's poetic ambitions begin to have greater power than the sheer experience of poetry, and that makes me sad. For a while, I thought that there was a community of writers, but I have seen divisions produced within that community based more on personal ambitions and pettiness and jealousy than on political ideas. Two of my dearest friends are poets, both poets' first books came out very recently. One is up in Boston and I see him twice a year if I'm lucky and the other is in Wisconsin, I see him once every two years if I'm lucky. But the reason they're my friends is because we all think very much alike, we all understand the war in similar terms, and we all feel isolated within our own culture.[7]

I think a lot of veterans have felt that way for different reasons, varying reasons, but over the last twenty-five years the government and those who form the government have worked very hard to reinvent Vietnam veterans as traditional American heroes. That's what the business of building a Vietnam memorial and having these welcome home parades is about. It allows alienated veterans to come back and once again feel a part of America. For myself, the price I would have to pay for this re-inclusion is too high. I'm not willing to walk away from what I believe about what happened and why.

SC. This is a question on "To Maynard on the Long Road Home" where you write at one point "they always assume the war is over, / not daring to imagine their wounds." Is this a civilian-veteran experiential gap? Are veteran histories and memories totally separate? If yes, how do you represent the Vietnam War to those who were not there? Can Vietnam be represented at all?

WDE. Well, I don't know. You've read a bunch of my stuff. Have I succeeded in representing it or not? Certainly one hopes to write accurately and honestly enough so that other people, by using imagination, can at least have some sense of what war and battle must be like. At the time that I was actually grappling with the war itself, the actual experiences that I had in Vietnam, I was still learning how to be a poet. By the time that I began to handle language, to write more effective poetry, I was no longer interested in the experience of the war itself. I was much more concerned with what it meant and the political and social implications, the moral dimension, what it meant for me and my country. I often wonder what I might have written if I had had the skill that I have now or had even by the late '70s. Might I have produced some poems that would have done a better job of communicating that experience? I do think it can be represented. The trick is to give people enough so that they can use their imagination and make some sense of it. Certainly no one can ever accurately tell me what it's like to have a baby, even though I was there right next to my wife while she was giving birth to our daughter. Nevertheless, writers have to try, that's their job. Anyway, that particular line, when I talk about people not daring to imagine their wounds, I was actually raising another question—what I was getting at was the moral abdication of responsibility by the civilian population in this country that allowed that war to go on, to do such terrible damage to us as a people, and to the Vietnamese.

SC. Can poetry counter more powerful representations of the war, like films?

WDE. Films are so absorbing. When you are staring at a screen larger than life and you've got surround sound with stereophonics, film is just the most manipulative medium imaginable. It's shaping the mythology. You go to a college campus and mention the words Vietnam War, and what they see in their heads, if they see anything, is what they've seen in Hollywood. It disturbs me, but there's nothing I can do about it. I can't make films go away but aside from a few documentaries, there are no films that will ever teach anyone anything worth knowing about the war in Vietnam or anything else for that matter. Film, certainly Hollywood cinema, is not a medium for teaching, not a medium for knowledge distribution. It's an artistic medium, but it's a fantasy world and finally it's entertainment, and you don't entertain people by giving them the truth; you entertain people by obfuscating the truth, even movies that are powerful and leave you thinking you've seen the real thing.

War is far too horrible, you couldn't put it on the screen. If you did, people would be throwing up in the theatre, they'd be demanding their money back, they'd be sick when they leave, not exhilarated, not pumped up, not those manipulative things that films do. And of course, real wars don't have sound tracks, or neat little beginnings and middles and ends, and they aren't over in 89 minutes. So of course, poetry can't compete with film, novels can't compete with that, nothing can compete with that; it is why film is the one activity that overwhelms our entire culture.

SC. You had some criticism in particular of literature of the Vietnam War, you said that all representation is a falsification of what happened, that you cannot represent the war.

WDE. Sure, but however imperfect the representation, you have to try.

SC. In "Bicentennial" I got the sense that the revolution was a glorious past corrupted by subsequent history. Is that so? What about earlier (and later) corruptions—issues of race, HUAC?[8]

WDE. One of the things to keep in mind is that this poem I wrote in 1975, maybe 1976, and it deals with the American bicentennial, I actually had my history slightly wrong. Crossing the Delaware and the Battle of Trenton took place about a year or so before the encampment at Valley Forge. But yes, obviously in that poem I'm idealizing the Revolution. I think you and I talked about this the other day, that really it was about taxes, middle class taxes, the last thing the leaders wanted was real democracy, so I am idealizing but I also think that if our culture is going to hold up those ideals we as a people supposedly represent then we have to make some attempt to live up to that ideal. For me, the other thing that you have to realize is that up until I joined the Marines, I believed the mythology of American history was the truth of American history so that once I began to see Americans doing certain things in Vietnam and when I began to learn about what really happened in American history, it was a terrible shock from which I have yet to recover. So yes I'm idealizing the Revolution partly deliberately, partly because of who I was twenty-two years ago, and I still needed to learn about both my country and human nature but I also think that I am writing in the voice of an average infantry soldier, the guy with a musket over his shoulder, the guy who was me 200 years before I went to Vietnam and I suspect that those men had the same ideals as I had when I went to Vietnam. That sense of how would a revolutionary soldier who had suffered that winter think about what future generations had done to the ideals he fought for.

SC. Okay, now I'll go back to the earlier poems and then on to the problems of writing poetry. When did you compile *Dark Seasons of the Mind*?[9]

WDE. I'll have to look at it, but I think sometime in the winter of '69, probably more likely in the spring of 1970. I should never have put those poems in Baky's collection.

SC. I really liked them.
WDE. I know, but that stuff is eminently forgettable.

SC. Could you give me a sense of how you developed the "Long Road" poems?
WDE. It's embarrassing to me to talk about such lousy writing but I guess you've got to ask.

SC. Yes. In "To My Mother" you talk about both the fear before going to war and the need to be a man. How do you connect the idea of manhood to the training that you received at the Marine Corps?
WDE. Oh, I don't anymore. I put that collection together during my first year of college, but the poems start in high school, so they cover about a four-year period and that one was surely written before I went to Vietnam. In those days, that was very much what we were taught—they are still teaching that to young men in our culture—that military service is a test of manhood, and of course the finest test of that is actually to be in battle, especially the Marine Corps. A Marine is a tough guy, if you want to be a real man, you join the Marine Corps, you don't join the Army, you don't join the Air Force. But there's no correlation at all, that was one of the things I learned in Vietnam. It doesn't have anything to do with manhood; it has to do with how well you take orders, you learn how to be Pavlov's dog, it's as simple as that, but I did not understand that thirty years ago.

SC. I want to talk to you about these early poems because I found some of them very good. Do you remember "Glimpse"? It is reminiscent of Wilfred Owen's war poetry in the graphic capturing of horrible realities.
WDE. If you see connections with Owen's poems that would certainly make sense, because I read Wilfred Owen's poetry, I had read it quite extensively. But obviously I missed the point, if I had understood what the man was trying to say I don't think I would have enlisted in the Marine Corps and gone off to war, but I did know his works so you can probably see his influences in my writing; though it's not deliberate, it's probably there.

SC. "The Living Christ" is again reminiscent of World War I poetry, particularly the soldier as Christ figure.
WDE. I think I told you about that one fragment where I use the image of Christ's tears dripping like blood, that's straight out of World War I, that was my knowledge of war poetry at that point in my life, the World War I

poems in particular. Even at the time I wrote "Christ" sometime in my first year of college I still haven't learned enough to find my own imagery, to go to my own war instead of reaching back two generations.

SC. "The Soldier's Return" seems to point to the idea of trauma, the fact that the soldier goes through experiences which sanction killing and yet because it was not a good war, it wasn't a victory, the soldier moves beyond the pale of social acceptance. I see it in a lot of other poetry by veterans—total alienation—you just don't belong because of what you've been through.

WDE. Actually, you know more about these poems than I do, I haven't thought about these poems in years but when I worked on those poems, I did not even begin to understand the political context of what was happening. All those poems pushed me into a search to understand my own history and consequently the history of my country and that's what *Passing Time* is all about. All those poems are still written by a guy who basically knows nothing. All I had was a bunch of raw emotion and I didn't know what to do or how to make sense of it. But what I would actually suggest is that you do not take these poems too seriously; they are written by a very young writer and a very young person. What finally led to the terrible alienation that has stayed with me all my life is not the experience of battle itself but the sense of no longer belonging to my own country. And that has to do with basically the politics of the war, the whole notion of mythology as opposed to the reality, the way in which people become comfortable with their lives and their country. I think you find in my poetry the real beginning in '72–'73. This early stuff you're asking about is just me still thrashing around like a fish that's been dumped on a sidewalk and trying to figure out where the water is, trying to get to something I can live in. As a poet, I knew very little; as a person, I was hopelessly lost, did not know how to make sense of anything, I didn't know which direction to turn to in my life.

SC. Would the collection *Winter Bells* represent a later development?

WDE. Oh yeah, that collection came out in 1988, the poem "Winter Bells" I wrote in 1985, we're talking a huge amount of development in me as a writer, as a person, as a thinker, as an emotional being, as an intellectual being.

SC. The poem "Waiting for Word from Alaska" seems to deal with friendship and betrayal.

WDE. That's literally about my brother. One of my brothers was an officer in the Air Force and in 1976 he and I went on a camping trip for several weeks and one night while we were out there in the middle of the woods with no one around for miles I began to talk about the bombing of North Vietnam.

I have always been angry about all this stuff: the angry raw-edged person that you run into in *Passing Time* is somewhat submerged, but back then it was right up on the top. And I remember talking to my brother about the Air Force and the U.S. government deliberately bombing civilians in Vietnam, which he fiercely denied—whatever civilian damage had been done was not deliberate. At that time, he was a captain in the American Air Force, and it caused a breach in our relationship that has never been fully repaired. So that's what the poem is talking about, I could hear the patients in Bach Mai Hospital, years later, on a Cascade camping trip, the Cascade Mountains. You won't find that poem in any of my collections because I don't think it works. If I didn't tell you what's going on in that poem, would you get anything like that while you were reading it?

SC. No, I thought it was a friend.
     WDE. Well, it was my brother; there are pieces of that poem that I love, there are some lines in there that are beautiful, but finally the poem doesn't work.

SC. It doesn't hold, I was wondering why, what happened.
     WDE. And of course the business of disappearing into the Arctic waste, at the time I wrote that poem, he had been sent to a radar site at the Arctic Circle and quite literally they spent 24 hours a day, these radar stations, looking for Russian missiles, waiting for the missiles. I did not successfully get all that information into the poem; the poem does not succeed.

SC. The sense of conflict and sadness is very well done but there's so much else that I couldn't figure out. The pathetic desire for recognition in poems such as "Parade" and "POW/MIA," is it part of the appropriation of the movement of the Vietnam veterans by the right wing?
     WDE. Yes, what you have is busted up poor sods who had to fight in Vietnam, could make no sense of it, came home totally confused like me. But the forces of conservatism, nationalist jingoism, those who control American policy, both foreign and domestic, have tapped into that personal pain and made it into a usable political tool. I hate talking in terms that could be construed as conspiracy theory—it's not quite that simple—but there are people who run the country and people who don't; most people don't, some people do, which is true anywhere. What they're faced with in the wake of the Vietnam War is played out in the '70s in several very embarrassing incidents for the U.S. government. Up until the Vietnam War, the government could inject American military forces as part of its policy almost anywhere in the world essentially without question. Look at the history of the United States in the Caribbean, Latin America, Central America; every time a country gives us a

hard time, send the Marines, and that remained true pretty much up to the Vietnam War.

The Vietnam War finally caused the American people to begin to question the government's use of military force in support of what government perceives as American interests, which are the interests of the rich and the powerful. U.S. government policy makers were deeply hampered by this restriction, this "Vietnam syndrome." Bush says during the [1991] Gulf War that we have finally kicked the Vietnam syndrome, and what he meant by that is the ability of the government to send troops out there is no longer a problem. They had to entirely relocate the notion of military service as an honorable thing, as a good thing, something to aspire to; they had to rebuild the image of the military. Well, you can't do that if you've got two million Vietnam War vets hanging around pissed off and alienated, and everybody thinks they are psychos and whack-jobs, so the first thing they do is to rehabilitate the military. So they've got to rehabilitate the Vietnam veterans and the whole notion of service. You see this beginning to play itself out with Reagan's speech about how our cause in Vietnam was a noble one. The speech he gave in September 1980, this is what I mark as the beginning of the rehabilitation of the Vietnam veterans, and they do it in traditional, patriarchal ways; they built a monument, they had ticker-tape parade in New York City, they do all this stuff for those who desperately want to feel good about themselves and what they did in Vietnam. The forces of conservatism play right into this desperate emotional need. You see this emerging in my poetry in the 1980s at the height of the Reagan years because I'm watching this transformation and seeing guys who should know better, who were used by their government in Vietnam, getting used by their government again twenty years later, and my dismay and amazement that my comrades can be so damned gullible, that they can let their government use them not once but twice.

SC. I saw the documentary *Hearts and Minds*[10] recently and listened to George Coker, a former POW, who has a lot to say. I couldn't believe that someone who's been through the war, who's been in prison, can actually say those things.

WDE. If you are really interested in exploring that topic, read Bruce Franklin's *MIA or Myth-Making in America* and Elliott Gruner's *Prisoners of Culture*. What you see over the body of my work is me having to make adjustments for changing political and cultural circumstances. For instance, when I wrote "A Relative Thing," I never imagined the kinds of veterans that I saw in New York City in 1985 at that ticker-tape parade. Thirteen years ago, I never imagined there would be guys who could go to the Vietnam War and now be willing to march in a parade like that, to be eager for, to bask in the admiration of the people lining up in the streets, because you have to trample history to do that. You have to absolutely turn on its head what actually happened in Vietnam.

SC. In "Twice Betrayed" you write about going back to Vietnam. What was it like being back there?

WDE. I wrote a whole book about that experience. What was it like? How to answer that question. Finally, it was wonderful, it was in many ways unnerving, it was disconcerting, you don't know what to expect but people were warm, people were friendly, curious, they were pleased that we had come all the way to visit them. I found that finally whatever difficulties there were, meeting people was always good, this was a very uplifting and beautiful experience. The thing was, no matter how I intellectualized, whenever I tried to imagine Vietnam, what I saw in my head was the war in 1967. Going back in 1985, I was able to replace those images with real life Vietnamese people, memories in color. I had no memories in color; all my memories were black and white. It also helped me to put my own experience in perspective. You go to their War Crimes Museum in Saigon, (Ho Chi Minh City officially but everybody still calls it Saigon, even the deputy mayor), and there's like nine rooms in this building, one and a half rooms are devoted to the American war, five rooms are Chinese crimes against the Vietnamese, and then there's two rooms with French crimes. You look at this and realize these are people with a history, they have a two-thousand year culture, they have been around for a long time, and however devastating the American war was to them, it was a tiny blip in their history. You begin to sense how hard they were struggling in 1985 just to live and you begin to realize all this emphasis, all this energy I've wasted all wrapped up in my experience, what happened to me, not what happened to them, and look what they've done, they are still going on with their lives, they've got important things to do, a country to rebuild. They are aware of this parade debate that's going on in the U.S. all these years after the end of the war and they don't understand it. They think: don't you guys have anything better to do? So all of that really is a healthy thing. I was there again in 1990 and in the poem "The Distance We Travel," I talk about "wearing the weight of what he has done / thinking his tiny part important." Going back there allowed me to put my own experience into perspective; it was a humbling experience, very uplifting.

SC. In "Some Other World" you write of watching "an egret ascend from a pond / with the grace of a whisper" and of a soldier turning away from violence while you cradle your daughter. Do you think that a private world of happiness, warmth, and integrity is effective to overcome the world of politics that we live in? You seem to say no, why do you think so?

WDE. No, sooner or later, except for the very, very, very lucky, sooner or later everyone has to deal with reality, no matter who you are, the world is out there and you cannot protect your children, the best you can do is love them and shelter them but you can't give them the world you would like them to have, no one can. That's life, it makes me sad, I wish I could.

SC. Do you think poetry is recuperative, regenerative?

WDE. I don't know. I write a poem and I feel good about it, wow look at that, I got it right, that's the way I feel about that, but then twenty minutes later some idiot is calling me on the telephone, trying to sell me steak over the telephone, interrupting my work to sell me meat. Meat by telephone. The world is still there, nothing changes because I've written another poem. Is it recuperative? Does it help me cope better? I don't know—the one thing I know is that when I don't write, I get crazier than I am when I do write. I am not an easy person, you aren't going to be around long enough to get any sense of that, you're seeing me at my best. I see at this point the writing of poetry as less a matter of relieving, I don't know what phrasing you use there, recuperating or healing, poetry keeps me from getting worse than I am. I have to write or else I go nuts. Beyond that I don't know what to say, I don't know what it finally does but it's just there. Poetry is an integral part of who I am, that's all.

SC. Were there many changes between *How I Live* [an unpublished manuscript] and *Just for Laughs*?

WDE. Not many changes. I think *How I Live* was a longer manuscript. I really winnowed down the manuscript, there are 46 poems in *Just for Laughs* and the earlier version might have run as high as 75 or 85, so the main thing that you'll find is that there are probably a number of poems in that manuscript that don't make it into *Just for Laughs* and also there are a few poems that got added that were written after I prepared the original manuscript. I started putting together that manuscript sometime in '88 and finally the *Just for Laughs* version was accepted for publication in September 1990, almost two, two and a half years—that manuscript kept evolving.

SC. In "Starting Over," there are multiple ideas of new beginnings, from Tet to the immigrant/exiles' life in America, and also you as veteran-poet-exile beginning anew.

WDE. When I tell you this story you're gonna think why doesn't Bill write a poem about that and I don't know the answer to that question. I did a reading in Boston, this must have been about 1987, and I met this young Vietnamese woman. Afterwards, somebody asked me a question about, basically, how do you feel about the war? My response was something to the effect that I felt it was a crime against humanity and none of us who had participated in it should ever be forgiven. It was one of my usual extreme statements. When finally the session ended, I noticed this one woman get up and walk straight at me, and I thought "oh oh." She walks up to me and says, "My name is ... and I am from Vietnam, I just want you to know that I forgive you," and then she reaches up and kisses me, and it was the most beautiful gesture. The war ended, she stayed there, finally left there with some hardship ten years later. She's twenty-eight years old, she'd been in the U.S. five or six years. It was that incident which triggered the poem. I actually began writing about that experience, but the more I worked on the poem, the more I realized it wasn't about me; this is a poem about this young woman, what it must be like for her, how weird it must be, how strange, how lonely to find herself in this alien culture.

This is another thing that bothers me about the way in which most Americans deal with the Vietnam War. What did it cost me? It cost me a lot, but it cost her her country. What a price to pay and she didn't volunteer, she just got caught in the middle of it so that's what I'm getting at. If you take away the particulars of the Vietnam War, this will be an experience of a lot of people who come to the United States, especially those who have come here in the wake of turbulence in their own countries, as refugees from war and disaster. I like to think that the poem does have some power beyond the Vietnam War, it's not a poem about the Vietnam War, it's a poem about trying to make sense of a country that is not your own.

SC. In "Responsibility," you see again the inability of America to imagine traumatic violence. Is it because it has never happened here?

WDE. Largely, yes. Of course, lots of Americans have had experience with traumatic violence—Native Americans, African Americans, women, other minorities—but on a national level, Americans have largely been spared.

SC. Do you compare this with an even more graphic prose piece "The Dream"? That is very disturbing.

WDE. I should have called it "Recurring Dream." I had that dream on many occasions for a number of years, for a good ten years. When you have a recurring dream, even in sleep you are thinking, oh no, do I have to go through this again, and you do because you're asleep. The two pieces—"Responsibility" and "The Dream"—do different things. The poem actually started out as a love poem for my wife. You can see it in the first stanza. I spent hours working on that and I'd be writing love stuff and suddenly this horrible imagery would come popping out of my pen onto the paper and I'd go, oh no, not that. I wrestled with that poem for four or five hours before I finally understood that it wanted to do something other than what I wanted to do, and then I let it go where it wanted to go. The last time anybody really suffered any serious consequences of war in this country was in the south in the American Civil War. We are a country that has been sheltered from that sort of thing, so it's easy for most Americans to ignore the consequences of what their government does.

SC. There is certainly anger and bitterness in your poems, but there is also sadness and the notion of regeneration through family. For example in "Winter Bells," these wonderful lines: "Woman with voice like a carillon / pealing the cold from my bones." In an interview with Ronald Baughman you said: "I think that those poets who are going to be durable are those who have managed not to transcend Vietnam but to incorporate it into the experience of their lives." I think that's true for your poems. Do you think so?

WDE. I hope so. All I can say is I hope that has happened and I would hate to think that I have gotten only as far as the Vietnam War. If one's writing is to have any durability at all, it cannot be topical. Someone who has never been to the Vietnam War, someone who's never been to war at all, has got to be able to read my work and find something common in it; otherwise why would they read it?

SC. Stateside protest poetry seems to be topical.

WDE. When I was doing *Carrying the Darkness*, when I was looking through the poems for that, I found myself startled and somewhat dismayed that most of the protest poetry that was written by really famous people like Robert Bly, Allen Ginsberg, little of it was good. Their hearts were at the right place, their politics, but I was not impressed with the poetry. There's one of Robert Bly's poems, he's a wonderful poet but the poems he wrote about the Vietnam War are the worst of his writing. In the poem "Asian Peace Offers Rejected Without Publication," he writes "Men like Rusk are not men: / They are bombs waiting to be loaded in a darkened hangar." There's nothing in there that explains why men like Rusk are bombs. I read that poem to a class of students in 1977. This is right after the war, but they had not even heard of Dean Rusk, they didn't know who he was, had never heard that name, a bunch of 18-, 19-, 20-year-old kids, so that poem meant nothing to them. If you already think that Dean Rusk was not a man but a bomb, then you think right on, but if you don't think that, then what? And I found that over and over again in those poems from the '60s, they're bad poetry and that's why you find so little of that stuff in *Carrying the Darkness*.

SC. A return to the representation question, if you haven't been there, can you write about Vietnam?

WDE. There's a poem called "The Peaceable Kingdom," by Marge Piercy. I wanted to include it, but the publishers were asking for too much money.

It's a wonderful political poem but it's not about the war; it's about the Johnson administration and their pursuit of the war; it stays within its proper bounds. In a later generation, Bobbie Ann Mason's novel *In Country* works very well because she doesn't try to be a Vietnam veteran in the book; the focus is on the young teenage girl Samantha, so it works. Had she tried to write that book from the perspective of Samantha's uncle, it probably would have failed.

SC. You write in "A Generation of Peace" about the irony of peace in America. Is this connected with the question of amnesty?

WDE. No, I don't think so because "A Generation of Peace" is a poem I wrote in the early winter of 1973. I don't think it's a very good poem, it finally didn't work very well, but it predates the whole issue of amnesty by about four years, so that was not part of my thinking at the time I wrote it.

SC. I found "Making the Children Behave" interesting because it expresses opinions from the other side—something you don't come across very often in poetry that I've read.

WDE. I think probably John Balaban does the best job as a poet of putting himself in their shoes, but it is also because he understood the people there, he spent three years there, learned and knew the language which gave him an entry into the culture. The only other writer who does that is the novelist Robert Olen Butler. He was in the military but he learned Vietnamese, he was a translator in Saigon. I had tried to make the Vietnamese a part of my poem, not as the Other out there, but to give them a sense of humanity and dignity. That poem was something I wrote in '75. It's funny, how things get written, it was a tiny little thing that didn't even take 25 minutes to write and it's turned out to be one of the most durable of my poems, one of the most powerful. Another thing that haunted me as I came to understand what I had done and been a part of is that I was the evil, I was the bad guy. I was eighteen years old and then I found out that it was for nothing, it was for worse than nothing, I was on the wrong side. That poem was written not because I am going to look at things from their point of view, but because I was haunted by the realization that I was the bogeyman; to them I was the bogeyman.

SC. Is it part of a problem? Well, not a problem but the limitation of a lot of this poetry, that it is concerned with exclusively American concerns?

WDE. Yeah, that's a problem, but it's inevitable, though it gives a skewed impression. You look at the literature, and pretty much you think that the Vietnam War is this thing that happened to a bunch of American teenage boys. The Vietnam Veterans Memorial is another representation of the same phenomenon, only I think much more insidious because it's much more deliberate. One has to look long and hard to find poems which offer different perspectives.

SC. "Money in the Bank" refers to Alfred Starr Hamilton. Who is/was he?

WDE. He was an American poet. I don't know if he's still alive or not. When I wrote that poem in 1975, he was 61 years old. I got a form letter from a poet and publisher named Jonathan Williams who had sent this out to hundreds of people explaining that here was this poor guy who lived in a boarding house in New Jersey, and he had no income, no nothing, and Williams was starting a fund trying to support this guy and I sent him 5 or 10 bucks. I didn't have a lot of money back then but I sent him some money. All I knew about him was what Williams had described in that letter. I subsequently wrote to him. Williams had published a book of his, the only book Hamilton ever published, odd poetry, curious stuff, but I got the book and I wrote to Hamilton and got back a very terse, strange letter, as strange as his poetry, saying that he didn't want to be bothered. I'm not sure he's still alive, but the thing is nobody's ever heard of him; he's hardly been published anywhere else.

SC. The end where you write, "I send it out of fear," is that a kind of solidarity?

WDE. No, a re-imagining of what happens if you take poetry seriously, if you try to make the life of a poet. And of course, you can see, while we are not destitute, I have no career as such; my wife basically supports the household. I knew when I was twenty-five, twenty-six years old that if I was really going to pursue poetry seriously, I could end up like Hamilton; that's what the fear is, that I'm going to end up like him.

SC. There is a theme I talked about earlier in "To Those Who Have Gone Home Tired" and in "Letter" related to ahistoricity and lack of responsibility. In "Letter" you write "we've found again our inspiration / by recalling where we came from / and forgetting where we've been." The poem refers to Ho Chi Minh as a poet—is that a kind of reaching out to the poet in politics, some kind of solidarity?

WDE. No, it's an actual, literal reference to the fact that Ho Chi Minh was an accomplished poet, technically very accomplished, and anybody who knows anything of Vietnamese language and Vietnamese poetry knows the value of his writings. He is not a famous poet in Vietnam just because he's Ho Chi Minh, so I'm making a literal connection as well. I wish that somehow my people and my society would be as thoughtful and poetic. Picture Richard Nixon trying to write a sonnet, or George Bush—the thought is almost comical. Someday I'm going to write a poem about Nixon writing poetry! Anyway, at that point in the poem I'm talking to the people of Vietnam. Hey, you won, make something out of this, and again I go back to a kind of idealized vision of our own revolution, but what I'm saying is, look what we've done to our revolution, we blew ours, you've got a chance to do it right.

SC. And it didn't, obviously it didn't work in Vietnam.

WDE. Well, they didn't get much of a chance. The United States actually waged a far more effective war after April 30th, 1975, it would strangle them to death, they would end up more or less where we wished them to be, they'll have McDonald's, they already have Kentucky Fried Chicken in Hanoi. I hope that the Vietnamese will somehow manage to keep their own identities in the face of the consumer culture invasion that's swallowing them up. It is a shame that in some places—I think of Cuba and Nicaragua and Vietnam in particular—what might they have done with their revolution if they had been allowed to do something with it. The United States wields so much economic power in the world that none of those countries ever had a chance of putting their revolutionary principles in practice. Maybe they would have blown it on their own, but the thing is they never got a chance, the world will never know what those three countries might have done if they had simply been allowed to try. Well of course, the United States does not want to have countries that believe in social equality and economic equality, and the last thing that anybody who runs this country wants to allow is for that to happen anywhere in the world; they're convinced it'll be disastrous. And for the rich and powerful, social and economic equity probably would be disastrous.

SC. In "The Farmer," do you see your poetic career as one of toil and patience? There's almost a Biblical quality in the line, "I have sown my seed on soil / guaranteed by poverty to fail."

WDE. Well, I'm a minister's son, my dad was a minister, I went to Sunday school and church every week for almost 16 years, so the Biblical overtones here and there are not consciously put there, but they are a part of my intellectual make-up. Certainly when I wrote that poem, again there's that sense of messianic vision that I am doing this good work in the world. Certainly when I wrote that poem, I imagined unrewarding toil. Pretty much got it right, it turns out, except for maybe the part about my not complaining.

SC. And yet you sound more resolute in a *Virginia Quarterly Review* article: "And if governments and nations remain impervious to the grace of poetry, I'll still pick poetry every time." You haven't repudiated that.

WDE. That's me having to recognize I can't change any of this but I don't take back a word I said, my heart and my intellect still reside with the poets, not with the politicians. After everything I have learned, I cannot unlearn it. I cannot imagine that a politician has more to offer to humanity than a John Balaban. The world would be better off if people paid more attention to Dale Ritterbusch. But I know that's not gonna happen. That's the difference: you go back to a poem like "To Those Who Have Gone Home Tired," maybe even in "The Farmer," although you can see the weariness in that poem, but I still really believed that significant change was possible. I no longer can make myself believe that. Nevertheless, I believe that significant change *should* happen, and the world is worse off because it's not happening.

SC. And silence is not the solution.

WDE. No. What's changed is only my perception of how effective a writer can be but the way the world is and the way I think the world ought to be, those things haven't changed. I don't think they will change.

SC. I just wanted to ask you some questions about the art of writing. Lorrie Smith in an essay says that your poetry is anti-poetry, a transfiguring metaphor. I am not sure about that, also the relationship between the didactic and the lyrical, can the two be combined? I feel they can be.

WDE. I don't mean to dodge your question or make light of it, but this sort of intellectualizing isn't part of my repertoire. I just write the stuff. It's your job and Smith's job to make sense of it. I don't think in terms of, well, am I going to write a didactic poem today or a lyrical poem, or let's see, I really want to combine those two. I don't think like that. The first time that somebody ever called my poetry didactic, I had to go and look the word up. Adi Wimmer, my Austrian friend, told me that he found so many oxymorons in my writing, and I was too embarrassed to ask him, but as soon as the conversation ended, I went to the dictionary and looked up "oxymoron" because I knew I had heard that in high school English class but I couldn't remember what it meant. I don't think like that when I'm writing; maybe other writers do but I sure don't. I'm just so pleased that anybody pays any damned attention at all to what I write that I try not to be critical of what those people write. Quite literally you are a better judge of her observation than I am.

SC. In your article "Soldier-Poets of the Vietnam War," you quoted Kennedy's speech at Amherst College in 1963 where he said that "when power corrupts, poetry cleanses." You've answered this question in different forms but do you think the language of poetry can cleanse the language of politics or has the language of politicians totally demoralized language? Have you felt the need to create "your own diction to tell the war, because the old diction doesn't work anymore," as Bruce Weigl says.

WDE. Well, I do think that language has been significantly debased over the course of my lifetime. Whether there were the good old days when politicians spoke the plain truth I don't know, I wasn't around at that time. I have a sneaking suspicion that the guys who were running the show in the 1840s were just as dishonest in their language, in their way of explaining events as politicians are now, but I don't know that for a fact. I do know that I have seen in my lifetime a degradation of language to the point where anyone who believes anything any politician says is a fool. I say that in public and people just strike me off as a radical, but they never tell the truth except by accident. Some event will happen and people in the White House and other politicians hire what they call spin doctors who explain what the President actually meant, and the news channels just report this stuff with a straight face. Then you find out a week later or ten years later that what they said happened didn't really happen, it was something else, and this goes on and on.

The Gulf War was a wonderful demonstration of the absolute irrelevance of language to what was actually happening. "Collateral damage" was actually dead civilians. But nobody says dead civilians, let alone dead babies; "collateral damage," that's all it is. Certainly the language of poetry can't compete with that because so few people read poetry. But the language of poetry is all I've got. I've no skill at playing the guitar, so I can't be a rock star, and I tried journalism, but I really don't like the ethics of journalism very much. (Two sides to every story? More like 22, or 42, or 102.) So I'm kind of stuck with poetry by default, but it's another one of those things that limits how much I'm going to effect change. I am working in a medium that very few people pay any attention to at all. We're talking tiny, infinitesimal segment of the population of this country reads poetry.

SC. To what extent did the collection *Winning Hearts and Minds* create a climate for veteran poetry particularly within the context of the early '70s, when there's very little interest?

WDE. It was a wonderful book and it had an impact largely due to circumstances. The three editors had tried to get commercial publishers, but nobody took it. They went to thirty or forty different places, but publishers said nobody wants to know about this stuff, so the editors got five thousand bucks from the mother of another guy in VVAW, Madeline Moore, I think her name was, God bless her, she or she and her husband gave these guys money, and they went to a commercial printer and printed the book themselves under their own imprint. They sold 10,000 copies in eight weeks by direct mail, no advertising, no nothing. It was reviewed in the *New York Times*, and in every major publication in the United States. They printed another 10,000 copies, and then some of the commercial publishing houses came back to them and said, "gee, fellows, about that book you have," and McGraw-Hill ended up doing an edition of something like 35,000 copies.

The attention was brief—a collection of short stories only a year later received very little attention. The Paris Peace Accords had been signed in January '73 and Americans were running away from the war as fast as they could go. So that was the end of that, but it did have a huge impact when it was first published and it did inspire other veterans to write. I think it generated a lot of writing and some of these guys became serious writers: Gus Hasford, Jerry McCarthy, Michael Uhl. What *Winning Hearts and Minds* did was to establish the very notion of a poetry of veterans. There was earlier stuff, not a lot, a collection of poems called *Vietnam Simply* by Dick Shea, who I think he had been with the Navy in Vietnam in '65, but nobody had paid attention; it was just scattered here and there. *Winning Hearts and Minds* really was the beginning of Vietnam veterans' writing.

SC. A lot of your poems were published in small presses.

WDE. Yes, tiny places that nobody had ever heard of, all through the '70s. Actually I still haven't gotten terribly far beyond that, every now and then *American Poetry Review* or the *Virginia Quarterly* will take something but for the most part, I don't publish in the prestigious literary magazines.

SC. Do you think that gives you greater freedom in some ways because you're not subject to editorial policy which you may not agree with?

WDE. No, I didn't really think in those terms, I didn't really know enough about these magazines to do that, or try to shape my writing according to someone else's tastes. *New Letters* took that poem "Money in the Bank," but they never took anything else I ever sent them, and after a while I stopped sending. I don't think it has anything to do with editorial policy. Maybe they didn't like my stuff, and all these magazines get bombarded with poems, tens of thousands of poems per year, especially to the most prestigious ones. There's no way the editors can really read that stuff; they have undergraduate students or assistants who do the initial screening, who can say no but not yes. It's a crap shoot, and if you have a name or recognition, that helps. Everybody tells you, "Oh no, we're very fair." I believe they try to be fair, but they just can't pay equal attention to that many poems. I do think that Lorrie Smith makes a good argument elsewhere about the way in which poetry is the most honest of all the literary forms because there's little commercial or financial incentive not to be honest, that's true of poetry in general. What it did for me, publishing in all these small places, the only places that would publish me, nevertheless gave me some sense of having an audience for my writing, of getting somewhere, that I wasn't just sitting there in a room talking to myself; it gave me a real sense of being a poet, getting a public, having somebody read my poetry. In many cases, we're talking about journals that maybe fifty people read, but there was somebody who liked my poem and would put it into the public domain. It kept me writing. So, it wasn't a sense of freedom; it was simply a sense of being.

SC. Do you think that the greater visibility of Vietnam literature in general, and of course poetry, was both a good thing because at least some people are listening and reading, questioning but also problematic because veteran literature becomes just another aspect of this great American cultural mainstream?

WDE. Finally, that's what it has become, mainstream, just a part of the grand American literary tradition and I think that's inevitable but it makes me uncomfortable. You're right, and what becomes most mainstream are those elements of the literature of the Vietnam War that least challenge basic assumptions, basic national mythologies. I do believe that's a lot of why my books have not received a wider reception, whereas a book like Philip Caputo's *A Rumor of War*—I hope Phil never reads this—I don't think it's any better a memoir than *Vietnam-Perkasie*. Caputo, while he recognizes the stupidity of the Vietnam War and the mistakes that were made, doesn't in any way challenge the underlying foundations of the government and the people that sent him to Vietnam. His bottom line message is: I wish I'd had a good war to fight instead of this bullshit. I can go through all these books. Tim O'Brien's a wonderful writer, and you get done reading his stuff and think, boy that war was really screwed up, but you don't get down to wow, this country's really screwed up, this country we live in is really screwed up. So the things that tend to be mainstream, that sell well, that get taught year after year in college courses and other things that tend to reinforce the mythology that has now grown around the Vietnam War that yes this was a terrible war, but this thing happened in isolation, it was a mistake and isn't the real America, that's the stuff that people are comfortable with. We now accept that the war in Vietnam was a mistake but why was it a mistake, what should have been done and what ought we to have learned from it? We have not as a people resolved those questions, and I don't think they will be resolved. Or rather, they will be resolved in the manner that you saw in the Gulf War: no pussyfooting around, no incremental squeeze, just massive force, overwhelming force right up front. Smash the enemy and go home. Of course, we'll see how it all works out in the long run, but the yellow ribbons and the big post-Gulf War victory parade in DC make it clear that the folks who brought us that war think they got it right this time.

SC. Your poems, some of them are taught in schools.
WDE. Occasionally. Oddly enough, there are two of my early Vietnam poems in a junior high school American history book. But they've chosen two that actually can fit into our current understanding of the war: isn't it

terrible how we treated the poor veterans and of course they killed civilians but how could they tell the difference, I mean the poems they used were "Guerrilla War" and "Coming Home." Those are poems that play into the developing mythology of the Vietnam War. They've chosen comfortable poems, they're not going to put "Making the Children Behave" in some junior high school history book, but at least those poems are there, it's something. There certainly weren't any poems in history books when I was in high school. I don't know that any of my poems have made it into English textbooks at the high school level. Generally, my stuff only shows up occasionally, someone might use *Carrying the Darkness* for a course. Occasionally a teacher or professor will choose to use a book. Colonel Joe Cox at the U.S. Military Academy is using *Just for Laughs* in a literature course on the Vietnam War, but I have not been taken very seriously by the mainstream, even among those people who pay attention to poetry. If you start looking at books on American poetry, general anthologies of contemporary American poetry, I'm not in any of them. I don't know how to explain that, maybe I'm not that good, maybe I don't go to the right cocktail parties, I don't know, but I'm not there.

SC. Do you think the problem is, the contradiction is, as soon as you become mainstream you become appropriated and yet when you are marginal, not listened to, the effectiveness is more, you're more subversive?

WDE. Yeah, it's an unresolvable dilemma and I think, the more prominent one becomes, the more careful one becomes in what one says. Having attention paid to you and the trappings which come with attention—even in the small and insular world of poetry, there's some money and some power to be had—some people want that, they start thinking, do I really want to say such and such. I think this about this person's poetry or I think this about the government, but can I say that out loud? I might offend somebody, and then I may not get that appointment. Such stuff happens. It's very awkward to me, I don't know how to answer these things, for me to explain why people don't pay attention to my writing; maybe I'm a lousy writer, maybe I have a bad attitude. I don't know, but I do see certain things happening and I find myself wondering. Maybe I just get what I deserve, who knows, all I can do is write the stuff. What others do or don't do with it is out of my hands.

SC. To return to the "Soldier-Poets of the Vietnam War" article, you said that most of the soldier poets were not poets, they were just soldiers hurt into writing poetry. Would this be part of the reason for the uneven quality of the poetry?

WDE. Yes.

SC. The other thing is of course that Vietnam War poetry has always been unfavorably compared to other war poetry, especially World War I. Paul

Fussell writes: "Whatever the reason, it seems undeniable that no one expects interesting poetry to emerge from the sad war. All we can expect is more of what we already have: a few structureless, free verse dribbles of easy irony, or easy sentiment, or easy political anger." I don't agree with that.

WDE. I don't either. Paul Fussell is a brilliant person and a wonderfully serious writer, about 80 percent of what he writes is just so sharp it takes your breath away but that other 20 percent just drives me crazy. Politically and socially, Paul's surprisingly almost radical, but culturally he is very conservative: if it doesn't rhyme, if you can't scan it, he's got a problem with it, and that's what you see in his reading of poetry from the Vietnam War. I don't agree with him, I think if he is going to dismiss the poetry of the Vietnam War, he also has to basically dismiss nearly all of contemporary poetry, from the beginning of the 20th century, but he may well be willing to do that. I have no idea but I don't agree with him, though I guess I'm not exactly an impartial observer.

SC. There's an article by Kali Tal, "Speaking the Language of Pain," where she writes that "national myths are unaffected by the exposure of these atrocities because the pain of marginal people is not *American* people, the American character is male, white, able-bodied, and over twenty-one (and not a Vietnam combat veteran.)"[11] Have nationalists in any way been altered by Vietnam?

WDE. Not a lot, no. Actually, this is another thing I have had to come to terms with and it's been very difficult. I thought that by the end of the Vietnam War there would be no way to repair the national myths and you would have to take an honest look at who we are as a people. But no, that has not happened and over the course of the last twenty-five years, you can see the war being recast to save the national mythologies. I think that Kali is basically correct and for all of our cultural diversity, essentially we still think about American culture as white and male. Why did we lose the war in Vietnam? What has now become the home-grown reality is that we lost the war because the meddling politicians didn't allow the military to fight the war, the media turned the people against the war, and the treasonous anti-war movement destroyed the morale of the troops. All three of those things are demonstrably not true, but that's become our national understanding. The so-called lessons we learned from Vietnam make it possible to believe that if we had done things differently, we would have won the war in Vietnam just like we won all our other wars. None of those three assumptions challenges what we were doing in Vietnam in the first place. What right did we have to try to determine what form of government that country should have? None of that comes into play, the idea that Vietnam was not ours to lose at all, that the outcome of the war might not have been affected in any way by anything we did. I don't think the war altered our cultural sense of what we are as a people in any significant way, and the impact of the Vietnam War in challenging those myths is rapidly diminishing and has diminished to the extent of vanishing.

SC. What do you think of Noam Chomsky?
WDE. I think Chomsky is right on the money on this point, I haven't found any reason to disagree with him.

SC. He's in mainstream academia.
WDE. No, he's very marginal, first of all, mainstream academia…

SC. I thought since he teaches at MIT…
WDE. He teaches at MIT but who pays any attention to him? They don't put him on the "News Hour," they don't use him on "Nightline." He's not mainstream; he teaches at a prestigious American university, but first of all, to say mainstream academia, academia already pushes you to the side of American culture and then you've got this professor who teaches at MIT, so what? Ring some doorbells and ask anybody if they ever heard of Noam Chomsky. There was actually a program on public television a few months ago, a series of interviews with Chomsky, an hour and a half, two hours, very big chunk of time, fascinating stuff, but less than one percent of the American people watch public television and that's as much attention as I've ever seen paid to Chomsky. No, Chomsky is not in any way mainstream; he is marginal and for precisely political reasons. They don't throw him in jail because they don't have to, but if anybody starts listening to him, they'd find a way to shut him up. That's what happened in the '60s and '70s, as soon as the government thought that anybody was paying attention to the Black Panthers and Vietnam Veteran Against the War [VVAW].

SC. In your book of essays *In the Shadow of Vietnam*, you write that Herr's *Dispatches* is "another paean to men-at-war, a glorious-grisly-romantic tribute to the ultimate insanity." Do writers get caught up in the excitement of war?
WDE. Michael Herr certainly did.

SC. Why did it become such a representative book on Vietnam?
WDE. Well for one thing, the writing is very, very good. He's the one who created this whole vision of Vietnam as rock-n-roll war and of course, once again, it's all about American teenage boys. You can hardly find a Vietnamese person in the whole damn book; it's like they are not even there. And Herr presents a vision of the war that has in many ways helped to shape what has become popularly accepted: the rock-n-roll war that was senseless and

stupid and the soldiers were good guys at heart and we misused them by sending them to Vietnam, we should have sent them to a good war. So the book in no way challenges the basic assumptions, even though he says really bitter things about Westmoreland. What does he say about Dean Rusk, what does he say about Lyndon Johnson? John Kennedy? Dwight Eisenhower? Harry Truman? General Waste-More-Land didn't start the Vietnam War.

SC. That brings me back to the question of how do you get to the Vietnamese point of view? Can there be a real debate?

WDE. Honestly speaking, I don't think there can be a real debate. The parameters of a debate in our free society are highly circumscribed, we get a choice between A and B, we never hear the choices C to Z at the end of the alphabet, they are not a part of the public debate, we have to find obscure, poorly read magazines like *The Nation* and *Mother Jones* and publications like that.

SC. But they're still in print.

WDE. Oh yeah, but as I said, it's not threatening in that sense. Look at what I've written; if anybody were paying attention to me, you think the government would let me talk the way I do? All you have to do is go back and look at dissent in the 1960s, and the federal government's and local governments' responses to that, you begin to see a whole sequence leading back to the '30s, you see similar phenomena dating back to the '50s, whenever somebody's presenting a truly dissenting point of view and people start listening, the forces of power step in and find various ways to crush that. Look at the labor organizing movements through the 19th and 20th centuries. Obviously, you did get labor organized, but look what it's cost, and what has happened to organized labor since the Vietnam War? The Republicans thought we should send the Marines to Nicaragua; the Democrats thought no, we shouldn't do that, we should squeeze them economically. Nobody says what right do we have to do either of those things in the first place; that's not part of the public debate. A free press means only that whoever owns the press gets to say whatever he wants. Who owns the media these days, who owns newspapers, magazines, radio, television? Money, power, they are not going to offer a point of view that challenges the foundations of their power. It takes an unusual person to be willing to do so.

SC. You can have a direct refusal, you can say no as you've said but it is eventually too powerful a system.

WDE. Well, it certainly seems that way. The power of that system has been increasing exponentially in the course of my lifetime. How does most of the culture, how do most people get their needs and their thoughts and what are they thinking, why are they thinking what they're thinking? You look at the actual companies and corporations and the people who control knowledge and it's an ever smaller number of very rich powerful people who also control a great many other things. What are you going to learn from them? Look at the consolidation of the newspaper industry. Rupert Murdoch and the Knight Rider chain, they own something like 90 percent of all newspapers in America. Who controls the dissemination of information controls the society and where does that control lie? In fewer and fewer hands. Take the publishing industry; even twenty years ago, there might have been seventy or eighty commercial publishers. I was looking at a book the other day by some publishing house I had never heard of, and then I read, Touchdown Books, a division of Simon & Schuster. Increasingly fewer companies and publishing houses. And bookstores, the city of Philadelphia used to have twenty-five or thirty independent booksellers; now there are one or two independent booksellers in all of Philadelphia, competing against these huge chains such as Barnes & Noble. You want your book in the front window in a Borders? Publishers pay a lot of money to get their books displayed in these big chain bookstores, so what books are they going to peddle? In all sorts of ways, power is increasingly concentrated in fewer and fewer hands, and one of the manifestations of power is dissemination of information.

SC. Would that be true for colleges and universities?

WDE. To a very large degree. You ought to read Bruce Franklin's autobiography, in which he's written a history of Stanford University, pretty appalling stuff. Many of the main universities are tied very closely to the military establishment, and state universities are obviously tied to the government because their budget comes from state legislatures. In science laboratories they are doing experiments that help develop new weapon systems and it's being paid for by the Department of Defense. The ties between university research and corporations are getting closer and closer; more and more focused money is being spent on university research. The University of Such & Such gets half a million dollars to do a study. Well, the professor-scientist-researcher says, "Oh, I'm perfectly at liberty to follow this investigation wherever it leads." But you can bet what professor so-and-so is going to get the next time around if he says that he's realized what he's doing is really a bad thing. Are they going to give him more money? It is very interesting how people can find ways to justify almost anything they do. I can't imagine that Richard Nixon got up there every morning and said that I'm a real evil guy but I don't care. He convinced himself that what he was doing was justifiable.

SC. So do you think poetry can be joined in the battle with all this?
   WDE. No.

SC. Can poetry create the space for a change?

WDE. You want an honest answer? I doubt it. Yet I keep writing, other people keep writing, somebody keeps publishing, somebody pays attention to them. Here you are all the way from India, sitting in this library, reading my stuff. I hate to give up because maybe I'm wrong. Maybe we can make a difference, but practically speaking, I still think that poetry will play a very, very small and very marginal role in shaking that collective consciousness. Yet for some reason poetry persists, even though nobody reads it. I've had editors tell me that more people write poetry than read it. How? In any case, poetry just keeps not going away even though the whole world is telling all of us poets, give up, forget it, nobody cares, but in spite of all of the signals one gets that this is a useless endeavor, people continue to do it. I do this because I have to do it. There was a time when I believed this could really make a difference; now I don't believe that, but I keep doing it anyway. Why? Just last week I wrote a poem for my wife and it made me feel good, and I think it made her feel good, too. The sense I get from creating a poem gives me a feeling of satisfaction that's unlike any other part of my life except perhaps having a child. And now a lot of my writing is about my daughter. It's also about squirrels jumping around in the trees, it's about the world I live in. Even if I cannot save one person in the world from being killed by the foolishness of American foreign policy or the lunacy of human nature, I can write a love poem for my wife that makes her feel good, and she deserves it because I do enough to make her feel bad, so I think that poetry has its place, has its function. How much that is true for the public sphere and how much of an impact it can actually have on the course of events? Probably not very much, but who knows?

Subarno Chattarji was a Ph.D. candidate at Wolfson College, Oxford University, at the time of this interview on February 6 and 12, 1997. Subsequently a professor at the University of Delhi, India, he contributed to The Last Time I Dreamed About the War: Essays on the Life and Writing of W. D. Ehrhart, *Jean-Jacques Malo, ed. (McFarland, 2014).*

Chattarji is grateful to Saumya Lal for her painstaking and excellent transcriptions.

NOTES

   1. Since this series of interviews Ehrhart was awarded a Ph.D. by the University of Wales, Swansea, UK, and has been teaching at the Haverford School, Haverford, Pennsylvania, since 2001. He was hired by Joe Cox, who became headmaster at the Haverford School after retiring from the U.S. Army.
   2. Ehrhart is referring to Adi Wimmer, whom he met at the 1985 Asia Society conference which took place in Manhattan, New York City, in May 1985.
   3. Kali Tal, *Worlds of Hurt: Reading the Literature of Trauma* (Cambridge: Cambridge University Press, 1996).
   4. "The guy" was Col. Joe Cox, who became headmaster of the Haverford School in 1998, and who subsequently hired Ehrhart to teach there.

5. Ehrhart spent six weeks in 1996 as Poet-in-Residence at the Downtown Detroit Metropolitan YMCA.

6. Ngo Dinh Diem (1901–1963) was the first president of South Vietnam (1955–1963).

7. Ehrhart is referring to Dave Connolly and Dale Ritterbusch respectively, both veteran poets of the Vietnam War.

8. House Un-American Activities Committee.

9. *Dark Seasons of the Mind* (Poems from the Service Years [1966–1969]). The original typescript of this and other early writings by Ehrhart are in the Imaginative Representations of the Vietnam War archive.

10. *Hearts and Minds*, a 112-minute 1974 documentary on the war in Vietnam directed by American filmmaker Peter Davis. On April 8, 1975, it received the Academy Award for Best Documentary Feature.

11. Kali Tal, "Speaking the Language of Pain: Vietnam War Literature in the Context of a Literature of Trauma," in Philip K. Jason, ed., *Fourteen Landing Zones: Approaches to Vietnam War Literature* (Iowa City: University of Iowa Press, 1991), 246.

I Myself Was the Evil

YOUSRA HASSAN RASHAD

YHR. Who influenced you the most when you first wrote poetry?

WDE. I was 15 years old when I first wrote a poem that a teacher didn't make me write. I have been writing ever since then. I was very fortunate to have two excellent English teachers in my last two years of high school who were able to convey to me their love of great literature. From those first few years, the writers I remember most are Whitman, Shelley, Wordsworth, Hardy, Edwin Arlington Robinson, Robinson Jeffers, Robert Frost, Emily Dickinson, Poe—goodness, I can hardly name them all. I was especially taken by the poetry of Stephen Crane. I think he's the one who made me first want to be a poet. He's better known for his short stories, but I loved his poetry, which seemed to speak directly to me. I also read just about everything of Kahlil Gibran. I read all of Wilfred Owen's poetry (although I didn't really understand what he was trying to say; if I had, I probably wouldn't have enlisted in the U.S. Marine Corps when I was just 17). After I returned from Vietnam and went to college, I took many poetry courses that gave me additional exposure to all kinds of poetry: the English Romantics, the Irish Renaissance, modern American poetry. (I especially remember W.B. Yeats.) Again, I can hardly list it all. By the time I was 25, I had read a lot of poetry. I took more poetry courses in graduate school in my late 20s, and the two poets who most influenced me then were W.S. Merwin and Richard Hugo. By then I'd already been writing for more than ten years, but every poet I read and liked influenced me in some way, however subtle.

YHR. I feel when reading your poems that they are universal, it is not even about the horror of only Vietnam but they send alarms that war was and is and will never be the way to peace. With the increasing amounts of wars everywhere, do you think that violence and terror are essential in us as human beings?

WDE. The American War in Vietnam certainly had its own particulars and peculiarities, but I think that all wars have much in common, that yes, as you suggest, war poetry is universal. I did a presentation a few years ago in which I compared the poetry of World War II (which the U.S. won), the Korean War (which was kind of a tie or draw), and the Vietnam War (which the U.S. lost) and in which I made the point that regardless of the wars' different outcomes, the themes of the poetry were the same: pain, grief, loss, disillusion, isolation, sadness. "Fighting for peace" is like making love for chastity. I am not, however, convinced that the world is any more warlike than it ever was since the human species first picked up rocks and sticks and used them against each other. The Hebrew Bible (what Christians call the Old Testament) is filled with war and slaughter. *The Iliad* dates back to Greek antiquity, and the *Epic of Gilgamesh* is even older. As Hayden Carruth writes in his poem "On a Certain Engagement South of Seoul": "A long time, many years, we've had these wars. / When they were opened, one can scarcely say." So I am not convinced that there are any more wars now than there ever were. That, however, is small consolation because if we humans are no more warlike than we ever were, we are certainly no less warlike than we ever were. In other words, as a species, we don't seem to have learned very much from our past experiences with war and violence. Are violence and terror essential in us as human beings? I don't like to think so—but even a cursory study of history makes that conclusion hard to avoid.

YHR. War occupied a huge space of your poetry. What were the most important points you wanted to emphasize through your war poems?

WDE. Well, firstly, I hope you've read enough of my poetry to discover that war is not my only theme. But it is nevertheless true that war occupies a prominent place in my poetry. That is because my own experience with war profoundly and permanently impacted on and changed my life, and not for the better. Moreover, when I was younger, I had (rather naïvely, it turns out) hoped that my country might learn something useful from the disaster of the Vietnam War, but as our subsequent wars (Reagan's proxy war against Central America, the invasions of Grenada and Panama, the Gulf War, the Afghanistan War, the Iraq War) have clearly demonstrated, those in power have learned nothing from past experience. I used to think that my poetry might somehow make some small difference, but I no longer believe that. So what are the most important points I wanted to emphasize? I don't honestly know how to answer that. No poem of mine ever starts out with my desire to emphasize some specific point. Poems begin as small sparks, or dim feelings, or maybe a few words or a phrase that resonate, fragment of a memory. And I begin to work whatever I've started with, add things, delete things, write and re-write until something begins to take shape. I seldom know what any poem is trying to say until the poem itself is well along toward being finished and all that remains to be done is the polishing. Indeed, I can't even tell you why I write at all. Why don't I paint? Or dance? Or act?

YHR. From your point of view, what are the technique and style features you use the most in war poems to achieve the full message behind each poem?

WDE. When I was starting out as a poet (long before I dared to call myself a poet, even to myself), I quickly realized that I needed to write in free verse. Maybe I just wasn't a good enough poet, but I couldn't manage to write in closed forms and still say what I wanted to say. (Every once in a while, I actually do write a poem that is rhymed and metered, but these poems remain a rarity in my writing.) I also have striven to be as direct and transparent as possible. I have never been a big fan of writers like T.S. Eliot and Ezra Pound and Wallace Stevens and some others of the so-called "giants" of modern poetry because I don't, frankly, understand what they are trying to say. I try to write for intelligent readers who can understand the English language, I try to be honest, I try to allow the reader to see and feel what I see and feel. Even if you have never been in a war, for instance, all humans understand fear, sorrow, anger, grief, joy, relief, love, all the range of emotions we experience not just in war, but in life.

YHR. How did the use of nature and the Vietnamese landscape help in the creation of your poems?

WDE. I can't think of any specific answer I can give you here. The landscape was there, nature was there, and I just put them in my poems when and where it seemed appropriate. Again, as I said, earlier, writing a poem is—for me, at least—more intuitive than calculated. One does something in a poem because it feels right, sits right, seems to belong. Writing a poem is more a process of trial and error, of groping in the dark for whatever one can get one's hands on. Try this. No? How about this?

YHR. In "Guns," you say that it is an absolute need that the future generation know what really happened. Do you think we are heading to a more peaceful future if we really learned from our past?

WDE. I'd like to think we are heading to a more peaceful future, but if the present is any indication, it is hard to believe that as a group we have learned anything from the past, and I have very little optimism about the future. As for putting an end to war, that would require those who have—both people and nations—to share with those who don't have, the overprivileged to give up some of their privileges to the under-privileged, the oppressors to cease their injustices and treat the oppressed with justice. For the root causes of war, in my opinion, have to do with the inequitable distribution of wealth. Will those who wield power and influence and privilege ever willingly give up their power and influence and privilege? Nothing in history suggests that this will ever happen. So why do I care? Why do I write? Two reasons: 1) I could be wrong about the future; maybe it's not as bleak as I think; and 2) I can't NOT write. I don't write because I think I will accomplish anything or influence anything or change anything. I write because I have to write; poetry is what I am, not what I do.

YHR. What do you think of the poetry of other Vietnam veterans. For example, how do you see the works of David Huddle, Walter MacDonald and Yusef Komunyakaa individually concerning approaching war experience?

WDE. All of the poets you mention here are very good and have contributed excellent poems to the canon of war poetry. As you may know, I included all three in my anthology *Carrying the Darkness: the Poetry of the Vietnam War*. Other good poets of the Vietnam War are Bruce Weigl, D.F. Brown, Gerald McCarthy. Perhaps the very best is John Balaban, who went to Vietnam as a civilian conscientious objector working with war-injured Vietnamese children and later returning (still during the war) to document and record Vietnamese folk poetry. I also like the work of Dale Ritterbusch and David V. Connolly.

YHR. In "Mostly Nothing Happens," you came across the issue of blacks and whites. Do you think and I quote from the poem that we are living in a "Hysterical, Realistic or just a Racist society"?

WDE. I don't know about Egypt, never having been there, but here in the U.S., we have come a long, long way during my lifetime with regard to race relations. I can remember segregated bus stations and other public facilities in the American South when I was still in high school, the violent attacks on blacks and whites who strove for civil and voting rights (sometimes perpetrated by the police themselves), vicious dogs turned loose on peaceful marchers singing religious hymns. For most of U.S. history, we have been a staggeringly racist society. Now we have an African American president, something I never thought I'd see in my lifetime. Blacks hold all kinds of positions they never were able to achieve even forty years ago: judges, pilots, engineers, TV broadcasters, you name it. But at the same time, African Americans still make up a disproportionate percentage of the poor, of those in prison, of those at the bottom of the educational achievement scale. And our racial stereotypes still too often take the place of reality (witness my initial response to that group of young black men in the poem). As a society, we have come a long way, but we still have a long way to go.

YHR. In the Vietnam war, there were a huge number of black soldiers enlisted. Do you think a black soldier looks at war differently than a white one?

WDE. I think Black soldiers in Vietnam looked at that war differently. As Mohammed Ali is supposed to have said in 1966, "No Vietcong ever called me nigger." Something along those lines. A great many blacks saw the war as a racist war against people of color, and why should they have to fight for the White man when blacks didn't even have freedom in their own country? I also think this feeling of "Our fight is at home, not in Vietnam" grew stronger among African American soldiers as the war went on longer and longer. A major turning point for soldiers and black civilians alike was the murder of Martin Luther King, Jr. Many young blacks in and out of the military gave up on America when that happened. As for our current wars in Iraq and Afghanistan, we now have an all-volunteer professional army (which I personally think is a very bad idea, but the generals like it well enough) with a culture of its own. Any African American who enters that culture and remains part of it has clearly accepted certain values that have more to do with the military community than the larger civilian realm. But I can't really speak to or for American soldiers today.

YHR. In many of your poems you portray the images of veterans haunted by the shadows of war. What do you think is the way for redemption?

WDE. It isn't just in my poems and my memories that the shadows of war haunt. Consider Weigl's "Song of Napalm" or Balaban's "Words for My Daughter"; from the Korean War, Reg Saner's "Re-Runs" or Keith Wilson's "The Ex-Officer, Navy"; from World War II, Howard Nemerov's "Redeployment" or Carruth's "On a Certain Engagement South of Seoul" (occasioned by the Korean War, but really about Carruth's experiences in World War II). This is a fact of war: the wounds of the soul never go away. If one is lucky, one learns to live with the shadows, but they never go away. As for redemption? I guess my poems are a kind of redemption, or at least a kind of atonement, a way of trying to apologize for what I did in the name of my country, for the lives I helped to destroy, for the damage I did. But how do I redeem myself? How do I undo the damage? How do I give back the lives? To be redeemed is to be saved from evil, but I myself was the evil.

Yousra Hassan Rashad was an undergraduate student at Mansoura University, Egypt, when she conducted this interview on March 13, 2001.

A Bowl of Alphabet Soup

TOM CHEN

TC. When did you start to write poetry? Who or what inspired you to write?

WDE. The first time I remember writing a poem that a teacher didn't make me write I was fifteen. By the time I was a junior in high school, I started to write very regularly. In fact, we're doing a unit on Stephen Crane in my Fifth Form class, and just today we were talking about his poetry. It was Stephen Crane's poetry that made me want to be a poet. He was the first poet that really spoke to me. I read these poems and I went "Wow! That's cool. I want to do that." I wrote very steadily through my last two years of high school. So the Vietnam War did not make me a writer.

TC. What did you write about in those days? How would you describe your early poetry?

WDE. Most of it was fairly typical teenage-angst poetry. I did a lot of highly imitative writing. I dig out my old high school literary magazine and there are poems in there that are almost virtual paraphrases of Crane, of Whitman, of the Lebanese poet Kahlil Gibran, whom I was quite taken with at one point, who wrote the famous book *The Prophet*.

But what I realized over a number of years as a writer is that what I was doing was learning how to write. You imitate those who you admire, and in the process you learn things. Eventually, you can incorporate certain aspects of another writer's style and make them your own. The parts of their style you can't make your own you let go of, and you go on to the next poet who fires your imagination. In fact, this is a process that goes on and should go through a lifetime.

For a long time I felt I wasn't a real poet because I wouldn't write anything, and then I would be reading W.S. Merwin or Richard Hugo and suddenly poems would pop into my head, and they would be sort of like their poems. I would feel this isn't legitimate. It wasn't until my daughter was born that I fully understood what was going on. Watching my daughter as an infant is what taught me that. The first conscious act that I saw her do, when she was still a baby on her back, was when I gave her this bottle, and she took that bottle and with the biggest grin on her face was shaking it. I realized that she had seen me shake it first every time I gave it to her, and it dawned on her, "I can do that!" So it's perfectly natural to imitate the writers that we admire; that's how we learn to write.

TC. Did you write poetry while you were in Vietnam? How did your experiences during the war affect your writing?

WDE. I did a little bit. When I first got there, I wrote some poems, a couple of which, much to my great consternation, have survived. Not only were they high school imitation Wilfred Owen, but my perception of what war poetry should be was shaped essentially by Wilfred Owen, and to a much lesser extent Siegfried Sassoon, I knew Owen's work very well. It's clear I didn't actually understand what he was trying to say or I wouldn't have gone off and enlisted in the Marine Corps. In fact, that was my perception of what war should be. And the Vietnam War was a very different kind of war. It didn't lend itself to that kind of thinking, at least not at that point.

I could make no sense of what was happening around me, I withdrew inside myself over a period of months, and I stopped thinking. If I thought about things, these ugly questions came up, and the questions themselves were frightening, let alone trying to grapple with what the answers might be, ultimately "What in the hell am I doing here? What have I gotten myself into? I thought we were the good guys."

I didn't want to be asking those questions, so I basically stopped thinking. And if you don't think, you can't write. So it isn't as if I chose not to write; it's simply the writing withered away as my introspection ceased, and then for the rest of the time I was there I did not write. I did not begin writing again until a few months before I got out of the Marine Corps. There was a period of about 2 years while I was in the Marines that I wasn't writing. I remember writing again the spring of 1969. The poems are still this bad Owen. In one poem I wrote the central image was blood dripping like tears from a bayonet. Well, that's an image straight out of the First World War. It was not an image that belonged to my war. Yet here I am reaching two generations back because I have not yet learned how to write about my experiences.

What I had to do in those early years was sort out how I felt about what had happened to me in Vietnam while at the same time learning how to write. Both grappling with the war and grappling with the process of writing was going on in those first 3 or 4 years after I got out of the Marines. But even during those years when I was writing about the war most intensely, I was writing about things other than the war. I have never just written about the war. I was still writing poems about geese in the autumn and broken-hearted love poems.

TC. Did you find yourself writing fewer war poems as time progressed?

WDE. I write about my life. I have a very pedestrian imagination. I can't invent things. I have to fall back on what actually happened to me. I don't even seem to have the skill to put myself into other people's experience, so my writing tends to be highly autobiographical. The Vietnam War and my encounter with it was a huge piece of my life, and not just a thing that happened in '67 and '68 and then ceased to happen. Its repercussions go through my life in one continuous stream. So it's always there; it's in and out.

The majority of my published poetry has nothing to do with the Vietnam War. If you look at *Beautiful Wreckage*, I think there are 128 poems in there, and only one quarter of them deal with war in any form, and the rest of them are just about all kinds of other things. I don't think there is a real pattern one can look at in terms of do I write more or less about war now. In general I'd say I write less about it now, but it just keeps weaving its way in and out of my poetry because it weaves its way in and out of my life.

TC. Did writing poetry help you to cope with your war experiences?

WDE. I think it was probably very therapeutic. It allowed me to sort out what I thought and how I felt. Inexperienced people think that writing is a mechanical process: you have these ideas in your head, and you put them down on paper through the mechanical process of pushing a pen across the table. That's not actually how it works. What you have in your head is a big bowl of alphabet soup, and you have to take your spoon and dip it in there. You have to make sense of what's up there, and in the process of writing, one discovers what one thinks. In fact, there have been a number of times when I'm writing poems and, three-quarters of the way through a poem, I suddenly realize what the poem is going to say, and I go: "Oh, I didn't know that! I didn't know I felt that way." So writing about the war was a way of coming to terms with it, of literally sorting out how I felt because I didn't know how I felt.

TC. When did you know for certain that you wanted to be a poet?

WDE. I guess it didn't quite come about in that positive way. I started writing poetry when I was fifteen, and I wrote pretty much continuously from that time on. When I was 25, I was working at a dead-end job, and had no particular ambition to be doing anything else. I was laboring under the feeling that I was kind of a lazy person, having one of those crises of my life where you look back on your life and figure what in the world have I done with it. And I seem to have that sort of introspective crisis about every six months or so.

This was when I was living in a house with five other people I had gone to college with, though this was several years after college. What I realized one night, thinking about what I have done with my life, why I am so lazy, so unambitious, was that the only constant thread running through that ten years of my life during which I developed from a teenager to an adult was the writing, that I did care about something. I cared about that, and I had worked at it already fairly diligently.

It wasn't a joyous discovery because I knew enough then to know that it's hard to make a living as a poet. It means you're going to have to do something, but you're never going to have a career doing that. I want to be this thing and my only ambition is to do this thing which guarantees that I'll be broke the rest of my life, or I'll be doing jobs I don't care about. So it was a recognition that was not a joyous moment, but I can distinctly remember the night that this came to me. In fact, it has worked out pretty much the way that I feared it would. I have always been out on the far margins of the economy. It took me years to understand what recession and inflation meant because I never had enough of an income to be at all affected by the ups and downs of economic cycles until I was well into my forties.

TC. Writing is a solitary activity. How do you incorporate it into your family life?

WDE. Before I was married and after I got married, the writing was always something that generally I did late at night, and because I have only periodically worked actual jobs where I had to get up and be somewhere in the morning, for much of my adult life I have been able to get the idea of writing a poem at one o'clock at night when I'm lying down. And the time when ideas tend to come to me most readily is when I'm in that transition between wakefulness and sleep, and all the cares of the day are gone. I can't go grocery shopping, I can't deal with the car. When all of that goes out of my head, then I tend to be more creative.

When my daughter was born, it entirely changed the cycle of my daily pattern. My daughter would wake up at 6:15 in the morning hungry. Whether I went to bed at midnight or 4 a.m., that little infant is going to wake up at 6:15; I'm going to have to deal with her, and because I started sleeping at night instead of being awake, it has forced me to change my writing pattern. There was actually another big change in the pattern of my day-to-day life when I quit smoking eight years ago.

I have never been as productive since my daughter was born. Much of the time, even since my daughter was born, I have had odd jobs. I worked part time for three years after she was born. I spent a semester at the University of Massachusetts in Boston, but for 8 months before I went up there, I wasn't working at all; I was home all the time. And for several years after that, I spent a lot of time at home without having a regular job.

So what I've had to do is teach myself to write during the day, to get creative ideas somehow going in the middle of the day because my family life allows for time to do that. It's just not the time I'm used to. Because my home is my workspace, my home is also the space filled with all these day-to-day cares that I have to address—things like when I get home today, I have to take out the garbage, I've got to do the laundry, I've got to do the dishes. Because my wife works a full-time job, I take care of a great many of the household responsibilities. If I spent three or four hours working on a poem, I'm still going to have to round up all the trash, and mow the yard, and trim the hedge out front. Plus now there's the computer and all this email and stuff. It's very hard for me in the course of my day to push all that aside and sit down and spend two or three or four hours working on a poem.

Some days I'm okay in keeping that stuff at bay and some days I'm not. My productivity as a poet has dropped exponentially over the last 15 years. I used to write thirty to forty poems a year. A lot of them were no good, but I was writing fairly consistently. Now I'm lucky to get eight or ten poems a year written. But it's always a great relief when I get a good poem written. If I'm writing only eight or ten poems a year, and nine of them are lousy, that's scary.

Though having to be in a family has certainly caused huge changes in my life as a writer, many of which make it harder to be a writer, there are also wonderful things that come out of those relationships. All you have to do is look through *Beautiful Wreckage* and you can see the point at which I got married and the point at which I had a kid because I begin to write a lot of poems that incorporate my wife and my daughter. They have been a tremendous source of inspiration, both in the abstract sense of my belonging in the world and providing the impetus for a lot of my poetry at this point.

TC. Do you write on a consistent basis, or only when you are inspired?

WDE. Do I write on a consistent basis? No, I wish I did. I know poets who do that. There's a fellow named Christopher Bursk, a wonderful poet, a bit older than me, and he gets up at about five o'clock several mornings a week and writes for two hours before he goes off to work. He just pushes the pen across the page, and whether it's garbage or good or whatever, he makes himself write.

I wish I had that discipline. My poetry has always been triggered by some kind of inspiration. A line may pop into my head, an image, a smell sometimes, a piece of music that resonates. And once that gets triggered, there's a lot of really hard work involved. But if there isn't that initial spark,

I can labor over a poem from now till the cows come home and it almost never will turn into a good poem.

Other kinds of writing I can write in a very workman-like manner. But that's because most of the other writing I do is nonfiction writing of various kinds where I know what I have to say. Okay, I just spent four days on this tugboat on the Delaware River, and now I have to produce an article about that experience. So it's a matter of the logistics of reducing a known body of information into a readable form. And that's just like going to work everyday, like building a brick wall.

But poetry doesn't work that way, so I don't write consistently. But I wish I did, because as I've gotten older, in the last 8 or 10 years in particular, the demands of my day-to-day life have become ever harder to keep at bay, to keep a little space in my own head for creative stuff. It isn't I don't have time to write poetry; it's that there's no space in my brain for that spark of inspiration to happen.

That's why I miss nighttime, where I'd lie in bed, and in that half-awake fog, ideas would percolate up to the surface. I always used to keep a notebook right by my bed. I'd flip on a light and start writing, but the older I get, the less willing I am, the harder it is to make myself turn on that light and work with a poem for an hour or two hours or three hours.

TC. What are the respective merits of metered poetry and free verse, and how do you decide which shape a poem will take?

WDE. When I was a much younger writer, I tried to work in fixed forms. This was when I was in my early twenties. I particularly remember doing this in a writing workshop with a man named Daniel Hoffman, a very, very fine poet, and he would assign a sonnet, and things like that.

What I found was that, probably because of my lack of skill as a poet, trying to work in a fixed form got in the way of what I wanted to say. Instead of looking for the right word that says what I mean, I'm looking for a word that rhymes with "alligator" or whatever. So I very quickly discarded fixed forms and wrote in free verse almost exclusively for twenty years.

I actually ended up with 3 or 4 poems in fixed forms that I liked enough that they're included in *Beautiful Wreckage*. I did a villanelle, "The Way Light Bends"; "How I Live," which is in couplets but in 5-line stanzas so that the rhyme breaks over the stanza every other stanza; and the one to my daughter, "A Small Romance," written in quatrains with rhyming couplets. Then the next book I did *The Distance We Travel* is all free verse again. But then at the tail end of *Beautiful Wreckage,* the new and uncollected poems back there, you'll find another couple of poems in fixed forms, including the tiny thing that I really love, "Nothing Profound," a little 5-line poem in which the title is part of the rhyme scheme.

"Sins of the Fathers" is blank verse. When the first line of that poem came to me, I immediately realized that it was an iambic pentameter line. So I thought, well, let's see what I can do with this. I ran out of steam at the end. In fact, Dr. Cox, with his class apparently, went through that poem and observed how the blank verse sort of begins to break down about half way through the poem, which he took as a deliberate reflection of the confusion that takes place in the middle of the poem where the poet suddenly realizes, "Holy Smokes! This is the stuff I used to do." Only I didn't mean that as a deliberate blending of form and content. It just happened because I couldn't sustain it effectively.

Oftentimes, if a poem opens for me in such a way that suggests you might be able to do this in a form, I'll try it, just for the fun of it, just to see if I can do it. There has always been this piece of me that has felt that it's not a real poem unless it's in a fixed form. Of course, that's not true, but every time I write something I like in a fixed form, I just kind of feel like, wow, I *can* do this if I choose to. The nagging suspicion is that you write in free verse because you're not good enough a poet to be able to do it in fixed forms. And that's, for me at least, an unavoidable sneaking suspicion I have about myself, because that was certainly true when I was much younger, when I just found that trying to find the word that rhymes or fills out the metric pattern got in the way of what I meant to say.

TC. What is your revision process?

WDE. I kind of work it over until I think I have it about where I want it. I'm actually revising almost from the moment I start writing. What generally happens is that I'll write as much as I can get written, which is sometimes two or three lines. Sometimes I might crank along for 6 or 8 lines, but sooner or later I reach a point where I don't know what to do. Then I generally stop writing at that point, tear the sheet off the tablet, and rewrite what I think I like so far. And I'm already doing revision at that point: I'll add lines to it, or I might realize that something needs to go in front of this. The first words that get written on the page aren't necessarily the beginning of the poem. It's just where the process of writing the poem begins. In fact, there are times when the initial line or image or phrase that triggered the poem will get written right out of the poem. By the time the poem has developed, you realize that this doesn't belong anymore; the poem has gone in a different direction.

Then I'll eventually get to where I think it's more or less a finished draft, finished enough to show somebody, and that might take me 3 or 4 of these stopping and rewriting on a clean sheet. Each time I do that it gets longer, but eventually I reach a point where I now know basically how I want the poem to end, and I'll type that up. Again in typing, I'll make changes all along the way. Then I'll show it to my wife, and over the years my wife has become a very good and thoughtful critic. When I first tried to get her to do this back when we were first courting, her response was "What do I know about poetry?" I said, "Well, do you like it or not? What don't you like about it?" You don't need to be a master carpenter to recognize a well-built table. And within a few years, she became a very effective critic. I have actually reached a point now where I'll show things to my daughter and ask her what she thinks.

I'll then send a copy to my old college roommate, which I have been doing now since he was my college roommate, almost 30 years now. He lives in Maryland, so I'll mail it down to him, and it'll generally take a week to two weeks before he gets around to looking at it and marking it up and mailing it back to me. It's less a matter of how effective his suggestions are than just putting it in the mail and waiting till I hear back from him. This gives me some distance and allows me to get away from it. When his suggestions come back, I'll open it up and I'm sort of looking at the poem fresh. Not only am I getting his opinion, but also I usually won't have looked at it for a week to two weeks, and so then I go through another process of revision at that point.

I still don't do nearly as much revising as I should. There are actually poems that when they get into print and I look at them, I just go: "Oh, how on earth did I let that get by me, what are those words or that line doing there?" That has happened to me more times than I would like because I haven't revised enough

TC. What advice can you give to a young person about writing poetry and being a poet?

WDE. Read everything you can get your hands on. Read, read, read, read, *read.* That's how you are going to learn to write. Eventually you're going to have to pick up a pen and do that part of it too, but it's the reading that'll teach you how to write. Read good writing, and don't be in such a hurry to publish—that is the other piece of it.

The reading part of it I understood. I've always loved to read. I'm a poor reader; I read very slowly. But I always read; certainly from the time I was in high school, I didn't need to be urged to read. I can remember in the Marine Corps reading Dostoyevsky's *The Idiot*, sitting in the barracks with this big fat book and guys going: "What are you reading? Look at the size of that print!"

But the bit about don't be in a hurry to publish has taken me well into my forties before I began to understand that I shouldn't have been in such a hurry. There are in fact poems of mine that I published in my early twenties that I wish had never seen the light of day, that come back to haunt me all the time. I can't make them go away; once you put them into print you're stuck with them. Just recently I had a book editor that wanted to publish a poem of mine, but he wanted to make significant changes to it, and I said thank you for your interest but no. You can publish it the way that I wrote it or not at all. And he chose not at all, but that's his right.

Again when I was young, in my early 30s, I allowed an editor to persuade me to alter a number of my poems in a little chapbook collection of about 15 poems. Because I wanted to be published, I said okay. And the moment the book was in my hand and I looked at those poems, I knew I had made a mistake. I didn't like what he had done; those weren't my poems anymore. I don't mind good critical feedback, but I changed those poems not because I believed the editor was right, but because I wanted to get that chapbook published. I don't even list that book on my list of publications because I'm ashamed of it. I don't like the poems that are in it and I don't like the trade that I made to get them published.

Tom Chen was a VI Form (12th grade) student at the Haverford School, Pennsylvania, and editor of the school's literary magazine, Pegasus, *which published this interview in two parts in v.1, #2, Spring 2001 (5–11) & v.1, #3, 2001 (4–14). At the time, Ehrhart was teaching as a long-term substitute, but the position became permanent in 2002.*

Every Day I'm Always on Patrol

ANNALISA BOVA

AB. In *Vietnam–Perkasie* I spotted two moments that seem to be some *turning point* in your view of the war: the death of your buddy Bobby Rowe and later, the news of the killing at Kent State. Actually my feeling, reading through the text, was that you gradually acquire a new awareness and that you didn't just change your opinions from a fact in particular, is that right?

WDE. The feeling you had, that my changing opinion was not caused by one or two specific events but rather by the gradual accumulation of experiences and insights, is correct. Bobby Ross's death (his real name was Ross) was certainly a shock to me because he was my age and worked with me and lived in my "hooch," but there were dozens of experiences that slowly but inexorably forced me to rethink my perception: that first load of detainees that Alpha Company sent in from the "Horseshoe" only a few days after I arrived in Vietnam was my first hint that I had no idea what I had gotten myself into. The day our ARVN interpreter,[1] whose real name was Suong, decided that we Americans were worse than the Vietcong—what a shock that day was. The dying woman with her dead child. The day that little boy tried to warn us about a VC attack and the man I called SSgt. Taggart treated the boy like a criminal. The lunatic logic of those "County Fairs." The absurdity of our Harassment & Interdiction artillery fire. The list is very long.

As for Kent State, that doesn't happen in *Vietnam–Perkasie* but rather in the second book, *Passing Time*. But if it is not possible to pinpoint an exact moment when I turned against the war, it *is* possible to pinpoint the moment when I decided to join the anti-war movement, and that moment was when I saw what the Ohio National Guard had done to those kids at Kent State. Do you know the English expression "the straw that broke the camel's back"? Well, Kent State was the straw that broke my camel's back.

AB. When you enlisted in the Marines you felt that you owed it to your country. At some point in *Passing Time* you said that you still believe it and that it's still worth something to be an American. How has your view of patriotism changed by now? If you had to do it again, and if you had the chance to choose, would you still leave for Vietnam?

WDE. I once wrote in an otherwise mostly forgettable love poem for my wife:

> duty, honor, country—rubbish;
> you're the only land I'll ever love

or something much like that, I can't even find a copy of the poem at the moment. What do we even mean by patriotism? Love of country? Should I love a country that has the highest murder rate in the world, the highest rate of incarceration, the highest rate of infant mortality in the developed world, the greatest maldistribution of wealth in the developed world, the worst health care delivery system in the developed world. Should I love a country where it's illegal to smoke marijuana but it's okay to wage unprovoked war against Iraq on the fabricated pretext that U.S. security is threatened by weapons of mass destruction? Should I love a country where politicians work for the people who pay for their obscenely expensive election campaigns? Should I love a country that spends more on military weaponry than the entire military budgets of all other countries in the world combined while 20 percent of its children go to bed hungry every night? What do we mean by patriotism? Blind allegiance? Willful ignorance of one's own history? I listen to the patriotic drivel that comes out of the mouths of people like George W. Bush and Dick Cheney and Donald Rumsfeld who were nowhere to be found when I was slogging through the rice fields of Vietnam getting my ass shot at, and I think of Samuel Johnson's dictum that "Patriotism is the last refuge of a scoundrel." I love my wife. I love my daughter. I love my friends. I love to go jogging in Valley Green. I love walking into my classroom every morning and engaging my students. I love it when I write a good poem. I pay my taxes. I vote in every election, even the primaries. I do what I can to make the United States of America a better country, a more honest country, a country I might be proud of. So far, my efforts don't seem to have made much of a difference. As for "patriotism," it's just a mushy abstraction that doesn't really mean much when you take a hard look at it.

AB. Having shared your experience with other Vietnam Veterans who, just like you, made a stand against the war after their homecoming and the fact that you succeeded in making people "listen" to what you had to say, the same people that today really admire you, has it helped in relieving the moral weight Vietnam has meant for you in all these years?

WDE. I don't feel as if all that many people have actually listened to what I have to say, let alone done something about it. Of course, I'm only one small voice in a very large world, but I don't think the world is any better off now than it was thirty years ago, which does not leave me feeling particularly successful. When I was younger, I wanted to transform America and the world, and actually had the temerity and naïveté to think that I could, but it doesn't work that way. Few of us ever manage to do more than move the world along one mind, one heart, one day at a time, often losing as much ground as one gains. I've done what I can as a writer, teacher and person to articulate and give meaning to the disaster we call the Vietnam War, and I will continue to do so, but I understand at last, I think, that the net result of my efforts is hardly significant enough to be measurable.

So I don't really feel like, "Okay, I did this terrible thing when I was young, was part of something I cannot now find any moral justification for (not to mention that the American policy in Vietnam and Indochina was shortsighted, arrogant, counterproductive, stupid, and incapable of succeeding), but I've succeeded in getting others to listen to me, so I no longer feel the moral weight so heavily." I've learned mostly to live with what I did in Vietnam and what I was a part of, but that's a matter of necessity. Moral responsibility isn't a balancing act. I did what I did and I can't change any of it. Lives were taken that cannot be given back. Lives were ruined that cannot be repaired. How does one atone for such things? Do I ever reach a stage where I can say, "Okay, the scales are balanced now. I've paid my debt to conscience"? I don't grind my teeth thinking about how evil I am, I don't lie awake at night remembering the ugly things I did, and I do take a certain measure of solace in having transformed an otherwise nightmarish experience into something worthwhile, this is to say into poetry and prose that might be of value to others. On my better days, I realize that's worth something.

AB. A question about history: I read that the U.S. never set out to "win" the war partly because they weren't allowed to use all the resources at its disposal and for this reason they had to fight under restrictive rules of engagement. Moreover, in *Vietnam–Perkasie* you said "government won't let us fight"; were there such limitations?

WDE. It's actually been years since I've read *Vietnam–Perkasie*. I'd have to go back and find the passage you refer to in order to be sure, but I expect my frustration had more to do with larger questions like the invasion of North Vietnam than with in-the-field tactical considerations. I do recall that in some areas, especially heavily inhabited areas, there were "no fire zones," but the rules of engagement were more often honored mostly in the breech (i.e. lip service was paid to proper procedures, but the rules were often ignored in practice), and along with the "no fire zones" also came many "free fire zones."

Let me give you an example. When a suspicious Vietnamese person was observed running, the rules of engagement said that we were first supposed to holler a verbal warning to stop, then fire a warning shot before shooting to kill. It was easy enough to ignore the first two steps in that process.

In point of fact, the magnitude of U.S. military hardware unleashed on Vietnam was staggering. More tonnage of bombs dropped in the Vietnam War than in all of World War II by all combatant nations combined. A country left littered with landmines and bomb craters and artillery shell craters and unexploded ordnance. Over half a million U.S. soldiers on the ground in Vietnam by 1969. To argue that the U.S. wasn't fighting to win is simply unsupportable by the evidence. The only real restrictions on what we did in Vietnam were our not using nuclear weapons on North Vietnam for fear that the Russians would feel compelled to retaliate in some fashion, and our not invading North Vietnam for fear that China would enter the war as it had in Korea in the 1950s in response to the U.S. invasion of North Korea. The notion that the American military was not allowed to fight to win is a myth; a convenient excuse for an unworkable policy and an unwinnable war.

AB. Why didn't you think about writing a work of fiction so far? Do you think your audience might get the same straight message that come out of your *memoirs* or maybe not?

WDE. I'm not sure why, exactly, but aside from a very bad short story I wrote in high school, I've never written fiction.[2] My poetry is almost all highly autobiographical with only a literal handful of exceptions. I wrote poetry for 15 years before I began to try to write prose (except, of course, for college papers, newspaper stories and the like). When I first set out to write what became *Vietnam-Perkasie*, in 1979, I wanted to try to explain what the war had been like. It never occurred to me to fictionalize it. I wanted to tell my story because I thought my story was, to a certain degree, the story of a lot of young men who volunteered for service in Vietnam and ended up colliding head-on with reality. I didn't like the movies that were then coming out about the war—*Coming Home, Apocalypse Now, The Deer Hunter*. I thought (and still think) they were Hollywood entertainment, not accurate depictions of the war in Vietnam (who wants to pay to see reality? People go to the movies to escape reality.). Here's hubris for you, real ego: I was going to tell the American people the real story of the Vietnam War, show them the reality, and then they'd understand and listen and help me change things.

Anyway, it didn't occur to me to fictionalize it because I just never thought in those terms, never had and still don't. I seem to have a very pedestrian mind. If it didn't really happen, I can't imagine it. About 14 years ago,

I sat down and attempted to write a novel about my days as a merchant seaman. I wrote about 80 pages. I had a great cast of characters (the crew) and a terrific setting (the ship), but I had no idea what the story should be, the plot. I'd heard writers say that once they get rolling, the characters tell them what to write, but after 80 pages my characters weren't giving me any help at all and I abandoned the effort. Same thing happened when I was commissioned to write a two-act play: I got the first act written, but had no idea what I ultimately wanted to say, what the point was. The artistic director of the theater company that hired me just said I should try to imagine the characters from Perkasie in *Vietnam–Perkasie* twenty years later and write about how they might interact. Not having seen most of those people in twenty years, I had no idea how they might have interacted if brought together again. Because it hadn't happened, I couldn't write about it. That just seems to be the way my mind works. I've always been interested in history (though I know that history books are as subjective as novels, in the end). I read much, much more nonfiction than fiction. Moreover, I read very slowly, so I have to make choices about what I read because I can't read everything I'd like to read or ought to read. So I read a lot more nonfiction than fiction, and of course one of the most powerful ways we learn to write is by reading. I can write nonfiction because that's what I read and thus what I've learned to write. This is an oversimplification, to some degree—I've just finished a wonderful novel called *Green Grass Grace* by Shawn McBride that one of my students recommended, but I read this in between a biography of Edna St. Vincent Millay, and a memoir by a Marine who fought in the first Gulf War.[3] In the end, I think, probably genetics determines what we write, or that we write at all. Why do I write but can barely cope with this computer upon which I am writing to you, while my wife works with computers every day as a programmer but finds it a chore to write a letter? Why does John McPhee write only nonfiction, not fiction? Why did William Wordsworth write poetry instead of novels? Why did Joseph Conrad write novels but not poetry? I've been trying to give you a rational answer to your question about why I don't write fiction, but the real answer is that I really don't know.

AB. I wonder how has the idea of the three "ghosts" in *Busted* come out. Should they represent the very conscience of yourself and a sort of guidance for you or is it something else? Why did you choose Bobby, Ski and Frenchie to "play" the ghosts?

WDE. Having just explained that I can't imagine something if it didn't actually happen, I'm going to contradict myself—at least it may seem so. When the University of Massachusetts Press was considering whether or not to publish *Busted*, the editor there asked, "How can you have ghosts in a nonfiction book?" I replied, "You go fight a fucked up war when you're 18 years old and see who you end up talking to for the rest of your life." I've had people ask me, with great concern, after reading the book, "Do you still see those ghosts?" As if to ask, *are you still crazy?* My ghosts have never appeared to me in corporeal form like that, but those ghosts are real. They are with me every day of my life. Think of it this way: Are there people in your life that you loved and cared about but who have died? A grandparent? A parent, sibling, uncle or aunt, friend? But just because they're dead, does that mean they are no longer a part of your life? Of course not. You think about them, remember them, love them still. They are always with you, aren't they? We all live with ghosts. It's the way life is. Both of my parents are dead, but last week when I was inducted into my high school hall of fame, I thought about my parents a lot and wished they could have been there at the ceremony. And thus, in a very real way, they were there with me. In *Busted*, I just had to give my ghosts a form that readers would understand. Bobbie, Ski, and Frenchie are really just these three teenagers who never got the chance to grow up. The way they behave in the story, what they say and do, is what I remember about their personalities. Of course, they do serve as a kind of "Greek Chorus," I've been told, or a sort of collective alter-ego or conscience, but I didn't plan it that way. I thought about what I could remember of each of them, and then tried to imagine what they'd say and do if they really could have been there with me.

I had a lot of fun writing them into the story. I really like my ghosts. They're not scary at all. They're just these kids, friends I knew once who died. If I were a novelist, I'd write a whole book about the ghosts of Bobby, Frenchie and Ski, but I'm not a novelist and don't have the spark of a clue what such a book would be about.

Annalisa Bova was an MA candidate at the University of Bergamo, Italy, when this interview was conducted in the summer of 2003. Her thesis was: "Everyday I'm Always on Patrol"—Testimonianza e trauma di W.D. Ehrhart.

NOTES

    1. ARVN: Army of the Republic of Vietnam.
    2. As a matter of fact, Ehrhart did publish an excellent short story, "The Dream" in *The Outer Banks & Other Poems* (Easthampton, MA: Adastra Press, 1984), 11–13.
    3. Ehrhart is referring to Clint Van Winkle and his *Soft Spots: A Marine's Memoir of Combat and Post-Traumatic Stress Disorder* (New York: St. Martin's Press, 2009).

Something Inside of Me
Amelia Moriarty

AM. I have found contradicting information about which parts of the Marine Corps you served in, where you served, what your rank was, and which honors that you received when. Can you please clarify that for me?

WDE. I spent a total of three years on active duty in the Marine Corps, from June 1966 to June 1969. For the first seven months, I went through various kinds of training in various locations in South Carolina, North Carolina, Virginia, and California. I fought in Vietnam from early February 1967 to late February 1968 as a member of 1st Battalion, 1st Marine Regiment. When I left Vietnam, I was transferred from the Marine ground forces to the Marine air wing (the Marine Corps has its own "air force": tactical fighter-bombers, helicopters, and transports) and served with several different units in North Carolina, Okinawa, Japan, and the Philippines. But my longest time of service with any one unit was my time in Vietnam, 13 months, with the infantry. I entered the Marines as a private, and worked my way up through private first class (August 1966), lance corporal (April 1967), corporal (July 1967), and eventually sergeant (April 1968). My occupational specialty was military intelligence. I received a Purple Heart Medal for wounds received while fighting in Hue City, Vietnam, during the Tet Offensive of 1968. I also received the Navy Combat Action Ribbon, two Presidential Unit Citations, a Good Conduct Medal, and the usual "junk badges" everyone gets just for showing up.

AM. When and why did you become interested in writing? (During high school, in Vietnam, after you returned?)

WDE. I started writing when I was 15, during the summer between my 10th and 11th grade years of high school, and I wrote steadily through those last two years of school. Why? I'm not really sure. I remember the first poem

I ever wrote that a teacher didn't make me write; I was angry with my parents and it was definitely a matter of venting. But as time passed, I saw other attractions to writing. I wasn't a great athlete or anything like that, but I realized that I could attract the attention of girls by being "a poet." (It is probably no coincidence that I started writing poetry about the same time I started paying attention to girls.) Finally, the more I read poets like Shelley and Keats and Wordsworth, Whitman, and Jeffers, and Poe, the more it sank in that these guys had "cheated the reaper"; they had outwitted death and made themselves immortal by writing poetry. I thought that was pretty cool. Put all of those things together and you get a kind of answer, though I don't recall ever articulating the reasons so clearly in my own head at the time. I just liked to write.

AM. What genre of writing do you prefer the most? Why?

WDE. My first love has always been poetry. I like the fact that I can express a complete thought in a short space and in a short time. When I started writing prose seriously, in 1979, years after I had been writing poetry (1964), I found it incredibly tedious and taxing to have to take six months or a year or even two years to finish a narrative book. I'm not really all that patient. And there is a delicacy about poetry, the absolute demand that words not be wasted, the challenge of saying something worthwhile in a few lines. Most of my poems are under 50 lines; many are under 30. Say what you have to say and be done with it. But in all honesty, I can't really say why I began with poetry—and have pretty much returned to it after years of writing prose as well as poetry. There was just a kind of affinity, something in my blood or my DNA or who knows what? I've tried to write fiction, but my few attempts have been miserable failures. Why did Fitzgerald write only fiction? Why did Keats write only poetry? Who knows?

AM. Why do you write about your experiences/feelings about the war? (To educate people, to vent your feelings, etc.) Also, many of your works are about your experiences in Vietnam, and your feelings towards the war. What else inspires your writing?

WDE. Even when I was writing about the war most intensely, during my years in college after my part in the war, the Vietnam War was not my only subject. I wrote broken-hearted love poems, and poems about geese in the autumn, a poem about seeing President Eisenhower in 1958, one about one of the dormitories on my college campus, all sorts of things. But of course, I was writing about the war as well. Why? Certainly to vent my feelings, but not only; rather, writing was a way to help me figure out what I felt and what I thought. I came home from the war in great pain, great emotional pain and confusion. I didn't understand what had happened to me or what it meant or how to cope with both the experience of war and the person I had become. Writing was a way to help me sort through all that. I didn't understand that at the time. Something inside of me needs to get out. I don't like to think of my writing as therapy—after all, it is my art, and I have spent a lifetime working at it—but in truth, the writing I was doing in those early years was indeed therapeutic. Over the years, the function has become less therapeutic and more educational. It is my way of trying to reach others—I wish I could write songs and play the guitar and fill the Boston Garden with 16,000 screaming fans, but I don't have that kind of skill—one uses the tools at hand, and my tools seem to be words on paper in the form of poems. There is also, often, still an element of venting in my writing, although the best poems get written after the violent emotions pass when one has time to contemplate, reflect, and articulate. I recently wrote a poem about my father's death—and that happened fully 20 years ago. Moreover, while the war certainly gave me a lot to write about, as I said, it is not and never has been my only source of inspiration. My wife and daughter have been major inspirations. I have a number of poems that deal in one way or another with nature and the environment, poems about friends living and dead, about experiences I've had through the years, all sorts of things. But the Vietnam War never goes far away. It is always there in one form or another. How can it not be so when our country steadfastly refuses to learn anything useful from that experience? One of my newer poems is not about the Vietnam War at all, but rather about the present Iraq War. It's called "Coaching Winter Track in Time of War." It's not a Vietnam War poem, but it's a poem that is entirely informed by my experiences in Vietnam. Here it is:

> The boys are running "suicides"
> on the football field today:
> ten-yard increments out to the fifty
> and back again, push-ups in between.
> It's thirty degrees, but they sweat
> like it's summer in Baghdad,
> curse like soldiers, swear to God
> they'll see you burn in Hell.
>
> You could fall in love with boys
> like these: so earnest, so eager, so
> ready to do whatever you ask, so
> full of themselves and the world.
>
> How do you tell them it's not that simple?
> How do you tell them: question it all.
> Question everything. Even a coach.
> Even a president. How do you tell them:
> ask the young dead soldiers coming home
> each night in aluminum boxes

> none of us is allowed to see,
> an army of shades.
>
> You tell the boys "good work" and call it a day,
> stand alone in fading light while
> memory's phantoms circle the track
> like weary athletes running a race
> without a finish line.

AM. Do you have any strong feelings about the war in Iraq? Have your experiences in Vietnam affected your outlook? Do you still write about war?

WDE. You can easily tell from this poem that I do indeed have strong feelings about the present war in Iraq, and yes, my experiences in Vietnam have much to do with those feelings. I learned as a result of the Vietnam War that governments lie, even our own, that killing is an ugly business and there had better be a damned good reason to ask decent young men (and now women) to become killers, that most folks back home have no idea what the cost of war is nor do they want to know, that soldiers are expendable (never mind the rhetoric of politicians), and that very few wars are fought in the interests of the people in whose name those wars are fought. I opposed the Iraq War before it ever began, believing it to be without legitimacy or justification, and it turns out (sadly enough, alas) that I was right: there were no weapons of mass destruction, and as evil as Saddam Hussein was, the chaos left in the wake of his demise is hardly any improvement. There are many, many differences between the Vietnam War and the Iraq War. But whatever differences there may be, these wars' two similarities make all the differences irrelevant: 1) in each case, the military was tasked by the civilian leadership with achieving goals that are simply not attainable by force of arms, and 2) when you send armed, scared kids into an alien and hostile environment they will never ever understand, bad things happen.

Do I still write about war? Yes. If we would stop fighting them, perhaps I could stop writing about them.

AM. Do you have a favorite piece(s)? Why?

WDE. Actually, when I look back over nearly 45 years of writing, I find myself pleased to discover how many of my poems I still like. Not all of them, but more than I have any right to expect. Favorites? Geez, I don't know. Maybe "A Scientific Treatise for My Wife" and "A Small Romance" because each poem deals with one of the two most important people in my life (my wife and my daughter) and because neither poem even hints at war. They are just love poems for the two people I love most in all the world.

AM. Are you well-known for any one of your particular works?

WDE. Actually, I don't think I'm well-known for anything. Within certain circles, however, primarily those who pay attention to Vietnam War literature, I am probably best known for a few early poems of mine, "Guerrilla War," "A Relative Thing," "Making the Children Behave," maybe some others. But these are not my best works. They just seem to get reprinted over and over again because most editors are unfamiliar with the vast majority of my work and tend to reach for what is readily at hand. I might also add that my two memoirs, *Vietnam-Perkasie: A Combat Marine Memoir* and *Passing Time: Memoir of a Vietnam Veteran Against the War*, seem to get used year after year in half a dozen or a dozen college courses—not a lot in terms of sales figures (a few hundred copies a year), but very consistent and steady over two decades and more.

AM. What are you working on at the present? What is your inspiration?

WDE. Well, for the past seven years I've been teaching high school full-time again (after a hiatus of 20 years), and most of my writing takes the form of quizzes and tests, essay assignments and lesson plans. But I do get a poem written now and then. And given that I started out as a poet, and poetry has always been my first love, if I can get a new poem written every now and then while teaching well and effectively, I'll die a happy man. My current ambition is to be a faithful husband, a loving father, and an effective teacher, and if I also manage to write enough good poems before I die to produce one more collection of poems, that will be—as they say—the cat's meow.

AM. Has your writing brought any unexpected outcomes to your life?

WDE. I'm 59 years old, and it has become apparent to me that I am a historical artifact, a piece of American history whether I like it or not. Students study me in college, and even in some high schools. Graduate students in the U.S., Italy, and Austria have written about my writing. Because of my writing, I've been invited to Austria, Germany, Slovenia, Spain, Canada, Britain, Japan, and most of the United States. Because of my writing, I was offered a research fellowship with the University of Wales, which went on for five and a half years and led to a doctorate. Because of my writing, I was offered the job I have now, master teacher at the Haverford School, a job that seems tailor-made for me at this stage of my life. Writing has brought me friendships in Britain, France, Austria, Spain, India, Algeria, Japan, and all over the U.S. Two of my dearest friends, Dave Connolly of South Boston and Dale Ritterbusch of Waukesha, WI, are poets I met through my writing. This barely scratches the surface.

Amelia Moriarty conducted this interview on April 1, 2008, for an English class assignment when she was in 8th grade at Fuller Middle School, Framingham, Massachusetts.

Lessons Learned and Not Learned

Luong Nguyen An Dien

LNAD. Thirty-four years after the Vietnam War ended, does what you have learned through your intimate and extraordinary relationship with Vietnam still shine through? Why?

WDE. I was 17 years old when I voluntarily enlisted in the U.S. Marine Corps, and only 18 years old when I arrived in Vietnam. I was, in short, very young. I thought I was going there to serve my country and to save the Vietnamese from the scourge of Communism. What I learned, ultimately, though it took many years for me to fully comprehend and understand it, was that my country is not always right, my government is all-too-ready to lie to its citizens, my leaders make highly emotional and irrational decisions divorced from knowledge or reason, and finally that I was the enemy in Vietnam, not the "liberator" or "freedom fighter." These are hard lessons to learn, especially when one thinks of the magnitude of the human suffering the Vietnam War inflicted on Americans, but more so on Vietnamese, Cambodians and Laotians. One does not walk away from such lessons, or forget them. Such lessons have shaped the way I see the world, my country, my fellow citizens, my government, and myself.

LNAD. Have you visited Vietnam regularly? What has changed?

WDE. I returned to Vietnam in December 1985, when I spent nine days in Hanoi and nine days in the Saigon area. I did not, at that time, get to visit any of the places where I had fought in what is now Central Vietnam. In 1985, Vietnam was still visibly suffering the effects of 80 years of colonial rule, 25 years of war, and 10 years of America's vindictive economic and political boycott against Vietnam. I returned a second time in June 1990. This time I was able to visit all the places I had been in 1967 and early 1968: Da Nang, Hue, Hoi An, the DMZ area, along with Hanoi, Haiphong, and Saigon. I was amazed at the changes even by that time. Already old French steam locomotives were being replaced by new Korean diesels on the railroads, one could find consumer products from all over the world in the marketplaces, the Australians and the Japanese were building resort hotels, and one no longer heard so often such phrases as the "American imperialist aggressors" and the "progressive American peoples." Vietnam was beginning to open up in all sorts of ways, and that was good to see. I have not been back since 1990, but I have many friends who have gone back—two friends as recently as last month—so I have kept in touch with contemporary Vietnam and know how vibrant and dynamic the country has been in the past two decades.

LNAD. What motivated you to come back to Vietnam? Did you find it easy at your first revisit to the country?

WDE. I was originally motivated to go back when I saw a TV documentary about the Vietnam War in 1983 in which an American veteran talked about his memories of how beautiful Vietnam was. I realized as I listened to him that I had no memory of beauty at all. Indeed, all of my memories were of war, and my memories were in black & white, not color. I developed an almost instant desire to go back and SEE Vietnam for the first time. I wanted to see a country, not a war. And my first trip back accomplished that goal. One of my fondest memories is of spending an evening in Hanoi eating and drinking with a former North Vietnamese soldier who was exactly my age and who had fought against me in Hue in February 1968. And now here we were: friends sharing an evening and a bottle of *Loa Moi*. I gained many good memories of that sort on my two trips back, and am very happy I had the chance to experience Vietnam the Country instead of Vietnam the War. I'd go back again if the opportunity presented itself.

LNAD. Is it easy for you to remove the stigma and escape the haunts of the war? What is the most difficult hurdle for you in this regard?

WDE. The war never goes away for long. I have been married for 28 years and we have a wonderful 22-year-old daughter. From the moment our daughter was born, I have never been able to see her without remembering that some Vietnamese young men no different than me were deprived of the opportunity to have a child because of me and because of my country. I don't lie awake at night dwelling on what I was a part of, but I am aware that I was a part of something that should never have happened. I am aware that the Vietnamese were fighting for their freedom from foreign domination, and I was part of the forces who tried to prevent the Vietnamese from gaining their freedom. I can't ever feel good about being a part of that. Moreover, I am reminded of the mistakes of the Vietnam War every time I turn on the TV news or read a newspaper because I am reminded that my country learned little of value from the disaster of the Vietnam War.

LNAD. Are there lessons America should draw from its experience in Vietnam? If so, has America learned those lessons?

WDE. Americans should have learned that their leaders often make decisions based on a terrible combination of arrogance and ignorance, and that Americans should always be skeptical when their government says, "We need your children to fight and die for their country now." Americans should have learned that what their government leaders tell them is not always the truth. Americans should have learned that the ones who start wars are seldom the ones who fight and die in them. Americans should have learned to mind their own business and stay out of the business of others. Americans should have learned to ask hard questions and pay careful attention to the answers. Americans should have learned that political questions cannot be solved by military means. However, the Reagan Wars in Central America in the 1980s, our current wars in Iraq and Afghanistan, and other situations the U.S. has gotten involved in around the world since 1975 clearly demonstrate that few Americans, certainly not those with access to the levers of power, have learned any of those lessons. It makes me very sad.

LNAD. Many American war veterans have said the rest of the world should learn from Vietnam, its bravery and endurance and dignity under terrible hardship. That is, however, the wartime lesson. What can Vietnam teach the rest of the world during peace time?

WDE. What my trips to Vietnam taught me is the power of forgiveness—I met very few Vietnamese who resented me or treated me badly because of what I and my country had done to them. And what Vietnam, I think, is teaching the world, is how resilient and resourceful and indomitable is the human spirit. A country that suffered so much at the hands of the French, the Japanese, and the Americans has resurrected itself, re-invented itself, and become one of the most dynamic and lively cultures and economies in the world.

LNAD. Given the lingering presence of Agent Orange and unexploded ordnance in Vietnam, what do American war veterans think when they meet affected Vietnamese victims and the suffering they have been bearing?

WDE. I can't speak for anyone but myself. When I see Vietnamese who have suffered the ravages of our American War in Vietnam, what I think is "What a waste." Like our collective American failure to learn from the disaster of the Vietnam War, it all just makes me very sad. Very, very sad.

By the way, you didn't ask me, but I am 60 years old. I joined the Marines in 1966 and fought in Vietnam from February 1967 to March 1968. I am now a high school history and English teacher. I have also written and published a great deal about the war and its consequences. I'm going to include one of my poems, written after my trip to Vietnam in 1985. It's from a book of mine called *Beautiful Wreckage*:

"Second Thoughts"
for Nguyen Van Hung

You watch with admiration as I roll
a cigarette from papers and tobacco.
Hanoi. The Rising Dragon. 1985.
You can't do what I can do
because it takes two hands

and you have only one, the other
lost years ago somewhere near Laos.
I roll another one for you. You smile,
then shrug, as if deformity from war
were just a minor inconvenience.

Together we discover what we share:
Hue City. Tet. 1968.
Sipping *Lua Moi*, we walk again
familiar ground when you were whole
and I was whole and everything around us

lay in ruins, dead or burning.
But not us. Not you and I. We're partners
in that ugly dance of men
who do the killing and the dying
and survive.

Now you run a factory; I teach and write.
You lost your arm, but have no
second thoughts about the war you fought.
I lost a piece of my humanity,
it's absence heavy as a severed arm—

but there I go again: those second thoughts
I carry always like an empty sleeve
when you are happy just to share
a cigarette and *Lua Moi*, the simple joy
of being with an old friend.

Luong Nguyen An Dien was a reporter for Thanh Nien Daily, *an English-language newspaper published in Saigon, when this interview was conducted on April 26, 2009.*

Institutionalized "Sour Grapes"

Jon Dillingham

JD. Media reports commonly congratulate Vietnam on "opening its doors to the world" as a result of its *doi moi* economic reform policies, its normalization of relations with the U.S. and more recently its WTO membership. But via embargo and sanctions, the world had in fact closed its doors to Vietnam and didn't open them for 20 years. Were these isolating measures justifiable?

WDE. Firstly, it is my understanding that the economic embargo against Vietnam after 1975 was fueled entirely by the United States. While other nations did participate in that boycott, it was only at the insistence of the United States, which threatened economic retaliation against any country that refused to participate in the embargo. Even with this kind of pressure, by 1990 many nations had finally decided that Vietnam represented an economic opportunity that was too good to pass up, and had begun to do business with and in Vietnam whether the U.S. liked it or not. I could see this change in the course of my two trips in December 1985 and June 1990. In 1985, there were few foreign products available in Vietnam, and those that were came from the Soviet Union and the Eastern Bloc nations. I remember especially a vile-tasting bottled Russian mineral water. By 1990, one could buy soap from Thailand, beer from Holland, Japanese tape decks, German film, Saudi Arabian bottled water, electric fans from Singapore, shampoo from Malaysia. Hyundai diesel engines had replaced the old French steam engines on the railroads. The Australians were building a luxury floating hotel on the Saigon River, and the Japanese had refurbished the old Metropole Hotel in Hanoi. I recall sitting next to a British oil engineer on a flight from Hanoi to Da Nang, and the man roaring with laughter as he pointed out that by the time the U.S. stopped behaving so petulantly, all of the opportunities that Vietnam offered would already be taken by other nations.

Were these isolating measures justifiable? No.

JD. Ho Chi Minh is known for saying in the 1960s "If the Americans stop bombing us today, we'll invite them for tea tomorrow." Vietnam was ready to normalize relations with the U.S. immediately following the war. Why wasn't the U.S. ready? Why did it take so long for the two countries to normalize relations?

WDE. U.S. refusal to normalize relations with Vietnam was, in my opinion, simply a matter of vindictiveness, revenge, institutionalized "sour grapes." Americans are not used to getting beaten, especially in war. The Vietnamese embarrassed and humiliated the U.S. and its most powerful leaders, and did so over a prolonged period of time. Lyndon Johnson was broken by the Vietnam War. Richard Nixon was destroyed by the Vietnam War. Fifty-eight thousand American kids came home from the war dead, and the men who sent them to die could not claim that those sacrifices had been worthwhile. The men who sent those kids off to die had blood on their hands, and they had to blame it on someone. They blamed it on the Vietnamese. Henry Kissinger once called Le Duc Tho[1] (pardon my language) a "shit." Do you think a man as arrogant and vain as Kissinger was going to recommend normalizing relations with people he considered "shits"?

JD. Initially a major obstacle to normalizing relations with Vietnam, and still a source of some tension for some in the U.S., is the return of the remains of soldiers lost here during the war. Why isn't there the same tension and outcry for the remains of the tens of thousands of U.S. servicemen still not repatriated from World War II?

WDE. And don't forget the several thousands of MIAs from the Korean War as well. Actually, though I know you don't have time to do so, you ought to read a book by H. Bruce Franklin called *M.I.A., or Mythmaking in America*, which explains in great detail the answer to your question. As simply as I can explain it, the Nixon Administration, elected in 1968 on a promise to end the war, never had any intention of doing so. As a means of excusing the continuation of the war, Nixon argued that he wouldn't leave Vietnam until the Vietnamese returned all of our POWs. He also, quite cynically, fostered the false idea that the Hanoi government was harboring the hundreds of Americans listed as MIA (most of which military authorities knew were actually dead). Moreover, the Nixon administration actively encouraged the families of POWs and MIAs to form a very public organization demanding that Hanoi "return our boys." Once the U.S. government had very publicly insisted that the Vietnamese knew where our MIAs were, who was going to be the U.S. president to stand up and say to those families of the missing, "Sorry, it was all just a political ruse. Your loved ones are dead, and we knew it all along"? For base political reasons, the U.S. government had created a monster that could not be easily gotten rid of.

JD. To this day, American leaders from the highest echelons of government (think George W. Bush, John McCain, John Negroponte and a long list of others) portray the North Vietnamese and the National Front for the Liberation of South Vietnam as the bad guys. Why did the government want to normalize relations with Vietnam?

WDE. My guess is that when normalization finally happened, it was for economic reasons entirely. There was, indeed, great pressure on the U.S. government from the American business community to normalize relations, and had been all through the 1980s and into the 1990s. Where there's money to be made, commercial interests don't care much about either history or politics.

JD. What right does the U.S. have to chastise Vietnam for human rights while Americans are spread out across the globe openly murdering hundreds of thousands (millions by some estimates) of civilians in Afghanistan, Iraq and Pakistan?

WDE. Well, of course the argument you'd get from official U.S. government sources is that the U.S. is NOT "openly murdering hundreds of thousands of civilians in Afghanistan, Iraq and Pakistan." When civilians die at U.S. hands, it's always "an accident," "collateral damage," the unfortunate consequence of the fog of war. And it's true that when the steel starts flying around, lots of people get hurt, not just the ones you necessarily intend to hurt. Does this make it okay? Of course not. But the real question, it seems to me, is: "What the heck is the US doing in those countries in the first place?" Nevertheless, if I were you, I'd be very careful about tossing around the accusation that the U.S. is "spread out across the globe openly murdering hundreds of thousands of civilians." Such glib accusations leave you open to being dismissed out of hand as "biased."

Beyond that, please don't ask me to try to justify U.S. actions and policies I myself neither support nor agree with.

I must ask you, however, what would happen if I provided answers as candid as these to questions involving the government and history of Vietnam? Would you be able to print them?

JD. Robert McNamara has died. Most obituaries said he had "apologized" for the Vietnam War. But in fact, he had never apologized. What McNamara concluded was "wrong, terribly wrong" had mostly to do with military tactics and political strategy. The errors, McNamara wrote, were "not of values and intentions, but of judgment and capabilities." McNamara never apologized for the results of the war: millions of dead and maimed Vietnamese, the ruined economy and scarred environment. Why do the media insist on perpetuating this myth that he had "apologized?"

WDE. Because, to this day, most Americans cannot cope with the idea that the U.S. had no business on earth making war against Vietnam, that a succession of leaders over a quarter of a century repeatedly made bad decisions based on arrogance and ignorance, and that those utterly wrongheaded decisions resulted in untold misery for hundreds of thousands of Americans and millions of Vietnamese, Laotians, and Cambodians. Most Americans cannot grasp the notion that the U.S. may not always be "the good guys," that the U.S. may often be the cause of evil rather than the solution. You hit upon the answer to your own question when you used the word "myth." All cultures thrive on myths. I'm sure the Vietnamese have many myths about themselves that may well be contradicted by a close look at the facts. People like to think the best about themselves, their nation, their government, and their history. If, in fact, the U.S. is responsible for "millions of dead and maimed Vietnamese, the ruined economy and scarred environment," what does that say about the U.S., its government, and its citizens? It takes a strong stomach to be willing to answer that question. Most of my fellow citizens clearly would rather avoid it.

JD. To this day, the most popular American media and films feature close to no Vietnamese characters when portraying the war. All the pain and sadness takes place in the hearts of American characters. Americans are compassionate people and surely care about the suffering of the Vietnamese. Do Americans know about the suffering of Vietnamese people? Do Americans know about what their government and military did here?

WDE. What makes you think that "Americans are compassionate people and surely care about the suffering of the Vietnamese"? I'm sure Americans like to think of themselves as such, and it may be true, but certainly no more so than might be said of the Vietnamese or the English or Japanese or any other nationality. I doubt that most Americans ever even think about the suffering of the Vietnamese people, nor do I think that most Americans know with any degree of accuracy or honesty what their government and military did there. As for American media and films—and indeed, for the American public at large—the Vietnam War was not something that happened to the Vietnamese, but rather something that happened to a bunch of American boys. Most Americans want to see themselves and their countrymen as victims of pain and sadness, not as agents of pain and sadness. This may well be human nature, not something particular to Americans alone, but it is certainly a phenomenon I have observed about my fellow citizens for decades.

JD. In line with the previous question, why is it that many Americans are so appalled that John McCain was tortured, but are not equally appalled by the fact (not denied by anyone) that he was bombing the capital city, full of defenseless civilian women and children?

WDE. Surely I've already answered this question. John McCain as victim of pain and suffering is palatable to most Americans; John McCain as agent of pain and suffering is not.

Jon Dillingham was a reporter for Thanh Nien Daily, *an English-language newspaper published in Saigon, when this interview was conducted on July 9, 2009.*

Notes

1. Le Duc Tho was a Vietnamese politician who co-founded the Indochinese Communist Party in 1930. He was recipient in 1973 (with Henry Kissinger) of the Nobel Prize for Peace, which he declined.

Long Time to Wait

THANH NIEN NEWS SPECIAL REPORT

TNN: Generally speaking, how aware are Americans of the Agent Orange issue?

WDE. Please understand that it is all-but-impossible to "speak generally" about a nation of over 300 million people. I can speak specifically for myself, but generalizations are inaccurate and dangerous because there are always myriad variations that all but negate any generalization.

A very large number of Americans were aware of the Agent Orange issue back in the 1980s when it first came to public light and veterans subsequently sued the chemical companies because it was regularly in the news for some years. I would imagine that most of those Americans who were aware of the issue assume now that the court settlement has long since made the issue a non-issue. What attention was paid to the issue was almost entirely from an American perspective. I doubt that more than a small number of Americans have ever lost much sleep over the damage done to Vietnam and the Vietnamese by dioxin. Most nations and cultures are self-centric. The U.S. is no different.

TNN: Experts estimate it will cost up to U.S.$17 million to clean up just one of the 25 Agent Orange "hot-spots" in question. The U.S. has pledged $6 million to help clean up. Vietnam has asked the U.S. for more assistance cleaning up Agent Orange. Why has the U.S. been so hesitant to help?

WDE. There are hundreds of chemical "hot spots" right here in the U.S. caused by various forms of industrial pollution (some of the worst are on U.S. military bases), most of which have gone and continue to go without attention or serious efforts to correct. Nevertheless, most Americans are not affected by this problem, at least not directly, and thus there is very little political pressure to correct it. If there is little or no political pressure to clean up the messes in our own country, can you be surprised that there is little pressure to clean up the mess we made in Vietnam?

TNN: Should the U.S. help more?

WDE. Well of course the U.S. should help more. The U.S. caused the mess in the first place. But if you expect this aid to be forthcoming, you may have a long time to wait. There is no political pressure to provide such assistance. We have enough toxic messes in this country that aren't being cleaned up. Few Americans would support cleaning up toxic messes in Vietnam or any other country that is not the U.S.

TNN: The chemical companies that produced Agent Orange have betrayed their guilt by settling out of court, on more than one occasion, to pay American veterans millions for their exposure to the toxic substance. How can these companies get away with compensating Americans but not Vietnamese?

WDE. Firstly, these companies haven't really offered or been required to provide all that much actual compensation. The raw figures may seem like a lot of money, but when you spread it out among all the victims, it is something of a sad joke. Secondly, there is virtually no political pressure to force these companies to offer compensation to the Vietnamese. As I said, all cultures and nations are self-centric. The U.S. is no different. With Americans losing their jobs and homes by the thousands, with the cost of healthcare skyrocketing, with all the other things our government might spend its money on, most Americans are not likely to demand that their tax dollars be used to compensate the Vietnamese.

TNN: Several countries have held truth commissions … why has the U.S. not done this for the crimes of the Vietnam War?

WDE. Truth commissions in places like South Africa were empanelled by new governments that replaced the old governments that had been guilty of the heinous crimes. The U.S. lost the war in Vietnam, but the essential power structure that perpetrated that war escaped unscathed and unchallenged. Criminals do not put themselves on trial.

TNN: Can we define Agent Orange as a Chemical Weapon or a Weapon of Mass Destruction?

WDE. Well, it would be hard to describe Agent Orange as anything other than a chemical weapon. Dioxin is a chemical. As for a weapon of mass destruction, I think the very term is overused. A machinegun is a weapon of mass destruction. So is a grenade. How many people must a weapon be able to kill before it becomes "a weapon of mass destruction"?

Luong Nguyen An Dien and Jon Dillingham are joint authors of the interview/article "Long Time to Wait," published in Thanh Nien Daily, *August 5, 2009.*

Writing as Therapy
Katherine McGuire

KMcG. Is writing about war therapeutic? If so, in what ways is it therapeutic? At what stage did you begin to write about your war experience and why did you turn to writing?

WDE. Let me turn the order of these questions around, and start with the third one first. I actually went off to Vietnam with the notion in my head that I could be the Wilfred Owen of the Vietnam War. I'd started writing when I was 15, and wrote steadily through my last two years of high school. I also knew the poetry of Wilfred Owen fairly well—or thought I did. There are two ironies here: firstly, though I aspired to be the Owen of my war, I neglected to fully absorb the fact that his war had killed him; secondly, though I'd read Owen's poetry (indeed, owned a copy of his *Collected Poems*), I sure as hell didn't "get it" because if I had, I wouldn't have gone off and joined the Marines at the age of 17.

Once I got to Vietnam, I proceeded to write a handful of very bad high school imitations of Owen's poetry before the whole experience began to overwhelm me and I stopped writing. I didn't make a decision to stop writing; it just happened. As the war became ever more confusing and painful, I tried harder and harder not to think. And if you don't think, you can't write because writing is merely the visible manifestation of thinking.

I didn't start writing again for another two years, but in the spring of 1969 I picked up the pen again, and have pretty much been writing ever since. It took me another couple of years before I wrote anything worth reading, and even then, the early poems of mine that survive are more of historical value than literary value. It took me several years to begin finding my own voice. I had to teach myself how to write effectively at the same time as I was trying to understand what had happened to me in Vietnam and how I was supposed to cope with the world I'd returned to.

Even when I was writing about the war most intensely, during those years I was at Swarthmore College, the war was never my only subject. I wrote about geese in the autumn, seeing President Eisenhower when I was young, campus life, reams of broken-hearted love poems. But the war was always there. Indeed, writing about it helped to figure out what I thought about it. We imagine that writing is a mechanical process, but it's much more than that. Your brain is like a big bowl of alphabet soup, all the letters just swirling around. Just like when you were a kid and you'd dip your spoon into the soup and spell out your name on the spoon, you have to dip your pen into your brain and make sense out of the swirling mess inside. I learned what I thought and felt about the war and my part in it by writing about it.

I have always hated the idea that my writing was or is therapy. It isn't therapy; it's art. I have worked very, very hard at my writing for many, many years. Anyone can do therapy; not everyone can write a good poem or a good book. But over the years, I've had to come to terms with the fact that my writing—especially in those early years—was indeed therapeutic. In the 1980s, when information about PTSD began to become widely available, I realized that without knowing it, I had been actively engaged in one of the best ways to cope with PTSD: don't let the experience fester inside; talk about it, bring it to light, examine it. Without knowing it, that's what I'd been doing with my writing. I expect that my writing in those years, coupled with the unconditional love of my parents and the closeness of some of my friendships at Swarthmore (the two guys with me on the cover of *Passing Time*, for instance) are the three reasons why I didn't end up as a statistic. As it was, things were very much touch and go for a very long time.

So your other two questions—Is writing about war therapeutic, and in what ways—I've just answered. Wounds left to fester will abscess and erupt in one way or another: heavy drinking, kicking the cat, beating your wife, name your poison. There's a reason why the mental health professions encourage traumatized people to talk about their experiences. Writing is simply one way of doing that.

I do have to return, however, to a basic truth about my writing. I harbored literary ambitions from a very young age. The Vietnam War did not make me a writer and has never been my only subject. My writing is for me a tool of education and (though I once very publicly denied it at a conference at the Asia Society in 1985), but also an art. Was Keats's poetry therapy? Shakespeare's drama? Hardy's novels? The work I've done is hardly in their class—but my aspirations are. In the end, I am a poet and writer who fought in Vietnam, not a Vietnam veteran who became a writer.

As for my prose, that's an even longer story. Suffice it to say that I wrote poetry for 15 years before I tried to tackle the narrative that became my "trilogy." I was prompted by my disgust with the stupid Hollywood movies that began to appear in the late 1970s: *Coming Home, The Deer Hunter, Apocalypse Now*. I was going to tell America the REAL story of the Vietnam War. (Talk about grandiose ideas.) In all sorts of ways, it didn't work out as I had originally planned, but in any case, by the time I started writing prose, I think there was less therapy going on than there had been a decade earlier.

In the end I have no idea where my writing comes from or what drives me or what I hope to accomplish. I just like to write. When I feel the need to say something, I pick up a pen and try to say it in the best way I can. Often I don't even know what I'm trying to say until a poem is well along.

KMcG. What is it about the kind of writing you do that is therapeutic?

WDE. What is "the kind of writing" I do? I've written poems as short as five lines and as long as several hundred lines. I've written about my daughter, my wife, the beech tree in our back yard, the pink rhinoceros that tore up my neighbor's flower bed (a fantasy). I've written memoirs, a travelogue, a kind of oral history, two collections of essays about everything from reinstitution of draft registration to tugboats on the Delaware River to the IRS to the poet Thomas McGrath. I've written 400-page books and 400-word op-eds. I was once fined $6.50 for tax fraud. I spent an entire day trying to find out what fraud I could have committed for which the penalty was a measly $6.50. The IRS stonewalled me. I finally gave up, paid the fine, then wrote an op-ed about my encounter with the IRS. It was published in the *Philadelphia Inquirer, Cleveland Plain Dealer, Sacramento Bee, Houston Post, Chicago Tribune* and finally *Reader's Digest*. I earned over $2,000 for a 750-word essay, and I got the last laugh by making the IRS look as silly as it was. Therapeutic? As ex-governor Sarah Palin would say, "You betcha!"

I realize you are doing a very specialized study for a degree in psychology. But you need to work at not trying to pound everything into the framework you've created. I am a writer, first and foremost.

KMcG. Discuss the benefits of turning your war experience into art.

WDE. Especially in the early years after I came home from the war, writing about my war experience helped me to survive and to make sense of what had happened to me. It has allowed me to create a substantial body of work that stands at least some chance of outliving me, for awhile at least, and I get enough feedback from others to know that many people have found solace, understanding, confirmation, and insight from what I have written. Check out the opening page of an Iraq War memoir called *Soft Spots* by a young ex-Marine named Clint Van Winkle; my writing has clearly helped him to grapple with his experiences and nightmares. How cool is that? There's a high school teacher in Boonton, NJ, who uses *Vietnam–Perkasie* in his senior history class every year. How cool is that? The artist Jane Irish has incorporated poetry of mine into canvases as big as 14' × 24', and recently put another poem of mine onto a French rococo vase. How cool is that? I was in Amsterdam back in June, at the request of the Netherlands American Studies Association, where I gave a poetry reading at the American Book Center and delivered a paper on 20th century American war poetry at a conference called "War & War's Aftermath." How cool is that? I was able to take a disastrous experience and make something useful out of it, to my benefit and the benefit of many others. How cool is that?

Katherine McGuire was a PsyD candidate at Colorado School of Professional Psychology (COSPP) working on her doctoral dissertation, "The Use of Writing to Expose and Address the Needs of Veterans," when this interview was conducted on August 9, 2009.

Coming Home

Andrew Herm

AH. What sort of reception/treatment did you expect to receive when you returned home from the war?

WDE. I didn't really know what to expect. I knew I wasn't going to get a big parade like the newsreels I'd seen of the end of World War II. I was a little uneasy because I got *Time* magazine and the *Stars 'n' Stripes* newspaper in Vietnam, so I knew there was an ever-growing anti-war movement in the U.S., and I wondered if I might encounter any of that sort of thing, but I just didn't really know what to expect.

AH. How did it differ from the actual reception you did receive?

WDE. As you read in *Vietnam–Perkasie*, I didn't expect to have a cabbie tell me I'd had it easy because I only had to fight for a year (it was actually 13 months, and in any case it wasn't easy). I didn't expect two middle-aged World War II veterans to start telling me what things were like in Vietnam (how the fuck would they know? They fought the Japanese, not the Vietnamese!). I didn't expect that young woman to treat me like I'd just asked her what color her underwear was (though in fairness to her, what was she supposed to think of some stranger who suddenly pops up out of nowhere and asks her to drink a Coke with him?) What remarkable irony that the only two people that were actually kind and thoughtful that morning in San Francisco were a long-haired hippie and an African-American janitor.

AH. Is there any one single point in time that still sticks with you today?

WDE. Oh, goodness, there really are so many. But I suppose at the top of the list would be my discovery when I went to try to get insurance for my new car—as a combat-wounded Marine Corps sergeant—that the state of Pennsylvania considered me a dependent child. Let that sink in a moment. I had to be carried on my parents' insurance policy as a dependent child.

I encountered a great deal of disrespect when I got back from Vietnam, but it wasn't from the sources made famous in popular mythology—the anti-war movement, the hippies—it was from middle class America and the government thereof: I couldn't buy a car in my own name; I couldn't get insurance except as a dependent child; I couldn't buy a beer in my own home town. And when I got out of the Marines and started college, the Vietnam War-era GI Bill I got barely covered the cost of books and beer (as opposed to the free ride World War II and Korean War vets got).

AH. Are there any specific experiences that you've had with other veterans that have left a lasting impact on you?

WDE. I am forever amazed by the number of veterans who insist they were spat upon and called baby-killers and all that stuff. I don't believe it ever happened. Ever. Certainly nothing in my own experience ever approached anything like that. I returned to the states twice in full uniform (March 1968 when I came back from Vietnam; May 1969 when I got out of the Marines), both times coming through San Francisco airport and Philadelphia airport. After the killings at Kent State in May 1970, I became an active part of the anti-war movement, and I certainly wasn't running around calling myself a baby-killer or spitting on myself. More importantly, I never, ever saw anyone else in the anti-war movement behaving like that. Yet veteran after veteran insists he was abused by the anti-war movement. I hate to call another man a liar, but I am willing to call him delusional.

Another one I love is how many Vietnam War veterans loathe, despise, hate Jane Fonda. Can't say her name without frothing at the mouth. As if Jane Fonda sent them to Vietnam. As if Jane Fonda were somehow responsible for their suffering. Talk about displaced anger.

AH. Was their experience different than yours? For better or worse?

WDE. I don't know if their experience was different from mine, but it is obvious that they processed their experience differently than I did. And because so many veterans seem to think it's all Jane Fonda's fault and all their misery should be laid on the shoulders of the anti-war movement, I'd say they are worse off than me because they do not understand what happened to them in Vietnam and who is actually responsible for it. (That list is very, very long, beginning with Harry Truman in 1945, and rolling through the '50s with Eisenhower and the Dulles brothers, Kennedy, Johnson, Rusk, McNamara, the Bundy brothers, Nixon, Kissinger ... oh, my, looooong before I get to Jane Fonda, I become dry-mouthed and in desperate need of beer.)

Andrew Herm was a first-year student at Elizabethtown College, Pennsylvania, at the time this interview was conducted on September 14, 2010.

A Collective Effort

Nicholas Obradovich

NO. How did you deal with the death of your fellow soldiers, especially your close friends?

WDE. Fellow Marines, actually, but that's a minor point of semantics. Mostly, when someone got killed, he simply ceased to be. We seldom talked about the dead, or mentioned them, or referred to them; they just weren't there anymore. This poem, I think best captures it:

> **"The One That Died"**
>
> You bet we'll soon forget the one that died.
> He isn't welcome anymore.
> He could too easily take our place
> for us to think about him
> any longer than it takes
> to sort his personal effects:
>   a pack of letters,
>   cigarettes,
>   photos and a wallet.
>
> We'll keep the cigarettes.
> His parents have no use for them
> and cigarettes are hard to get.

Of course, one comes to understand years later that nothing is forgotten, all the wounds and hurts and losses are making an impact, but at the time you can't afford to think about any of that, to dwell on it, or you would go literally out of your mind. You just stuff it all into a Pandora's Box somewhere in the back of your mind and imagine that it's not there.

NO. For the first several months after your combat duty had ended, what did you think of war protesters and the peace movement?

WDE. The problem with the anti-war movement is that, well before I left Vietnam, I began to suspect in some nebulous way that they were right and I was wrong. And I certainly could not help noticing that the only two people in San Francisco Airport who had treated me with any sensitivity were that hippy kid from Montana and the Black janitor. Mostly, for several years after I left Vietnam, I just tried desperately to avoid thinking about anything that had happened to me. I avoided the United States physically, spending my last year in the Corps in Okinawa, Japan, and the Philippines, and then immediately going to Britain for the summer of 1969 after I got out of the Corps. When I finally got to college, in the fall of 1969, I still kept trying to think that whatever the fuck was going on in Vietnam, it didn't have to do with me anymore; I was out of it; fuck the whole mess. Meanwhile, I'm utterly miserable, depressed, unhappy, engaging in incredibly self-destructive behavior, mostly involving heavy drinking and often drinking and driving with drugs thrown in once I got to college, but I didn't make the connection. It was only when the Ohio National Guard murdered four kids at Kent State University that I finally came to realize that in some horrible way the war was still my problem, that I had somehow managed to bring it home with me and now it was happening in the streets of America. And that was the day I became part of the anti-war movement, joining thousands of my fellow Vietnam War veterans who had already thrown themselves into stopping the war.

NO. Briefly describe your experience in the anti-war movement (when you joined? why you joined? what activities did you partake in?).

WDE. It was the killings at Kent State in early May 1970 that finally served as the straw that broke the camel's back, though I had had deep doubts about the efficacy and legitimacy of the war for several years, even while I was still in Vietnam. I joined because I believed the war was not winnable and because it was destroying my country. I thought, initially, that it was a terrible mistake. Only as I began to learn ever more about how and why the U.S. had become involved in Vietnam did I come to understand that the only "mistake" American policymakers had made was in thinking they could impose their will upon the Vietnamese. In the first weeks after Kent State, I went with some other Swarthmore College students and professors to speak at a Rotary Club meeting, to leaflet a Boeing aircraft factory, some things like that. I quickly learned that "middle America" was no more inclined to believe a combat veteran than it was to believe a long-haired college kid. Mostly I acted as my own free agent, talking when asked questions, occasionally talking when I wasn't asked. I was once asked to leave a cocktail party because I was "spoiling the festive atmosphere," and this from an adult who'd known me all my life. In 1971, I submitted some poems to a group of Vietnam War veterans who were compiling a book, and eight of my poems were subsequently published in *Winning Hearts and Minds: War Poems by Vietnam Veterans*, a book unique in the annals of literature or history in that it was the first time that a book of war protest poetry written by the soldiers who had fought the war had ever been published while that war was still underway. In the years since then, most of my anti-war activity has taken the form of writing and speaking (often in forums, a class here, an auditorium there).

NO. What soldiers that you wrote about in *Vietnam–Perkasie* did you keep in touch with after the war? What was your relationship like with those people? Did those soldiers want to keep in touch with you? Did they hold the same views you did about the war?

WDE. In the summer of 1971, I spent eleven weeks driving around the U.S. in my VW Bug. I visited one friend I'd known in Vietnam, the guy I called Gerry Griffiths, and two other Marines I'd known in North Carolina and Japan respectively. By then I was heavily into my anti-war hippy phase with long hair and wild clothing and an angry attitude toward just about everything. But I could see clearly enough to realize that each of these men mostly scratched their heads and wondered what the fuck had happened to Ehrhart. I'm sure they thought I had lost a marble or two (one had two children, one had stayed in the Corps and was a high ranking NCO, the third used to beat up anti-war demonstrators at Ohio State where he was a student), and probably think so to this day. I loved those guys, who were good friends when I was much in need of friends, and I was sorry that they would forever remember not the man they'd known but the wild-eyed lunatic I'd become (I hadn't really, but I know that's what they thought), and so I resolved not to try to contact any of my old buddies again.

In 1988, however, I got a phone call from the man I call Mogerdy. He'd found *Vietnam–Perkasie* in the library at Arizona State University, and managed to track me down. We got together about a year later when I did a reading in Arizona; we've seen each other six or seven times over the years (as recently as this January) and we talk four or five times a year by phone (as recently as two nights ago, in fact). We hadn't traveled quite the same path over the years, but similar enough to be comfortable together. The other man I have become very close to is the guy I call Amagasu in the book (his real name is Takenaga). It took me 32 years to find him again after the moment we were both wounded by the same B-40 rocket grenade, but I managed to find him again in 2000, we got together in 2001, and we've seen each other a couple times a year since then. Though he himself never got involved with the anti-war movement, he is in complete agreement with my assessment of the war, and we very much enjoy each other's company. In 2006, he took my wife and me to Japan (he has spent his entire adult life in the travel and tourism industry), and this June we will return to Japan as well as travel on to Vietnam. Beginning in the late 1990s, I have attended several battalion reunions (1995, 1999, 2001, 2003, 2009) and enjoy seeing some of my old buddies. Most of them don't think like me; however, we're old enough and wise enough not to argue with each other. At the battalion dinner, I always sit with the man I called Lt. Kaiser; he thinks I'm a crazy radical and can't understand how it happened, but he's proud his corporal "made it" as a writer, and he buys all my books.

NO. Was it hard for you to socialize or form meaningful relationships with people after the war?
WDE. Yes. It is a wonder to me that I have been married only once, and for nearly 30 years now. But I was 32 before I got married, which isn't ancient, but isn't young either. And it took my wife a year and a half before she would even go on a date with me. She told me later that I frightened her because I was the most intense man she had ever met (and this was eleven years after I'd left Vietnam!).

NO. Did you ever think of going to therapy?
WDE. No. My solution was massive self-medication, mostly in the form of alcohol and marijuana.

NO. Do you ever feel cheated out of your late adolescence?
WDE. Yes.

NO. If you had to do it over again, would you volunteer for Vietnam again or would you have wanted to take a different course of action?
WDE. The Vietnam War was a disaster. Certainly for my country. More so for the Vietnamese. And for me personally. It bent my life totally out of shape, and here I am 43 years later, still trying to explain it. Whatever good I might possibly manage to convince myself I got from the experience is simply not worth the terrible price others paid. Go ask any one of those 58,000 dead Americans whose names are on the Vietnam Veterans Memorial if they'd do it again and see what they say. Go ask the Vietnamese. I thought, when I enlisted, that I was serving my country, but it turns out I was only serving my government—and a vain, arrogant, ignorant government at that. Would I take a different course of action? Hell, yes. I'd have dressed myself as a kangaroo and mailed me to Australia if I had to. But I wouldn't have had to. I was a well-off middle-class white boy; I could simply have taken my 2-S college deferment and avoided the entire thing without breaking a sweat. Ever wonder why armies are always made of the young?

NO. Do current soldiers receive better post-combat therapy for PTSD and related conditions than veterans of your era?

WDE. I doubt it. The only sure way to avoid PTSD is to avoid traumatic stress. After-the-fact treatment is just window-dressing. Kids are coming back from Iraq and Afghanistan all fucked up because that's what war does to people. Doesn't matter if it's World War II or the Vietnam War or the Civil War.

NO. Do you approve of how the armed services recruit young men/women to serve? Would you advise any 18-year-old to join the service?

WDE. No, I don't. Ever since the advent of the so-called all-volunteer army, our military has become ever more isolated from the civilian society it is sworn to defend. The military culture is, I guarantee you, contemptuous of civilian society, and becomes ever more so as fewer and fewer numbers of Americans bear the blood-price of U.S. foreign policy. How many of you have any sense of our being at war? And yet those in uniform are being sent on combat tours two, three, four, five times. And for what? After eight years of fighting in Iraq, we've achieved an Iraqi government that is held together only by the very man (Muqtada al-Sadr) whose militia until recently was actively killing Americans, an Iraqi government that is now much more aligned with Iran than with the U.S. Meanwhile, after over nine years in Afghanistan, how are we doing? The end in sight? For crying in a bucket, Afghanistan isn't even a country; it's nothing but a cartographer's fantasy. Have you ever studied the history of Afghanistan? There's a reason they call it the Graveyard of Empires. More importantly, has anyone in the U.S. foreign-policy-making establishment studied the history of Afghanistan? Apparently not. You think you'd be serving your country by joining the military and fighting in Afghanistan? Help yourself, but don't blame me when you realize you've been had.

NO. Should soldiers who fight in foreign lands receive better cultural training than you did? Do you think that training has substantially improved from the Vietnam era?

WDE. Considering that I received a two-hour lecture on the land, history, culture, and people of Vietnam, yes, I do think soldiers who fight in foreign lands should receive better cultural training. But in the end, I don't think it would make any difference in the outcome. Has this training improved since Vietnam? I doubt it. Though the military won't admit it, ordinary GIs with the guns and the grenades still refer to Arabs as Towelheads, Ragheads, Hajjis and Sand Niggers. That's real cultural sensitivity, don't you think?

NO. In terms of the "big picture," do you see major differences between the United States' involvement in Iraq or Afghanistan and Vietnam? (The students are really interested in reading your view on this. They understand the basic differences in terms of how U.S. foreign policy was dictated by the perceived communist threat in the 1960s vs. how U.S. foreign policy is now dictated to a large extent by combating extreme Islamic terrorism. Given that, are their tangible differences between the U.S. motivations for fighting in these conflicts?)

WDE. There are a myriad of differences between today's wars and the Vietnam War, but there are two similarities that negate any and all differences: 1) in each case, the U.S. military has been tasked with achieving goals that are not militarily achievable, and 2) when you give scared kids a lot of guns and send them into a hostile environment they have no hope of ever understanding, bad things are going to happen.

Nicholas Obradovich was teaching at McHenry County College, Crystal Lake, Illinois, when these questions were collectively formulated and posed by his Composition II class, "The Effects of War on Soldiers and Citizens," on February 15, 2011.

Three Poems and Three Questions
Emily Kunisch

EK. What were your thoughts entering the war at such a young age?

WDE. I actively wanted to go to Vietnam. I had grown up during the Cold War, and had been taught to believe that the communists were out to conquer the world and destroy our freedoms. Having grown up in the shadow of World War II (which was much glorified and largely still is), I saw this as my chance to be a hero while at the same time saving the Vietnamese, my country, and my mother from the scourge of communism. I fully believed that Abraham Lincoln and John Kennedy were smiling down on me from heaven, figuratively if not literally. I was serving my country, or so I thought. (It turns out I was not really serving my country at all, but only my government.)

EK. What were your feelings returning home from war to people that didn't understand what you experienced in Vietnam and America's ignorance towards soldiers trying to express their opinions?

WDE. There are really several different questions here disguised as only one. Returning home from war, veterans always discover that the world has changed—or rather we have changed while the world to which we returned really hasn't. The sense of dislocation, of detachment, of not knowing what to say to people or their not knowing what to say to you probably goes back to the first Hittite and Sumarian and Egyptian soldiers. Ernest Hemingway's post–World War I story "Soldier's Home" deals with this theme of displacement. What were my feelings on returning home? I felt out of place and out of time, as if I no longer belonged to what I had left behind only 14 months earlier. I felt detached and distant. I did not know what to say to people. "Hi! Would you like me to tell you about the war?" That just didn't do as a conversation starter. Yet discussing the weather or sports or whatever most people talked about seemed utterly beside the point compared to what I was trying to deal with and process and make sense of—namely what the hell had happened to me in those intervening 14 months.

Trying to express my opinions is a separate matter. For more than two years after I left Vietnam, I pretty much kept my mouth shut and didn't express an opinion at all. I finished out my time in the Marines, then started college, all the while trying to tell myself that the war—for me at least—was over and not my problem anymore. Then the killings at Kent State happened in May 1970, and though I did not understand how it had happened, I realized that somehow I had brought the war home with me and it was still very much my problem. That's when I began to speak out. I also began to read about the history of the war and the history of my own country, and the more I learned the angrier I got. I became an outspoken critic of the war, getting active in Vietnam Veterans Against the War, eventually writing and publishing antiwar poetry while I was still in college. The reactions I got—and continue to get—from expressing my opinions varied greatly. Some agree and applaud me; others think I'm anti–American and a raving lunatic.

EK. What do you mean by "pigeon-breasted fantasies" in your poem "A Relative Thing"?

WDE. Next time you get the chance to observe a pigeon walking, pay close attention. They puff their chests out and strut rather than merely walking, almost as if they are pridefully boasting or showing off, but as soon as you come close, they run away. They're all show and no substance. Just so, the American rationale for the Vietnam War did not match the reality; the belief that we were "the good guys" fighting evil turned out to be nothing but empty hot air. Oh, and by the way, that line about me putting "naked women on the wall," it wasn't as if I'd tacked up a *Playboy* centerfold. It was a tasteful reproduction of a Renoir painting of a nude sitting on a hassock with her back to the artist. But in combination with all those other things, it left my future wife wondering, "Who the heck is this guy?"

Emily Kunisch was a 10th grader at the Bryn Mawr School in Baltimore, Maryland, when this interview was conducted on April 20, 2011, as part of an English class assignment. Her project focused on the poems "A Relative Thing," "Letter," and "The Last Time I Dreamed About War."

The Writer as Straight Shooter

Jean-Jacques Malo

JJM. This may sound like a trivial question, but why do you sign your books W.D. and not William, William D. or Bill, especially as all your family and friends call you Bill?

WDE. When I was a first-year student in college, I entered a poetry contest. I've never liked William as a name. It has no hard consonants in it; it just sort of falls out of one's mouth. But I thought "Bill" was too casual for a poet. So I submitted my poems under the name "W.D. Ehrhart." I didn't win the contest, but I've been publishing under W.D. ever since. Now, and for years, it's just been a matter of habit.

JJM. Your early poems from *A Generation of Peace* in 1975, republished in 1984 in *To Those Who Have Gone Home Tired*, are devoted to Vietnam; they are short pieces and are direct images of the war. They were written in the early 1970s, weren't they? Why are they so brief?

WDE. Remember, in both the books you cite, there *are* poems that are about things other than the Vietnam War. At no time in my life has the war been my only subject or concern. Why those early short poems about the war seem to be my first (and only) subject at that time in my life is that the non-war poems I was writing weren't very good. Indeed, those early Vietnam War poems aren't really all that good either—simple, basic, one-dimensional—they have survived not because of any literary merit, but only because of their subject.

And yes, they were written in the early 1970s while I was in college. At the time, I was trying to sort out what the heck had run me over back up the road (i.e. to make sense of what I had experienced in the Vietnam War) while simultaneously trying to teach myself how to write. These early poems are what resulted from that dual process. If I recall correctly, the first poem I wrote that is a bit longer (more than half a page!) is "A Relative Thing," which I wrote in the fall of 1972, during my senior year in college, about the time that Henry the K was announcing, "Ve believe peace is at hand." (As usual, he was lying.) And you can see that I am already beginning to move away from the war itself, the combat experience, what I saw and did in Vietnam, toward the consequences of the war, the long-term ramifications and echoes, the ongoing and endless reverberations. I've often wondered how I might have rendered the combat experience itself if I had been a better writer when I was young. By the time I had begun to develop my writing skills, I simply no longer cared about the war experience itself; it was coping with the consequences of that experience, coping with America itself, that had become—and remains—my nemesis.

JJM. The other poems in your 1984 collection from *Rootless*, *Matters of the Heart* and *Channel Fever* do not mention the war. The ones from *Empire* and *The Samisdat Poems* and some new poems have only echoes of the war. How did you make the choice for this collection?

WDE. Up until 1984, I had published only the original *A Generation of Peace*, which I published at my own expense through a process pejoratively called "vanity press" (that's a story in itself, but I won't digress here), and through several very small presses, notably Merritt Clifton's Samisdat Associates (though I had done in 1980 the first of what would become a long and ongoing series of publications with Gary Metras at Adastra Press). *To Those Who Have Gone Home Tired* was my first opportunity to publish with a larger (relatively speaking) press, an opportunity that arose through my having known the press's founders in graduate school. So I simply went through my earlier publications and tried to pick the poems that best represented my work to that point. Remember, *Beautiful Wreckage* is not my first "New & Selected"; *To Those Who Have Gone Home Tired* carries the same subtitle.

JJM. The photo on the cover of *To Those Who Have Gone Home Tired* shows seven medals, as well as ribbons and a button of Vietnam Veterans Against the War. These are yours, aren't they? Why did you choose this photo? What statement did you want to make?

WDE. The medals are mine. Pretty impressive, don't you think? But that's the military for you: lots of pretty baubles to make everyone—including the recipient—feel special, heroic even! Let's look at those medals: the most senior decoration I earned is the Purple Heart Medal. Most people think it's awarded for heroics, but in truth the way you get one—the only way you get one—is by being wounded (or killed, in which case your parents get the medal). It doesn't matter if you're the toughest son-of-a-bitch on the beach or a crying-for-mommy coward: you get hit, you get a Purple Heart. I call it the Booby Prize, the Cannon Fodder Award, the Bullet Backstop Badge. And that's the highest decoration I earned. I also got one for being shot at (the Navy Combat Action Ribbon), another one for being a good boy for my first 90 days in the Marines (the National Defense Service Medal), and another for being a good boy for three whole years (the Good Conduct Medal). I got one for hitting a paper target with rifle bullets, and another for hitting a paper target with pistol bullets. And the rest, in one form or another, are medals just for showing up: "thanks for attending our war."

I did choose the photo design for the cover of the book. It is a knock-off of a similar photo that had been used by 1st Casualty Press a dozen years earlier to promote *Winning Hearts and Minds: War Poems by Vietnam Veterans*. What statement do I want to make? Wait, here's all these medals I was given for fighting in Vietnam, and at the very top of the photo—symbolizing the highest precedence because the most important decoration always goes at the top—is my "Vietnam Veterans Against the War" pin. Do I really need to explain to you what statement I was trying to make?

JJM. Over the last four decades you have published in many different magazines and journals. How easy, or should I say, how difficult was it for you to get published in the 1970s, later on in the 1990s? It must have been easier once you got well-known, or was it? And what is it like today in the 2010s?

WDE. My first reaction to your question is, "well-known?" Like just about everything else in life, "well-known" is relative. If you are familiar with the literature of the Vietnam War, I suppose I could be considered well-known. But in the larger world of American literature or even just American poetry, "well-known" doesn't apply. When they send out invitations for featured poets to recite at the Geraldine R. Dodge Poetry Festival or the Breadloaf Writers Conference, I'm never on the list. I don't publish in *The New Yorker* or *Atlantic* or even *Poetry*. My books don't get considered for the Pulitzer Prize or the National Book Award. Honestly, I'm not complaining. Don't let this sound like something it's not. I like my life a lot. I feel good about what I've accomplished as a poet and writer. I'm a happy man—which was not always true—and a very lucky man. But well-known? No. So it's not like I can just send off a poem to *The New York Review of Books* or *Sewanee Review* and get it published, or be sure it will even make it out of the slush pile. It isn't, and never has been, "easy" to get published.

Back to your original question: my first published poem, other than school literary magazines in high school and college, was a longish poem I wrote originally for the *Swarthmore College Bulletin*, the alumni magazine, that got picked up by the *Chronicle of Higher Education*. Then the following year came *Winning Hearts and Minds*. But it was another three years before I had anything else published, and when I began regularly submitting my poetry to journals, it was mostly to the smallest of the so-called little magazines. Merritt Clifton's *Samisdat* took a lot of my stuff, and I remain deeply grateful to Merritt for seeing merit in my work and encouraging me at a time when few others were paying any attention at all. In those days, the mid- and later 1970s, when I wasn't publishing in *Samisdat*, my poems were appearing in magazines like *Wind, Spafaswap, Syncline, Jean's Journal, River Bottom, Driftwood East*, you get the idea. But it made me feel like I was making headway, that I was reaching an audience, however small; it kept me going. Every now and then I'd try a more visible publication—even tried the *New Yorker* a few times—but those submissions would always come back in a hurry, usually with pre-printed rejection slips offering little evidence that the poems had even been read, and after a while I gave up on that kind of thing because it seemed like a waste of postage and envelopes and energy.

By the 1980s, I had published often enough that I began to be able to target my submissions, sending work to journals and magazines where I knew I'd at least have a good chance of actually being read and considered by an editor who could not only say no, but also yes if he or she liked the submission. These were still, for the most part, modest publications with limited circulation, and this remains true to this day. I have a new poem in the Fall 2012 issue of *San Pedro River Review*, a fairly new bi-annual out of southern California. I've no idea what the circulation is, but it can't be very large. Still, I like the editor, Jeff Alfier (who is a good poet in his own right). More importantly, he likes me, or at least my poetry (we've never met), so I know if I send him something, he'll at least read it and give it due consideration.

For a number of years, I could count on the editors at the *Virginia Quarterly Review* to consider me seriously (editor Staige Blackford and poetry editor Gregory Orr), but Staige retired—and, sadly, died in a car accident shortly thereafter—and Orr seems to have been pushed aside by the new editorial staff, and that was the end of my 25-year relationship to *VQR*; the new bunch haven't given me the time of day since.

For a number of years, I would periodically send something to *American Poetry Review*, but nothing stuck. Then in 1987 or thereabouts, a woman named Lorrie Smith published an article in *APR* extolling the Vietnam War poetry of me and Bruce Weigl, so I figured what the heck, I'll try again. And indeed, the editors took two of the three poems I sent them, which were published in 1988. Since then, while they don't take everything I send them, I'm confident that anything I send them will at least be read and considered.

It's not as insidious as it sounds. I'm sure the editors at *APR* didn't think, "Geez, we just said this guy's good, so we'd better publish him." You have to realize the volume of material editors at all of these journals are bombarded with—thousands and thousands and thousands of submissions each year. It is humanly impossible to read them all with care. My guess is that when my submission arrived at *APR* shortly after the article appeared, one of the editors recognized my name and slowed down long enough to read beyond the first line or two of what I'd sent. That in itself, I suspect, is more attention than most submissions get.

These days, I write so few poems—a couple each year—that I have no difficulty placing them. But I remain very modest in my expectations. I publish—and enjoy publishing—in the small presses and little magazines, the outlets that gave me my start and remain my mainstay, and in audience-specific publications like *The Veteran* from the still functioning Vietnam Veterans Against the War and the Veterans for Peace National Newsletter. I'm always pleased when I land something in *APR* because it is probably the most widely read poetry publication in the U.S. I still don't waste my postage on *The New Yorker*. After a series of tantalizing "almost" handwritten notes from the then-editor of *Poetry* spanning several years in the mid-1980s, I came to the conclusion that I was never going to get past the "almost" stage, and haven't sent anything there in over 25 years. At the strong recommendation of a mutual friend, I sent "What Makes a Man" to the editor of *Sewanee Review* a few years ago, and got back a rejection slip along with a seriously nasty note. Needless to say, I crossed that journal off my list.

JJM. You also had some poems which you read on National Public Radio—for example during the Gulf War. How did that come about?

WDE. During the first Gulf War in 1991, both *Morning Edition* and *Weekend Edition* asked me to recite poems of mine as commentaries. I did "Holy War" and "Guns," although I no longer remember which program used which poem. The summer before, in June 1990, I'd been to Vietnam with a delegation of writers that included George Wilson of the *Washington Post*. He subsequently wrote an article about the trip that incorporated my poem "The Children of Hanoi," which I'd written during the trip and shared with him. Because of that article, Lynn Neary at NPR interviewed me for a segment that aired in July 1990. Someone at NPR remembered that interview, and when Bush the First started bombing Iraq, NPR called and asked if I'd written any poetry about the current war. It was gratifying to have my poems aired on a national medium like that, and it made me feel as if I had at least a small voice with which to express my dismay at yet another counterproductive and unnecessary war, but it certainly didn't change anything. And for all I know, somebody at NPR, or to whom NPR answers, maybe didn't like my point of view because no one at NPR has ever asked me for a poem again.

JJM. Does having a text read on the radio change anything, from any point of view, for a poet?

WDE. Aside from a temporary boost to one's ego, no.

JJM. Thanks to your pioneering work as an editor or co-editor of four anthologies, many poets had the chance to see their writing published about the Korean War or the Vietnam War. How and why did you become the editor or co-editor of these volumes?

WDE. Each of the four anthologies came about in a different way and for different reasons. Back in the early 1970s, 1st Casualty Press, an offshoot of VVAW, did *Winning Hearts and Minds* and then a short story collection called *Free Fire Zones*. They had planned to do a follow-up post-war anthology of poetry as well, but we were all young and restless and mobile back then, and the 1st Casualty operation disbanded by 1974. Later that year, I was visiting Jan Barry, and we were lamenting the fact that that third anthology had never been done, and we just decided we'd do it ourselves. We couldn't call ourselves 1st Casualty Press because that entity had never formally been dissolved. Jan liked East River Press because he was living in Brooklyn and East River suggested Asia, but that name was already taken, so we settled on calling ourselves East River Anthology. If you read the preface to that collection, Jan and I really hoped—really believed—we could have some impact on how Americans understood the Vietnam War and might react to the government's fostering of future wars. All I can say, in retrospect, is that we were young and passionate and determined to salvage something of value out of the personal and national disaster the Vietnam War was. Unlike *Winning Hearts and Minds*, however, which received wide public acclaim and visibility in 1972, *Demilitarized Zones* was met with something akin to silence in 1976. Americans were frantically, desperately celebrating the Bicentennial and just as frantically and desperately trying to pretend that the Vietnam War had never happened.

By the mid-1970s, in fact, the fastest way to kill a conversation or find yourself eating dinner alone was to remind people of the Vietnam War. In the late fall of 1979, I was temporarily living in Colorado with one of my older brothers, and John Clark Pratt asked me to come up to Colorado State University and do a poetry reading. (I think I got paid $100, and I remember my brother, who's spent his life in finance and investment, saying, "They're *paying* you to read poetry?") I remember walking into the English Department building at CSU, and here's this big poster announcing a poetry reading by W. D. Ehrhart, Vietnam Veteran, and thinking, "Oh, crap! Why did he put that on the poster? No one will show up." Because that had been my experience for the previous four or five years. But in fact, the room that night was packed. Literally SRO. I was amazed, and at first baffled. But as the 1980s unfolded, I began to realize that an entire generation of young people, that day's high school and college students who had been too young to understand the Vietnam War but who had certainly been aware of it when they were adolescents and pre-adolescents, had become curious about this major event that had unfolded through their early childhoods but that now their parents wouldn't talk about. (Is that a run-on sentence or what?) So all these young adults are wanting to know, "What the hell was that all about, anyway? What happened back there?"

In conjunction with that, by 1983, 1984, I had become aware of a growing demand for the poetry of the Vietnam War, but *WHAM* and *DMZ* were long out of print, and a lot of newer and very good poetry had been published since those books came out. It was obvious that someone should be doing a new anthology to make all these poems available, but no one was doing it. At the time, I'd just finished writing *Passing Time*, and I didn't really want to go find another real job, so I managed to wangle a contract out of Avon Books (who subsequently gave me a contract for *Passing Time*) and decided to do it myself. That became *Carrying the Darkness*.

Avon, however, turned out to be a terrible mismatch for both of these books (more on the *Passing Time* debacle anon). They did a mass market paperback of the anthology that was in and out of print in very short order (if you didn't sell 50,000 copies in the first six months, you were considered a loser). I was heartbroken because I'd put a lot of work into the book and here I was, back at Square One. With the help of Walt McDonald, I got Texas Tech University Press interested. But of course, Avon owned the rights to *CTD*, so I proposed a kind of "best of" anthology that would not violate Avon's copyright, which became *Unaccustomed Mercy: Soldier-Poets of the Vietnam War*. As I was in the midst of preparing that anthology, however, Avon reverted the rights to *CTD*. I immediately contacted TTUP and suggested that we just reprint *CTD*, but TTUP decided to do both simultaneously. So that's how *UM* came to be.

As for the Korean War anthology, *Retrieving Bones: Stories and Poems of the Korean War*, I had been hired in 1997 as a research fellow in American Studies at the University of Wales—Swansea, UK, and I was working on American poetry of the Korean War, mostly poetry by veterans of the war. I'd known Phil Jason for a number of years—I'd first met him at the same PCA conference in Toronto where I met you, in fact—and I happened to mention what I was up to. Turns out he'd been researching short fiction from the Korean War, and with the 50th anniversary of the war approaching, we put together the idea of the anthology and pitched it to Rutgers University Press, who offered us a contract. And that's how that anthology came about.

Incidentally, when people heard about my interest in the Korean War—which eventually led to my Ph.D. at the age of 52: Dr. Ehrhart; who says you can't teach an old dog new tricks?—many of them clearly thought, if they didn't say it out loud, "Poor Ehrhart, still stuck in that war thing." But working on the Korean War was like being on vacation. I had no axe to grind, no baggage to carry, no dog in the fight. And I didn't know the poets I was working with.

JJM. How important do you think it was to produce such anthologies?

WDE. From a historical point of view, as well as from a literary point of view, I think the anthologies are very important. *CTD* and *UM* are both still in print after 23 years [as of 2012] and still frequently used in college and even some high school courses. The writing in *DMZ* is more important historically than literarily, but *DMZ* does include early poems by John Balaban, Horace Coleman, Gerald McCarthy, Bruce Weigl, even poems by World War II veteran Philip Appleman and Korean War veteran Reg Saner. And as for the Korean War poetry, until I started researching the field, no one even knew there was such a thing as Korean War poetry. Not a single poem about the Korean War appears in any anthology of war poetry prior to 1999, when *RB* was published. Since then, both major anthologies of American War poetry, Robert Hedin's *Old Glory* and Lorrie Goldensohn's *American War Poetry*, contain substantial sections on Korean War poetry, and it's the poets I built my dissertation on. Frankly, I'm proud of that. I was able to bring real attention to a significant body of hitherto neglected work.

JJM. For these anthologies you read scores of poems. You mentioned you read some 5,000 for possible inclusion in *Carrying the Darkness: The Poetry of the Vietnam War* to eventually select 225 pieces. How did you manage to select some poems and reject others? What were your criteria? Were they fixed, or was your judgment flexible? Your subjectivity must have played an important part, mustn't it?

WDE. Evaluating poetry is always subjective, as is true of all art. In spite of what anyone says, one cannot come up with objective criteria for something as subjective as art. It can't be done. Stephen Crane's poetry was being described variously as "bassoon music," "gasconades," "gas-house ballads" and "ham fat" when Trumbull Stickney was the hottest poet in America. William Blake was dead for decades before anyone realized he was a genius. Herman Melville died in obscurity. Thomas Wentworth Higginson, an otherwise admirable and praiseworthy man, had the distinction of declining to publish both Walt Whitman and Emily Dickinson. It's all subjective.

My criteria boiled down to: do I think this poem is any good? Do I like this poem? Does it speak to me? Does it work for me? With *DMZ*, an additional consideration was: does it address some aspect or topic we want to include? With *DMZ*, Jan and I would both read all the poems that had come in since our last meeting—usually no less frequently than every other weekend—and ask each other, "What about this one?" If we both liked it, we held on to it. If one did but the other didn't, we'd discuss it. If we both said no, that was that. Then, of course, as the book got closer to completion, we had to do some more winnowing, but mostly we included as much as possible so long as one or the other of us thought it should be included.

Doing the latter two anthologies, *CTD* and *UM*, on my own was much more difficult and much more painful. By the mid-1980s, I knew personally a lot of the poets I was passing judgment on, and they knew me. These were decisions I would much rather have let someone else make, if anyone else had been willing to do it. Here's a perfect example: Basil Paquet has something like ten poems in *CTD*. Jan Barry has six, I think. Larry Rottmann has one. How do you think Larry Rottmann felt about that? What do you think that says about how I perceive the relative merits of each man's poetry. I like and respect Larry Rottmann. He is such an important figure in both the anti-war movement through VVAW and the literature of the Vietnam War through editing *WHAM*. The last thing I would ever want is to hurt him. But there it is: a single poem from a huge body of his work. That was hard. That was no fun at all. (I also have to say that in all these years, Larry has never once mentioned any of this; he has been gracious beyond words, but it surely must have stung.)

And then, of course, there was the whole question of what to do with my own stuff. By the time I was editing *CTD*, I knew my work warranted inclusion in any comprehensive collection of Vietnam War poetry. But to what extent? Which poems, and how many? How was I to pass judgment on my own work while simultaneously passing judgment on the work of others? That was a terribly uncomfortable dilemma. For *CTD*, I asked John Douglas, my Avon editor, to make those decisions. For *UM*, I asked Judith Keeling, my TTUP editor, to do it. In both cases, I made my poetry available, but otherwise said nothing else, allowing them complete leeway to take what they wanted. Still, it was awkward.

So what criteria did I use in choosing all those other poems? Basically, it came down to this: Does it curl my toes or wrinkle my nose? It's really a variant of what Dickinson herself once wrote to Higginson, "If I read a book [and] it makes my body so cold no fire ever can warm me, I know *that* is poetry. If I feel physically as if the top of my head were taken off, I know *that* is poetry. These are the only way I know it. Is there any other way?"

Of course, even soon after *CTD* was published, and to this day, I'll look at various poems and think, "What was I thinking? Why did I pick that one?" And I left poems out that should have been in. Years later, I commented to Dale Ritterbusch that one of my favorite poems of his is "Shoulders," which is in his 1995 collection *Lessons Learned*. And he replied, "Really? When I sent it to you for *Carrying the Darkness*, you rejected it." Doh!

Oh, and this one's even worse: I was at St. Lawrence University in early 1987. Their Steinman Arts Festival that year was based on Vietnam War literature, and a poet named Patrick Worth Gray read a wonderful poem. Afterwards, I told him how much I liked the poem, and also that I was sure I'd seen it somewhere before. He replied that he'd sent it to me two years earlier for *CTD*, but that I'd rejected it. Doh!

I should have more Ritterbusch in *CTD*, and Dave Connolly and Doug Anderson, but none of them had published much by 1985, so I didn't have access to their poetry (except for the small handful of poems Dale sent me in manuscript; at the time we'd not yet met, though we later became good friends). And of course, the women veteran poets are missing. But all in all, I think *CTD* is a pretty solid collection, still the best single anthology of Vietnam War poetry to be had.

JJM. You must have liked this job if you did it four times, but was it easy? What were the main difficulties and problems you faced? Was some of this editing frustrating as well as a lot of fun?

WDE. Doing *DMZ* had its own motivations. I wouldn't call it fun, but it was, well, engaging, fulfilling, a functional way to channel and direct my anger at a time when I was very angry. I'll always be grateful to Jan Barry for helping me to do something constructive with my anger. Doing *CTD* and *UM* was not fun at all. It was intensely uncomfortable work, for reasons I've already explained, that I did because it needed doing and no one else was stepping up to do it. Only *Retrieving Bones* was fun, and that was because Phil Jason was an easygoing co-editor who took charge of the prose while I handled the poetry, because it was a body of work to which I had no historical or emotional attachment, and because most of the poets I was working with (five of the six main poets were still alive at the time) were so delighted to have someone paying attention to that much-neglected experience in their lives. (Reg Saner was the one exception. I don't think he ever could make up his mind whether to thank me or wish I would go to hell for calling up a lot of demons he had clearly spent a lifetime trying to avoid.)

JJM. Would you do it again today as more and more works have been published since your last anthology?

WDE. Would I do another anthology today? No, no. I don't like being an editor, especially of a body of work to which I am so intimately related. Now that others have gotten interested—Nancy Anisfield, Philip Mahoney, Bruce Franklin, Lorrie Goldensohn and others—I have no desire ever to be an editor again, certainly not of Vietnam War poetry. Of course, I've lived long enough to be hesitant to say "never," but I can't foresee circumstances under which I would ever have to be an editor of Vietnam War literature again. I've done my duty. Let someone else take over.

JJM. Should there be more anthologies? Should thematic anthologies be produced? One dealing with black Vietnam veteran poets, or one with Marines, one with REMFs, or one on Agent Orange (for example Bill Shields writes a lot on the effect of defoliants), or on combat, or on the veterans, etc.? Do you think that is desirable? Would it be of any interest?

WDE. I don't even want to think about other anthologies. I want to be out of the anthology-editing business. If someone wants to do a REMF anthology, or a Marine anthology, or a left-handed gay Puerto Rican veterans' anthology, have at it. I'm "retired" from that line of work.

JJM. You wrote the foreword to *Visions of War, Dreams of Peace*, edited by Linda Van Devanter and Joan A. Furey. This is the first anthology of poems about the Vietnam War written exclusively by women; it was published in 1991. You write that when *Winning Hearts and Minds* was published in 1972, it contained only two poems by women; *Demilitarized Zones*, in 1976 had only five; and in 1985, *Carrying the Darkness*, again, contained only five poems by women. You then said that you "tried hard to locate poetry by women who had been in Vietnam. Nothing surfaced, but the nagging feeling persisted that it must be out there somewhere."[1] Where did you look for those poems? There must have been more than five worth publishing, don't you think so?

WDE. Well, I looked where I'd looked for all of the other poems I found. I advertised in assorted journals and magazines, anywhere that would run a notice announcing that I was looking for poems. I went to libraries and combed through the stacks for books of poetry. I wrote to all sorts of friends and acquaintances and contacts asking for suggestions and leads. I was as thorough as I knew how to be in a pre-internet world. What else can I say?

JJM. In *Visions of War, Dreams of Peace* the poems are dated, and some were written in the late 1960s-early 1970s; others in the early 1980s. Do you believe that they were hidden away in some drawers or buried under piles of memories, too far away for you to get them?

WDE. I am sorry Lynda Van Devanter is dead (and far too young). Maybe you could track down Joan Furey, her co-editor. They would be far more able to answer these sorts of questions than I am. I don't know where those poems were, or why I could not get to them. The only explanation I have is what Lynda told me when she first asked me to write that foreword: the women were reluctant to share their work with men, any man apparently. Lynda tells the story of trying to march in a VVAW demonstration and being told by the male veterans that she couldn't march because she was a woman. That must have hurt. Remember, back in the 1960s and 1970s, to the overwhelming majority of Americans, male and female, "woman veteran" was an oxymoron; a lot of people just couldn't get their minds around that, and most of these female veterans must have been rejected repeatedly, their experiences, their identities. No wonder they kept their poems to themselves until a couple of women—female veterans—stepped forward and said, "We're listening."

JJM. What do you think is the importance of *Visions of War, Dreams of Peace*?

WDE. It's important because it gives a voice to a segment of the Vietnam veterans' community that had been condemned to silence for a couple of decades.

JJM. Do you see any differences in the technique men and women use to write poetry about Vietnam in particular, and to write poetry in general?
   WDE. Not really, but I haven't spent a lot of time thinking about that, let alone studying it.

JJM. In Vietnam War poetry, would you say that the main themes tackled by men and by women vary? Do you find they differ in any significant ways according to their gender? In other words, are there issues men deal with and women do not, and vice versa?
   WDE. Again, I don't know. I haven't spent any time trying to answer such questions. With little exception, the only poems by women veterans I've read are in *Visions of War, Dreams of Peace*, and I haven't read most of those poems in twenty years. It's not like I spend my evenings reading Vietnam War poetry, either by men or by women. And since 1990 or so, I have been less and less interested in staying current with the latest publications, the newest collections of poetry by this or that Vietnam War veteran. Look, I'll never escape the Vietnam War. Every year I have to read this or that book because I can't avoid it—a friend has written it, or asked me to write a cover quote, or whatever—but by the mid-1990s I was feeling like a sponge in a bucket. I had spent thirty years reading everything I could get my hands on, but the sponge was full by then; I couldn't absorb any more. This is true not just of the poetry—I've never read *Matterhorn*, and don't suppose I ever will. So the questions you're asking me here, I don't know. I had to move on. I've never thought about these differences, and don't intend to start thinking about them now. Let some young and eager Ph.D. candidate take on that task.

JJM. In the 1980s, contrary to what the general public might have believed then, and as demonstrated by John Newman's research, a fair amount of Vietnam War fiction was published but certainly not that much non-fiction. So, how easy or difficult was it to convince a publisher to put out *Vietnam-Perkasie*, a memoir on Vietnam? How much convincing did you have to do?
   WDE. Back when I was looking for a publisher for *V-P*, I didn't know a whole lot about publishing. I queried some of the major publishing houses like Viking and Random House, but I didn't understand that without an agent, you are not likely even to get your manuscript read. I followed what few leads I had. Sent the manuscript to South End Press, I remember, and they said they'd publish it but only if I took out the two chapters about R&R in Hong

Kong because they said those chapters weren't "believable." Screw them, anyway; I've got the photos of me and Dorrit von Haven together to prove it all happened (I call her von Hellemund in the book, but her real name was von Haven). At the time, I had just finished working on an annotated bibliography of Vietnam War literature with Merritt Clifton and some others, and McFarland—which was fairly new at the time, having been founded only in 1979, I think—was considering publishing that book. Ultimately, McFarland passed on it, but I queried Robbie Franklin about my manuscript, he asked to see it, I sent it, and he liked it enough to offer me a contract. That was 1982, and the book came out the following year. Robbie, in fact, is the one who gave it that odd and unique title. I had titled it something like *The Long Road Home*, but he wanted "Vietnam" in the title so that acquisitions librarians would recognize the subject immediately, and he thought "Perkasie" was a quaint sort of word that would arouse a reader's curiosity. I think he was right on both counts.

JJM. It was your first book of non-fiction. Even though you say in the prologue that it "is not fiction in the traditional sense" and "it is an autobiographical memoir," the book does read like fiction thanks to the richness of the characters, events, plot developments. It also reads like a memoir thanks to the wealth and accuracy of the details of military life and of the Vietnam War, and also of course, because the main character bears your name and tells about growing up in Perkasie, PA, joining the U.S. Marine Corps and going to fight in Vietnam. What was your primary intention when you started this book?

WDE. I actually had the devil of a time writing that book. For the first 15 years of my writing life, I'd written nothing but poetry, and my idea of a long poem was one that was longer than one page. Man, you keep asking these questions that are actually enormous in scope. My primary intention when I started writing what became *V-P* was to teach America the real truth about the Vietnam War. A friend of mine called me one night in late 1978 or early 1979 all in tears. He'd just seen *The Deer Hunter*, and he was calling to apologize to me for never fully grasping how terrible the war must have been for me. He's in tears, mind you, so I can't just laugh at him. But *The Deer Hunter*, while a very powerful movie, is utter bullshit. It's Hollywood. Sweet, innocent American boys go to Vietnam where they are brutalized by the evil Asian commies. We're the victims in that movie (and virtually every other commercially successful Hollywood movie ever made about that war), not the Vietnamese. Moreover, the movie's central image, the Russian roulette stuff—none of the U.S. POWs ever claimed their captors even once did that. It's fiction. I couldn't tell Daniel he'd been suckered by Hollywood, which he had, but by the time I hung up the phone that night, I had decided that I was going to teach America the truth. Can you imagine how full of myself I was in those days?! But that's what I set out to do. It has taken me a lifetime to accept that I am only a little man in a very big universe.

Anyway, I finished that year of teaching in a small Quaker boarding school and set out to write my story. The trouble was that I had no idea what I was doing. I wrote furiously for six months, but after amassing a series of discontinuous essays in different voices—hundreds of pages—that didn't hang together at all, I finally ran out of steam and didn't know what to do next, so I simply stopped writing. I did nothing at all with the material for nearly a year. Then I came back to it in November 1980, threw out everything except what became the opening two chapters with some revision, and started writing a straight-line narrative. But after another six months, I had still barely gotten myself out of Vietnam and back to the States, I had over 400 pages of finished manuscript, and I had just barely begun to get to the real story I wanted to tell: trying to cope with America after fighting in Vietnam. That was the hard part—still is, after all these years—in Vietnam, I had a rotation date: I knew if I were still alive on March 5th, 1968, I could go home. But I get back to an America that is utterly changed, utterly alien, doesn't feel like home anymore, and I'm looking around and wondering, "What the fuck? What planet is this? When's my rotation date out of this madness?" And of course, there isn't one. You're stuck here until you get "rough pine parole" (i.e., until you die). This is home, like it or not. So I had wanted to explain that struggle, how and why America had changed—or rather, how and why I had changed and how that impacted my relationship with the land of my birth. And here I was, after two tries and two years, and I wasn't even close to finishing the story. I got discouraged again and stopped writing again. I gave the manuscript to a good and trusted friend and said, "I'm sick of this; find me an ending." He called me back a week later and said, "End it at the shower scene." So I threw out about 75 pages I'd written beyond that point, and that's how the book got its ending. (An accidental ending, and the best ending I ever wrote as it turns out.)

Oh, by the way, as for that "qualifier" bit at the beginning of my foreword to *V-P*, I was concerned because I was writing from memory alone. I had not kept notes or anything like that, and here I was trying to reconstruct the experience after a decade and a half, complete with verbatim dialogue. I was worried that someone would accuse me of making stuff up or of writing fiction and calling it nonfiction or whatever. But if I could revise those prefaces (to *PT* as well), I'd remove that stuff. What I've written is autobiographical memoir. It is what it is. A number of the people I write about in both books have read the books, and no one has complained to me that I screwed anything up. My memory, it turns out, was pretty damned accurate.

JJM. Once you completed the book, did you feel you had achieved the goals you had set forth?

WDE. No, I didn't feel as if I'd achieved my goals. I felt like an utter failure. I hadn't come close to succeeding. I hadn't wanted to write a book about the Vietnam War; I'd wanted to write a book about America, about the United States of America. Only after *V-P* was published did I decide that I was going to try again to write the book I'd meant to write, which became *Passing Time*. And only in retrospect did I realize that *V-P* was just me teaching myself how to write more than 25 lines at a time. *PT* is, it turns out, the book I meant to write all along. And *Busted* really should be the last 100 pages of *PT* except that at the time I was writing *PT*, Nancy Reagan was telling everyone to just say no, and I wasn't, so I didn't really feel comfortable explaining in print how I lost my job as a merchant seaman. Only after I realized that no one was paying any attention to anything I was writing did I decide to tell the rest of the story, which is how *Busted* got written six years after *PT*. If I'd known what I was doing from the start, there'd be only one book, not a "trilogy."

JJM. *Marking Time*, your second volume of memoirs was published by Avon in 1986; it was then republished as *Passing Time* by McFarland in 1989. It is a sequel to *Vietnam-Perkasie*. In this new book you cover the few years that followed your tour of duty in Vietnam. Did you feel you had not said it all in *Vietnam-Perkasie*?

WDE. Let's start with the most important point here: my title for this book had ALWAYS been *Passing Time*. Geez, at the end of the very first chapter, the 3rd engineer asks me what a college graduate is doing working as a wiper (a seagoing janitor) in the engine room of an oil tanker, and I reply, "Just passing time." "Marking Time" implies something very different from "passing time," but at the last minute the assholes in Avon marketing said they couldn't market a book with my title because it was 'too passive," so they changed it on me without asking or caring what I thought. And the great irony was that they published it in mass market format and didn't spend ten cents to market it anyway, and it was in and out of print in less than a year. The only reason I'd approached Avon in the first place is because Robbie Franklin told me he'd publish the book but thought I could "do better" than McFarland. Turns out I couldn't. (And eventually I learned that I didn't and don't want to do better than McFarland. I've been very happy with, and very well served by McFarland.) Anyway, I managed to get the rights to the book back from Avon, and asked Robbie if he'd do a new edition, this time with MY title, not Avon's abortion.

JJM. On your website you do not mention *Marking Time* but only *Passing Time*. How important was it for you to see it in print with another title in a different house just years after its first publication?

WDE. As I said, *Marking Time* was **never** MY title. If I could, I would wipe out every trace, every shred of evidence, every reference to a book titled *Marking Time*. The title of the book is *Passing Time*. And McFarland's willingness to re-publish the book was and is very, very important to me. One of many reasons I keep coming back to McFarland book after book. They've been loyal to me, and deserve the same from me.

JJM. In December 1985, you were invited by the Vietnamese government to return to Vietnam, and you went for about three weeks. Why did you go back? At the time, did you really want to go back to Vietnam, to this country which disrupted your life so much?

WDE. I very much wanted to go back to post-war Vietnam, especially after *Vietnam: A Television History* was broadcast in the fall of 1983. In the segment I'm in, Episode 5: "America Takes Charge," another of the interviewees talks about how beautiful Vietnam was, and I sat there listening and thinking that I had no recollection of beauty. And then he talked about the colors, the greens, how they seemed to vibrate they were so vivid, and I was shocked because I realized that all my memories were in black and white. I even went and dug out some of my old Kodak 104 photos, and some of them were in color, when I could get color film. And I also knew intellectually that the war was over, but in my head, whenever I thought of Vietnam, all I could see was Vietnam at war in 1967 and 1968, and it was all in black and white. By the time that hour program was over, I told myself, "Pal, you missed something. You gotta go back and take another look." It took another two years and two months to arrange, because the U.S. and Vietnam did not have diplomatic relations then, so it was difficult to get access and permission, but eventually with the help of John McAuliffe of the U.S.-Indochina Reconciliation Project, I was able to go back with John Balaban and Bruce Weigl. We were hosted by retired Major General Tran Kinh Chi, vice chairman of Vietnam's War Crimes Commission, who turned out to be a wonderfully gracious host and traveling companion.

JJM. In 1987, you published an account of this trip, *Going Back: An Ex-Marine Returns to Vietnam*, which you wrote as a diary of your journey. Why did you choose this literary form?

WDE. I helped defray the cost of that trip by writing a piece for the Philadelphia *Inquirer Magazine*. It was about 25 pages long. I sent a copy to Robbie Franklin, saying it had been tough to write because I could easily have written 150 pages. Next thing I know, a signed contract arrives in the mail. By that time, my wife was pregnant, I was supposed to travel to Nicaragua in July with the Central America Organizing Project and then write a piece about that trip, and I was going to start teaching again at another

Quaker high school in September. I had about six weeks to write *Going Back* before I left for Nicaragua, so I just wrote it in the most straightforward and efficient manner I could.

JJM. In the summer of 1990, you went back again to Vietnam with a group of veteran-writers. Were you eager to visit Southeast Asia again? Didn't you accomplish in 1985 what you had set out to do?

WDE. The trip I took in 1985 was the one I had to take for myself, for my own soul; it was my "trip of the heart." In 1990, I traveled with a delegation of writers sponsored by the William Joiner Center for the Study of War and Social Consequences, University of Massachusetts, Boston. All my expenses were covered by the Joiner Center and by a grant from Bobby Muller's VVA Foundation, and I was contracted to *The Virginia Quarterly Review* and *Gallery* to write articles for them (by the way, you could not get an odder pairing of publications than those two, but *Gallery* published what I sent them uncensored, and paid very well). So I actually made several thousand dollars on that 1990 trip. Heck, I'll go just about anywhere within reason if you're going to pay me. As it turns out, however, there was another bonus. In 1985, I was not able to visit any of the places I had actually fought in during the war, but in 1990 we went to Da Nang, Hoi An, the DMZ, and Hue, in addition to Hanoi, Haiphong, and Saigon. That was the first time I found the building I'd been in when Ken Takenaga and I had been wounded, and it still looked pretty much the same after 22 years. And I found where our battalion CP had been when we were based in the Hoi An area.

JJM. Was it an easier trip than in 1985?

WDE. In most ways, yes. Compared to a number of the guys on that trip—Phil Caputo, Larry Heinemann, Yusef Komunyakaa—I was an "old hand."

JJM. Were you writing while on these trips? Poems, letters, notes, diary, etc.?

WDE. I kept a daily diary/notebook kind of thing during both of those trips, and relied on them when I was doing post-trip writing (also true of my 2011 trip to Japan and Vietnam with Takenaga). A few poems have come out of those trips, but only "The Children of Hanoi" was written while I was still in Vietnam.

JJM. Your first three non-fiction books are composed of short chapters (sometimes just one page or two): 53 for *Vietnam–Perkasie*, 59 for *Passing Time*, and *Going Back* is divided by days and places where you went. Why did you choose these narrative structures?

WDE. For *V-P* and *PT*, each chapter is a day's worth of writing. I would figure out what I wanted to cover, then write it down, whether it took two hours or six hours. I worked initially in longhand then. The next day, I would type up what I'd written, revising as I went. Meanwhile, I would have basically two days to figure out what chunk of material I wanted to cover next. As for *GB*, as I said, I was in a hurry to get that one completed, so I just made each day of the trip its own chapter.

JJM. You went back to Vietnam a third time in June 2011 with fellow Marine Ken Takenaga. There is a strong bond between the two of you, particularly as you were wounded in action at the very same time and place in a building in Hue City during Tet 1968. You wrote an account of this journey which you published first on your website, then as well in *Dead on a High Hill. Essays on War, Literature and Living, 2002-2012*. Why did you choose the Web first, rather than a journal or a magazine, before having your piece in a book?

WDE. There is a very strong bond between Ken and me, and it has much to do with the fact that we seem to have processed our experience in Vietnam in very similar ways. I am in touch with a handful of the men I served with in Vietnam, and it's always good to see them and to hear from them, but we don't really have a whole lot in common beyond the war. I spent several days with one guy whom I love dearly to this day, but the whole time I was at his house, he had Fox News on; he's listening to Rush Limbaugh and Glenn Beck and all this stuff, and seriously relating to it. Not exactly where I'm coming from. (You should also know, however, that he brought out a stack of my books a foot and a half high, and asked me to sign them all. He's clearly proud his corporal became a published author, even if he can't figure out how my head got so twisted up! And if he can tolerate my politics, I can certainly do the same for him.) Anyway, after that RPG exploded, it took me 32 years to locate Kenny again, but when I did, it was as if no time had passed at all. We just picked up where we'd left off. That was a dozen years ago. We see each other several times a year. He's spent his life in the travel and tourism business, and he arranged a trip for my wife Anne and me to Japan in 2006, and then this trip to Japan and Vietnam in 2011. I got a fair amount of publicity for Japan tourism by writing about that 2006 trip, so the people he works for were willing to underwrite this second trip.

This 2011 trip was, of course, very, very rich. Ken is Japanese by birth, and spent the first 16 years of his life in Japan before coming to the U.S. (he was still a Japanese citizen without dual citizenship when he served in the Marines), so during the Japan portion of the trip, he took us to Yatsushiro, where he'd grown up. And then we went to all those places in Vietnam where the two of us had fought. So there was a hell of a lot to write about, but I knew that no print journal would be willing to take more than a few thousand words. (Ultimately, five different print outlets ran articles about the trip, but they all varied between 800 and 1,600 words. Meanwhile, my main article runs to 7,000 words with 100 photos.)

I'm not very techno-savvy, but I do know enough to understand that length is not an issue on the Web, and I am aware that the Web seems to be the way of the future, so right from the start I decided that my primary outlet would be a Web-based essay that I could post on my own website (thanks to my amazing wife, who knows how to do this stuff. Go look at that website; Anne built it) and that other sites could link to, which is what happened. There are something like two dozen other sites that link to "Ken & Bill's Excellent Adventure," everything from the Japanese National Tourism Office to Swarthmore College to Veterans for Peace. And even though the full essay appears in *Dead on a High Hill*, McFarland could include only a fraction of the photographs that appear with the Web version. I struggle with technology, and often find it a distraction rather than a boon—especially in the classroom when I'm trying to keep a bunch of teenaged boys focused—but it does have its advantages.

JJM. Did choosing the Web first influence your writing?
WDE. Only in that it allowed me to write until I'd said all I wanted to say without having to worry about space limitations.

JJM. You really wanted to go back to the very place where you were wounded, didn't you? You wrote about your being wounded in your poem "Letter." Why was it so important to revisit that very place, especially with Takenaga?
WDE. As I said, I'd actually found the building in 1990. And I found it again in 2011, though this time it looked very, very different. It's now the business and administrative offices for a four-star hotel that was built around it in 2004. It looks as new as the hotel itself. And as for why we wanted to go back there: geez, we were both nearly killed there. I mean, you're always at risk when you're in combat. But there it was. We were both hit by a powerful explosive weapon. We both could have died in that instant. My life could have ended right then and there at the age of 19. You want to stand on that spot and just marvel at the great good luck that allowed you to have the next 43 years, a wife, a daughter, a career, a life. You just shake your head and think, "Wow." Ken and I spent a lot of time on that trip whacking each other in the ribs with our elbows and going, "Can you believe this? Can you believe this?"

JJM. In "Letter" you sound like you wish you had been killed that day. How did you feel over 40 years later when you were back on the premises which had totally changed your life?
WDE. It was cool. It was fun. It was profound. It was exhilarating. It

was awesome. My life is very, very different now, and in 2011, than it had been in 1977 when I wrote "Letter." It took me most of my adult life to learn how to be happy.

JJM. Are you planning more trips to Vietnam? With some of your high school students, for instance?

WDE. No, no more trips, unless someone else is willing to pay the freight again. Traveling with Ken is so easy. He does all the planning and makes all the reservations and figures out how to finance it all, and all I have to do is follow him around and go where he tells me to go. Travel doesn't get any easier than that. I'll go anywhere with Ken. But on my own initiative, well, my idea of a great vacation is to drive an hour and a half to the New Jersey Shore and play in the ocean for a week. Taking a bunch of high school students to Vietnam—are you nuts? Do you think I'm nuts? I love teaching them, but I'm sure as hell not going to take them half-way around the world.

JJM. In 1991 McFarland published your first collection of essays which you entitled *In the Shadow of Vietnam: Essays 1977–1991*. Why such a title?

WDE. Well, mostly McFarland markets me as a Vietnam War writer, and the majority of the essays in that first collection are about or in some way influenced by the Vietnam War, so the title seemed to be an accurate reflection of the contents.

JJM. In 2012, McFarland—again—published your third volume of essays: *Dead on a High Hill: Essays on War, Literature and Living, 2002–2012*. At first glance the title sounds strange. It refers to one of your essays on Korean War poetry. Can you explain this choice?

WDE. My first choice for a title was *The World Is Watching: Essays on History, Literature and Living*, but as I said, McFarland markets me as a Vietnam War writer, so they wanted something more "warlike" as a title (and you'll notice they changed the subtitle as well). I wasn't going to argue with them. What the heck. McFarland is probably the only publisher on the planet willing to publish a collection of essays by a writer who is, as I've already explained, not exactly famous. They want a warlike title, fine with me.

When I choose titles, I generally try to pick something that will catch a reader's attention. Of the various essays in the book that deal with war, it seemed to me that "Dead on a High Hill" was the catchiest-sounding (it's actually a line from a Thomas McGrath poem), so I suggested that and McFarland liked it.

JJM. You selected 25 essays for this opus which covers ten years. Some are short (a couple of pages), others are much longer (up to 23 pages). Some contain poetry or photos. There is a great variety of subjects too. And I suppose you left out a number of other pieces you wrote during this decade. So, how did you make your selection for this book?

WDE. Actually, I didn't leave out very much. This mostly represents all the essays I wrote during that decade. And I just put them in the book in chronological order. And that was that. The great variety of subjects reflects the great variety of my life. While one might get the impression that I am primarily a Vietnam War veteran and write primarily about the Vietnam War, in fact I am rather more multi-dimensional. I can't help other people's perceptions, but even a cursory examination of my poetry and essay collections ought to suggest that the war is only one facet of my life.

JJM. The covers of all your prose books have a photo related to Vietnam. Again for *Dead on a High Hill*. We see yourself with your friend and fellow Marine Ken Takenaga near Quang Tri, Vietnam, in October 1967. The focus of this book is not on Southeast Asia. After all, one of your essays is "What's the Point of Poetry?" Another one, "The World Is Watching," deals with Rwanda, the Mountain Gorilla Project, the importance of wilderness in our lives. Did you pick this photo because Vietnam is still—at least partly—in the background of your writing nowadays?

WDE. Actually, a few days before the book went to press, McFarland sent me their cover design. Someone there took his or her cue solely from the book's title, and had obtained a photograph of American soldiers on a hill in Korea standing over several dismembered and decaying North Korean soldiers. When I saw the photo, I practically threw up. It was, literally, hideous. And it did not reflect accurately what a reader would find in the book. To McFarland's credit—yet another reason why I love the folks at McFarland—they immediately discarded that design and asked me what I suggested. Now the book was literally waiting on the cover to be sent to press, so I hastily offered a few suggestions including this photo of Ken and me, which is also in the book so they already had it in hand. And the design the art people came up with using this photo was the one we all liked the best.

JJM. So far you have not published any fiction, about the war or about anything else. In November 1982, in the prologue to *Vietnam-Perkasie*, you wrote that you were not ready yet, literarily or emotionally, to treat Vietnam as fiction. Thirty years later, are you ready to do it?

WDE. At this point, it's not a matter of being ready or not. I have discovered over the years that I'm not very good at writing fiction. If it didn't happen, my brain is too pedestrian to make it up.

I don't read a lot of fiction, relative to the amount of nonfiction I read. And the best way to learn how to write is by reading. So if you don't read fiction, it's hard to write it, I think. Why do I read so much nonfiction? Just the way I'm wired. Years ago, must have been late 1977, I went to see a college friend of mine, Steve Lang, in G.B. Shaw's *Saint Joan*. I'd never even read anything by Shaw, and it was a wonderful play, so the very next day I went to a bookstore. Did I buy some of Shaw's plays? No. I bought a biography of Saint Joan because I wanted to know how much of that play was true. That's just how my brain works. I don't know why.

JJM. If not about Vietnam, are you ready to write fiction about any topic?

WDE. No, I really don't expect to write fiction about anything. It's just not my genre.

JJM. Would not short stories, instead of a novel, be a good way to start writing fiction? After all, this is what many authors did before you, then assembled their short stories into a collection.

WDE. Short stories, novels, plays—doesn't matter. I'm not a fiction writer.

JJM. Even if you say you don't read a lot of fiction, do you have any favorite authors?

WDE. Favorite authors? As in when they publish a book, I just have to read it? I guess not. There are lots of authors I like, both living and dead. I've always enjoyed the books of John McPhee (he's a nonfiction writer, of course). I got on a kick a while back and read virtually every one of the Cadfael mysteries by Edith Pargeter (a.k.a. Ellis Peters) because I saw a BBC production of one of them staring Derek Jacobi and he was just wonderful. Now and then I'll read some science fiction by C.J. Cherryh, whom my wife reads constantly, and I always enjoy them. I have read a number of the books in the StarFIST series by David Sherman and Dan Cragg—utterly escapist and lightweight stuff, but good fun. (They even dedicated one of their books to me, although they IDed me as a scout-sniper instead of a battalion S-2 scout. Maybe that's why I like their books: they like me!)

A few years back, when I was teaching an 11th grade English class, I had the boys read a fairly recent novel called *Green Grass Grace*, which a former student of mine had recommended, saying I would like it, and I did. It's set in Philadelphia in the mid-1980s, and it literally begins: "Hellfire hallelujah and halitosis. Mike Schmidt sits to pee. How you doing, fuckface? My name's Henry Tobias Tooey." I tried to get the other 11th grade teachers to use the book, but they didn't dare, so finally I just taught the book on my own. What was the school going to do? Cut my hair off and send me to Vietnam? The boys loved the book, and it's actually a wonderful novel. I think it was Shawn McBride's first. I don't know if he's done anything since.

But this question—what am I supposed to do with it? There are so many,

many good writers out there. I think *Moby Dick* is the greatest poem in the English language. I quote from the book in several of my memoirs. Which leads me to a digression, but I gotta tell you this story.

Back in 1995, the reviewer for the Philadelphia *Inquirer* absolutely panned *Busted*. The book clearly pushed all of his buttons. I looked him up, Norman Russell, and he'd written a book called *Suicide Charlie: A Vietnam War Story*. So I think he didn't like my politics very much. One of the things he said in his review is that I was "no prose stylist." He then proceeded to demonstrate my lack of prose style by quoting me thusly, "Thar she blows! Thar she blows! A hump like a snowhill! It is Moby Dick!" Well, that's not my writing; I'm quoting Herman Melville and *Moby Dick*. But apparently neither the reviewer nor the *Inquirer*'s book review editor knew enough to realize Russell was quoting Melville, not Ehrhart. What can one do in the face of that kind of ignorance? Not much.

Anyway, back to your question. I can't teach *Moby Dick* because it would take more time than I have in a high school curriculum, but when I teach American lit, I always do *Billy Budd*. I love Stephen Crane's short stories (along with his poetry): "The Open Boat," "The Blue Hotel," "The Bride Comes to Yellow Sky." Wonderful stuff. There's a brilliant book by the Welsh writer Duncan Bush called *The Genre of Silence* that I just love and use whenever I teach my European Dictators course. Graham Greene wrote some good stuff. Alan Furst is writing good work. And I've recently had occasion to remember how much I enjoyed *The Good Earth* when I read it years ago. I may have to re-read it. William Golding's *The Inheritors* has to be the most poignant (and depressing) book I've ever read. I loved it, but I could never bear to read it again. Seriously, I've been reading for 55 years or so. How does one pick a "favorite"?

I guess over the years I have read a lot of fiction simply because I read all the time (though I am a painfully slow reader). But again, on balance, I read much, much, much more nonfiction, and I usually choose books for topic rather than author. Earlier this summer I read *Along the Way*, a memoir jointly authored by Martin Sheen and Emilio Estevez because Sheen sent it to me (it's a long story; suffice it to say that he encountered my poetry while narrating a documentary nearly 30 years ago, and we've kept in loose touch since). I then read a history called *Slaves in the Family*, and am currently working my way through another one called *Slavery by Another Name*. I can't even tell you who the authors are; it's the subject matter that interests me. Next up is a new (2011) biography of Smedley Darlington Butler I just got. No novels in sight at the moment.

JJM. Who did you read—whatever the genre—when you were in high-school and when you started writing poetry?

WDE. When I was in high school, and even in the Marines when I could get books, I read widely. In addition to the curriculum, which included the usual suspects for the early and mid-1960s (dead white guys, mostly, but they were good writers), I read Gibran, Owen, Thomas Hardy, Dostoyevsky, Conrad, Salinger. I read Ayn Rand's books—two or three of them—because my oldest brother said I should (though I ultimately did not become a convert!). Camus (in translation) while I was still in high school. I remember reading Updike's *Rabbit, Run* when I was up at Con Thien. I remember reading *Candide* in Vietnam, again in translation. Somebody had a copy, and you read what you could get your hands on. I remember reading *The Lewd Librarian* in Vietnam, too. As I said, you read whatever came your way.

JJM. Are there authors who had or have today any major influence on your writing?

WDE. I think I told you that Stephen Crane's poetry was the first poetry to really grab my attention. But I was enamored of many other poets, too. And I spent a lot of time imitating the ones I admired, even to the very precipice of plagiarism. I mentioned Kahlil Gibran. Walt Whitman. At one point in high school, I remember being much taken with Lawrence Ferlinghetti's *A Coney Island of the Mind*. In the long run, I'd say Crane was the most influential. He's the guy, I think, who made me think, "Hey, I want to be a poet, too. I wanna do that." Since then, lots of poets have been influential for me. I especially remember being greatly attracted to W.S. Merwin's *The Lice* in my mid-20s, and a few years later Richard Hugo's *What Thou Lovest Well, Remains American*, and I spent time imitating both writers in turn. But *major* influence, who can say? I don't know. One ends up as the sum of it all, the grand stew of living, a kind of stone soup.

JJM. From past conversations and what you say in our conversation about *The Deer Hunter*, I know you are not keen on Vietnam War movies. My research[2]—as well as John Baky's[3]—shows that so far about 1,500 motion pictures have been produced worldwide which deal directly or indirectly with Southeast Asia, the French and/or the American wars. Do you think such films perform any important artistic, political or sociological roles, and that Hollywood should keep cranking them out until they explore all the intricate aspects of the effects of the Vietnam War on the American psyche?

WDE. Come on, you know how I feel about these films. As I regularly tell both my students and just about every audience I ever speak to (because they all ask about the films), "If Hollywood were in the business of education, we'd all be over at King of Prussia Mall eating popcorn and earning our diplomas." Hollywood is in the business of parting you from your disposable income, which filmmakers do by entertaining you. What you are seeing is entertainment, period. You want to be entertained, go to the movies, but for God's sake, don't imagine that you are actually learning anything. Unfortunately, people think they *are* learning something. When you have no frame of reference for the Vietnam War, and someone begins to talk about the Vietnam War, your only reference becomes the films, be they *The Deer Hunter, Platoon, Apocalypse Now* or *Rambo: First Blood, Part II*. Personally, I'd be happy if every film ever made about the Vietnam War simply vanished, and I'm not eager to have Hollywood keep cranking out more of them. Only one is worth a flying fig, and that one was a box office flop because it was too damned honest: *Go Tell the Spartans*. I also like Pierre Schoendoerffer's *The 317th Platoon*, but that's about the French War and was made by a Frenchman. Anyway, what makes you think that Hollywood will ever "explore all the intricate aspects of the effects of the Vietnam War on the American psyche," no matter how many movies they crank out? I'd say you're being rather optimistic there.

JJM. There are now Iraq and Afghanistan Wars films, from various countries in the world, not just the USA. Do you see any value in them?

WDE. I haven't seen what other countries are doing, but as for American films, the answer is: No. As I said, Hollywood is in the business of entertainment, not education. Take *The Hurt Locker*. The film has those demolition guys doing stuff no real demolition units would ever be doing. It's fiction. It's dramatic. It's cinematic. It's bullshit.

JJM. We have talked about poetry and prose but how about theatre? Have you seen any plays about Vietnam, and if so what did you think of them?

WDE. I saw a production of *Tracers* once and thought it was pretty good. I've taught David Rabe's *Sticks & Bones*, and I like it a lot, though I've never seen a production of it. Never saw *Miss Saigon*. I'm not much of a theater person, although I'll go see Shakespeare almost any time the opportunity arises. But he didn't write anything about Vietnam.

JJM. Do you have any heroes of the Vietnam War? Or in life in general? Who would they be and why?

WDE. Hugh Thompson because he had the courage to do the right thing in the midst of evil. Ron Ridenhour because he had a conscience and could not let it go. Ho Chi Minh because he devoted his entire life to freeing his people from foreign oppression. Muhammad Ali (though I think he was duped and badly used by the Nation of Islam) because he was willing to give up the best years of his career rather than fight in Vietnam. Wayne Morse and Ernest Gruening because they wouldn't be fooled.

As for life in general, my mother because she was the most tolerant, forgiving, and forbearing person I have ever known. My mother was the kind of person Jesus had in mind when he gave his Sermon on the Mount. If every Christian were as Christian as my mother was, Christianity wouldn't be half bad. Also my wife because she has put up with me for 32 years; indeed, come to think of it, while she's not a Christian, she reminds me very much of my mother in her ability to tolerate and forgive. And my daughter because she's been strong enough and resilient enough to survive having me for a father.

Other heroes? That's a strong word. There are many people I admire. Almost too many to enumerate. Whenever I begin to despair of the seemingly unlimited number of jackasses and dickheads there are in the world, I just remember all those people who are doing their best, often at great sacrifice, to make up for the jackasses and dickheads. I had a friend—he's dead now, died too young of cancer—who spent his entire career as an EPA lawyer. The usual pattern for these government lawyers is that they learn the ropes, the rules, the regs for a few years, and then they hire out to the very corporations they were regulating, knowing now how to beat the regs and getting paid five and ten times what EPA could pay (this is true of the FTC, the FCC, all these regulatory agencies). But Ben spent his whole career with the Environmental Protection Agency. I asked him about it once, and he said, "Hey, I'm earning enough to keep a roof over my family's head and send my kids to college, and I can look at myself in the mirror every morning." That man was a hero. His name was Ben Kalkstein.

JJM. Forty-five years later do you remember what you were told about Vietnam before you joined the USMC? What would you tell a young man or woman who would like to sign up today?

WDE. Oh, it was all quite cut and dried. Eisenhower had laid it out in 1954 or 1955: the Domino Theory—if Vietnam falls, Thailand will fall, etc., etc. It was all, of course, part and parcel of the worldwide communist conspiracy to conquer the world. Wasn't this obvious? Just look at Eastern Europe 1945–48. And then China 1949. And Korea. And all those uppity Commie revolutionaries like Patrice Lumumba and Fidel Castro. The Hungarian Revolt and its brutal suppression. Well, it was obvious, wasn't it? As Lyndon Johnson said in a speech while I was still in high school, "If we do not stop the communists in Vietnam, we will one day have to fight them on the sands of Waikiki." Early in my time at Parris Island, we recruits were herded into an auditorium and shown a film narrated by Jack Webb of *Dragnet* fame. What I remember of it was a graphic of the world as a globe and a bucket of red paint being dumped over it to symbolize the Communist struggle to conquer the world. It was up to us young recruits to see that the Commies didn't succeed.

What would I tell a young man or woman today? Don't believe the bastards.

They won't go, but they'll send you. You're expendable. It's what I do tell them. But they don't listen any more than I listened to the few people who tried to tell me that maybe my enlisting wasn't such a good idea. You've got a whole culture that propagandizes and distorts and dissembles. A few voices of sanity mostly don't stand a snowball's chance in hell of being heard. Young people are, by nature, trusting, optimistic, naïve. It's why armies are made of the young.

JJM. In "Letter" dedicated "to a north Vietnamese soldier whose life crossed paths with mine in Hue City, February 5th, 1968," you again described how you felt after being wounded. This poem was first published in *Empire* in 1978, was it not? It was then published again in 1984 in *To Those Who Have Gone Home Tired*. Did you modify or want to modify anything in this piece for the 1984 edition? Did you personally and literarily feel the same half-a-dozen years later?

WDE. By 1984, I didn't feel the same way I had in 1977 when I wrote "Letter," but I didn't change the poem because the poem was a true reflection of where I was when I wrote it. Actually, however, most of the feelings expressed in the poem hadn't changed—certainly the feeling that my own country had learned nothing from the disaster of that war, and the hope that the Vietnamese would create something better.

JJM. The second verse goes: "But I lived / long enough to wonder often / how you missed; long enough / to wish too many times / you hadn't." This is a rather strong feeling. Did you ever *really* wish you had died in Vietnam?

WDE. It's this part that had changed in the intervening seven years. By 1984, I was married and on my way (albeit slowly) to a more healthy and happy life than I'd been living through all of the 1970s. Did I really wish I had died in Vietnam? There were many, many times in the long (seemingly endless) years between 1968 and 1980 that I at least *thought* I wished I had been killed. I was a very unhappy man for a very long time.

JJM. Do you remember when and why you wrote this particular stanza?

WDE. Yes. I wrote it on the ninth anniversary of the day I was wounded. I was living in a tiny apartment in Chicago, living about as close to the poverty line as I would ever get, alone and lonely, and seeing no brighter future ahead.

JJM. If you were to write today another letter to this NVA soldier, would you still include such a dark thought in a verse as your life seems to have been rather successful as far as your writing is concerned?

WDE. No, I'd probably write that I'm glad he missed me—or at least didn't manage to hit me head-on, which really would have killed me instantly, (and painlessly I might add; I never would have known what happened)—but I'm still sorry that my country has remained so steadfastly resistant to learning anything of value from that war, and I hope he and his country are doing okay these days.

JJM. You had a number of different and varied jobs in your life. You were on and off a teacher at the high school and college levels from the mid–1970s till the 1990s. You now have been teaching full-time English and history at the Haverford School since 2001 This is an old school for boys founded in 1884. What do you like about teaching? What do you try to accomplish in a classroom?

WDE. I originally taught for a single semester at the Haverford School, January-June 2001, as a temporary long-term substitute for someone who had to retire suddenly for medical reasons. I was then gone for a year, though I did a two-week session with the entire senior class in the spring of 2002. Finally, I began as a fulltime regular faculty member in the fall of 2002. So I generally just say I started in 2001.

I've taught college on a number of occasions, and it's okay, I guess, but at that level all you're doing is teaching a subject. You see your students three times a week over the course of a semester (if you're lucky and they show up), and maybe you have one one-on-one during office hours if you require it, and that's about it. High school, you've got these kids five days a week from early September to early June. The last thing you're doing is teaching them an academic subject. That's almost beside the point. These are emerging adults trying to figure out who they are, what they are, how they want to be in the world, which end is up. And of course, many of these kids, I coach them in winter track six days a week for four months, I work with the school's literary magazine (next year, 2012–13, I'm trading that job for the faculty sponsor of the poetry club instead). I have nine to ten boys who are my advisees for three years, whether I teach them or not. So I have all kinds of contact with my students. I'm helping them discover themselves, helping them decide how they want to navigate the world around them. That's fun. It's rewarding. It's damned hard work, relentless, day in and day out, six and seven days a week for nearly ten months, but it's fun. It's the next best thing to staying young forever: each year I get older, but each year, when I walk into my classroom in September, the boys sitting in front of me are the same age they were the year before.

JJM. Do you recall teachers and instructors who had a great effect on your schooling?

WDE. I had two remarkable English teachers my junior and senior years of high school. Robert F. Hollenbach I actually had in 7th and 8th grades, and then again in 11th grade. Three of my six years of secondary school. In junior high, we read Guy de Maupassant, Marjorie Kinnan Rawlings, Saki, O. Henry, Ole Rolvaag, Willa Cather. Imagine reading those authors today. I'll bet half the English teachers in America today have never heard of most of those authors. Hollenbach was a stern taskmaster, but he was a terrific teacher. Probably more than any other one person, he taught me how to write well. And of course, we read more great literature in 11th grade. We read *Catcher in the Rye* at a time and in a school district when he could have gotten in serious trouble if the Powers That Be had known what we were reading. We read Hawthorne and Fitzgerald. And a host of American poets: Whitman, Bryant, Longfellow, Emerson, Robinson, Jeffers, Frost, Bishop, Millay—he was especially fond of Millay, and to this day I love "Renascence" and always teach it when I teach American lit. We read Seeger's "Rendezvous."

And in my senior year, I had John B. Diehl. Another remarkable man. A great humanist. He'd been in the Marines during the Korean War, though he hadn't deployed to Korea. He'd taught my oldest brother in the early 1960s, then joined the Peace Corps and spent two years in what was then Tanganyika. Then he came back in time to teach me. He taught World Cultures, so we read a lot of other-than-U.S. literature. He's the one who introduced me to Camus. And Osip Mandelstam, the great Russian poet who was silenced by Stalin. And Jaroslav Hasek's *The Good Soldier Svejk*. One day Mr. Diehl brought in a full-page ad from the *New York Times* that was protesting the war in Vietnam. This was 1965. And he told us how much a full-page ad cost, and how much this one individual—a Japanese businessman—must have believed in what he was saying that he would be willing to use his money like that. This was dangerous ground for a public high school teacher in Perkasie, Pennsylvania, in the mid-1960s. I actually did not fully appreciate what Diehl was trying to do, and how much he was risking, until years later, but he was trying to get us to *think*. Not to accept the empty bromides and vacuous clichés that filled our lives. Obviously, he failed with me, as he did with most of us, but he had tried his best to be a true educator. I don't step into a classroom ever without thinking of Hollenbach and Diehl, and I hope I have half the skill and passion and commitment that they had.

JJM. For about thirty years you have been giving regular readings from your work and lectures, all over the USA, and even overseas (for example at the EVAC Conference in Manchester, England, in September of 1986; at the NASA Conference on War and War's Aftermath in Amsterdam, The Netherlands, in June 2009). How important are these readings and lectures for you and your audiences?

WDE. How important are they to my audiences? Well, you'd have to ask my audiences. I have no idea. As for myself, I enjoy giving readings. Lectures are a bit more challenging—I actually have to do some work to prepare for those, whereas the readings are just me reading what I've already written—but I'm happy enough to get up in front of an audience and tell people what I think. And it is, truth be told, gratifying when the Netherlands American Studies Association or the Universidad de Sevilla or Wayne State University or Wor-Wic Community College thinks enough of me to ask me to come and speak. I'm not a closet poet. I like to be heard. I want to be heard. So when people and institutions give me that opportunity, I'm grateful.

JJM. At the end of the ground war in the Persian Gulf in 1991, George Bush, Sr., declared that the Vietnam syndrome was over. What did you think of his statement at the time?

WDE. I've been hearing that the Vietnam War is "finally over" ever since Gerald Ford was president. There's an essay of mine in *The Madness of It all* called "The War That Won't Go Away." It was a talk I gave at the Austrian Association of American Studies Conference in 1993, and in it I detail how every American president since Ford had made similar statements—Ford, Carter, Reagan, Bush the 1st, and Clinton—and all of them, it turns out, had been pipe-dreaming. Now we can add Bush II. And as for Obama, instead of trying to pretend that the war is over, he's actually inaugurated a decade-long Vietnam War Commemoration to "thank and honor veterans of the Vietnam War." Is this progress? (A rhetorical question.)

JJM. Did you write much poetry related to the Gulf War, apart from "Holy War"?

WDE. There are a few other poems that I wrote at the time or shortly thereafter, but most of them weren't very good. I did write "Guns" at the time, and that's a very good poem (in my opinion, at least). I had originally titled the working draft "Desert Shield," then changed the title to "Desert Storm" when it became clear that King George I was going to have a war no matter what. But soon after I finished the poem in the winter of 1991, it became clear that the Gulf War wasn't going to be much of a war (for us at least, seeing as we killed more of our own troops than the Iraqis managed to kill), so I changed the title to the more generic "Guns," and now I can haul the poem out for whatever war happens to be going on at the time (of which there seem to be an endless supply).

JJM. In 1991 U.S. Iraq War soldiers got the parades Vietnam veterans never had. Do you believe it was important to have such parades for these soldiers on their return?

WDE. In *Beautiful Wreckage* (I think it was originally in *Just for Laughs*) is a poem of mine called "Parade" about the so-called "Welcome Home Parade" held in New York City in the spring of 1985. That poem sums up what I think of parades. They can take their parades and shove 'em where the sun doesn't shine. What am I supposed to do with a parade? Put it in the bank? Serve it for dinner? How about decent health care? VA benefits without having to jump through hoops and prostitute oneself? Maybe fewer no-win dead-end wars that accomplish nothing except to enrich the arms merchants and Pentagon contractors. How long have we been in Afghanistan now? How are we doing so far? Christ almighty, Afghanistan isn't even a country. Lines on a map. What the fuck do we think we're doing there? God help us. Parades certainly won't.

JJM. What are your feelings regarding the Iraq War and Afghanistan War veterans who went through a different kind of war from yours? Has the USA created a new kind of veterans? Or are they similar to past ones?

WDE. Your question assumes that these younger veterans have fought "a different kind of war." On what premise do you base your assumption? No war is the same as any other, but every war does lasting damage to everyone touched by it, soldier and civilian, wounded and physically unscathed. What we have now is literally a warrior society, a tiny fraction of the population that is bearing the entire blood burden of American military adventurism while everyone else goes about our business as if none of this is happening. I don't know what the long-term consequences of this will be, but the high incidence of PTSD, the epidemic levels of suicide among active duty soldiers and recent veterans, the broken families, the backlog of disability claims awaiting adjudication by the VA—none of this is new. Give the troops some parades and medals and public genuflection, and then toss them aside: this is the history of military service in America. Read a book called *The Wages of War*. It only goes up to the 1980s, but it starts back with the American Revolution. The parades, the rhetoric, the Memorial Day commemorations, the solemn return of flag-draped caskets, it's all just bullshit. The fact is that we have already deemed expendable those that we send to fight our wars. That hasn't changed in 250 years.

JJM. The Vietnam War lost the support of the people in the late 1960s-early 1970s. The Gulf War did receive the endorsement of the American population in the early 1990s The U.S. involvement in Iraq and Afghanistan in the 21st century has been dragging on for ten years. Popular backing is down. Many veterans of these two wars suffer from PTSD, suicides, and alcohol. The Veterans Administration does not seem to do enough for them for a number of reasons. These vets appear to be in a situation much more similar to Vietnam than to Gulf War vets. Would you agree with this? What should be done?

WDE. Well, I'm not sure Gulf War vets really got all that good a deal.

Their war was much shorter and didn't involve the same degree of combat with its consequent repercussions. But to this day, I don't think the VA or the U.S. government has ever acknowledged responsibility for what came to be known as "Gulf War Syndrome." And it became clear within a year of the war's conclusion that nothing had actually been "concluded," so the seeming closure that occurred in the summer of 1991 must soon have appeared more than a little hollow to at least the more perceptive of those who participated in both the war and the parades.

JJM. You have read Iraq and Afghanistan Wars poetry and memoirs, haven't you? How do they compare to their Vietnam counterparts?

WDE. From the first Gulf War, I have read only *Jarhead*, the Swofford book, and I thought it a bit too slick and calculated. It read like something an Iowa Writers Workshop student might write, which, as it turns out, is exactly what it is. As for these more recent wars, the only memoir I've read is Clint Van Winkle's *Soft Spots*, which I read largely because I've been corresponding with Van Winkle since well before he ever began his book. He had found my writing when he was an undergraduate student, and felt an affinity with it and me. He opens his book with a quote from one of my poems, so I read his book, which I thought was very good. But I am sure I would never have read the book if I didn't have a personal connection to Clint. In general I'm not interested in reading these books. What am I going to learn from them? The horrors of war? The difficulty of telling friend from foe? The tragic consequences of sending scared kids armed to the teeth into an alien culture they can never hope to understand? I don't mean to sound callous, but this new generation of vets has nothing to teach me. As for the poetry, I've read some of Brian Turner's stuff. It's okay, but I can't get excited about it, probably for the reasons I've given above. I've also read all three of the anthologies published by the Warrior Writers Project. I applaud what the folks who run this program are trying to do—provide a constructive outlet for veterans to come to terms with what they experienced—but the actual writing I've seen so far is not terribly impressive. But it's early yet, literarily speaking. There is perhaps much more yet to come.

JJM. In your collection of essays *Dead on a High Hill*, you refer twice to *Soft Spots*, Clint Van Winkle's 2009 Iraq War memoir. This book was praised by *The Washington Post* and *The Marine Corps Times* amongst others. You also recommend it. Why?

WDE. It's a good book, that's why.

JJM. And how about *Here, Bullet*, Brian Turner's 2005 poetry collection you also mention along with *Soft Spots* in *Dead on a High Hill*?

WDE. Turner's book is the only poetry I've seen that rises to the level of art. How durable these poems will be remains to be seen.

I have to tell you that I don't like talking about other people's writing and this younger generation's wars. Look, I'm an old fogey, for one thing. My experiences probably seem no more relevant to these kids than were the experiences of the World War II generation to me. Only in my later forties did I begin to fully appreciate the commonality of experience (and I largely have Paul Fussell to thank for that). For now I'm sure these younger vets, whatever they hear or read from me, are thinking, "What does that old fart know about my experience?" And it's a fair question. And as for the writing that has come out of these wars, I am really uncomfortable being judgmental. I have so many of my own demons and dragons and baggage to haul around that it really isn't fair for me to be pontificating about what these younger vets are writing.

JJM. What are your views on today's politics of the U.S. government regarding foreign affairs? Do you see any parallels with the politics from the 1960s that got America in the Vietnam quagmire?

WDE. Good God Almighty! You've got to be kidding me. I'm really supposed to try to answer this question? In how many words? How long is this book allowed to be? Where do I even begin? Okay, let me try something concise but accurate. The differences between the Vietnam War and our wars in Iraq and Afghanistan are myriad. But there are two overriding similarities: in all three cases. Firstly, in each case American policymakers tasked the military with achieving goals that were and are simply not achievable by military might (and probably not achievable at all. Do we really imagine that Afghans will all convert to Christianity and register Republican?) Secondly, when you send heavily armed scared kids into alien environments they cannot possibly hope to understand, no good will come of it. Obama is claiming to have kept his campaign pledge to end the war in Iraq, but he didn't end anything. The Iraqi government refused to renew a treaty exempting U.S. service personnel from Iraqi jurisdiction and told us to get out instead, leaving the country fractured and its government largely dysfunctional and strongly aligned with the Iranian government. Some victory. And as for Afghanistan, how long have we been there? And how are we doing so far? It's called the arrogance of power, and it's fueled by a lucrative and pervasive military-industrial complex that now includes the mainstream media as well (since mainstream media are now owned by corporate America).

JJM. What is your view on the artist in the light of a traumatic event?

WDE. The role of the artist is to be an artist, traumatic event or not.

JJM. Would you be the writer you are today, would you have written as much if it were not for your experience in Vietnam? Would you have not been even more of an essay author?

WDE. I wouldn't be the writer I am today, I wouldn't be the person I am today, were it not for my experience in Vietnam. However, what I would be is utterly unanswerable. If I had wings, maybe I could fly, but I don't and I can't. I only know what was and is, not what might have been.

JJM. What are your thoughts on being stereotyped as a Vietnam War writer? Isn't it actually a burden on your shoulders, especially as for at least twenty plus years your poetry, even though it is still occasionally influenced by Vietnam, embraces many other themes, some quite distant from Southeast Asia?

WDE. For years, I really chafed at being identified as a "Vietnam poet." You say that my writing began to diverge from that topic "at least twenty plus years" ago, but in fact the war has *never* been my only subject. Even when I was writing about the war, in poetry, most intensely, during the years I was in college, I was also writing poems about spaceships, and love poems (almost exclusively broken-hearted love poems in those days!), and walking through the campus late at night. All sorts of things. I remember writing one that was in my college literary magazine about seeing President Eisenhower's motorcade pass by while I was picnicking with my family at Gettysburg Battlefield in 1958. Here it is:

Gettysburg

Yankee day
picnicking by an old stone wall
where cannons ranged once in fury.
Waving colored flags
and blue felt hats,
we interrupt our meal
to watch
the President's long black motorcade
pass by.
He doesn't notice,
but his wife does,
and smiles at us
from behind the closed window.

I wrote that during my second year of college, 1970 or '71, at the same time I was writing all those short "snapshot" poems about the war. The war has *never* been my only subject.

So yes, it's a burden to be so identified with the war. But as I got older, into my 40s, I began to realize that most writers never get recognized at all. As I said before, I wasn't getting invited to the Geraldine R. Dodge Poetry

Festival or the Breadloaf Writers Conference, but I was getting invited to the West Side YMCA's "Back in the World: Writing After Viet Nam" and Tulane University's "My Lai: 25 Years After." So if I weren't associated with the war, I wouldn't be getting invited anywhere. I probably wouldn't be recognized as anything. I'd just be another minor poet writing in total obscurity instead of a not-quite-so-minor poet who's at least known to those who pay attention to the literature of the Vietnam War. And maybe a few people along the way will notice that I actually have a large body of work, both poetry and essays, unconnected to the war.

JJM. Do you have a definition of poetry?

WDE. If the person who wrote it says it's poetry, then it's poetry. Whether it's good poetry or not is a different question. I think I've already quoted for you Emily Dickinson's definition of poetry, by which she meant *good* poetry. That's good enough for me.

JJM. Along the same lines, do you have definitions of non-fiction and of fiction?

WDE. If it's more or less true—true to the best of the writer's ability and recollection—then it's nonfiction. If it's made up, then it's fiction.

JJM. Do you agree with the statement by the French poet Aimé Césaire that essentially we are a composite of all our experiences—love, hatred, understanding, misunderstanding—and that consequently we rise out of those things like a phoenix?

WDE. The part I would disagree with is the phoenix bit. Doesn't the phoenix actually die, then rise again from its own ashes? I am indeed the composite of all my experiences, but I have not yet died (as far as I know), let alone risen again.

JJM. Yusef Komunyakaa said: "The way we are, perhaps today, might be entirely different tomorrow." Do you agree with that? Is it your case? Are you any different today from who you were yesterday?

WDE. This question begins to drift into the realm of the esoteric (I am struggling to avoid the term hoity-toity). I doubt that I have ever become an "entirely different" person in the space of a single day and night. One does change over time, but how much does one change? I'm pretty certain I'm the same person today that I was yesterday, except that I'm a day closer to my mortal demise. Just as surely, I have changed a lot over the 63 years I've been wandering around Planet Earth. But what those changes are, well, I'm not inclined to puzzle my brain trying to figure out what about me has changed. I like to think I am wiser, more accepting, more tolerant. But at the same time, I think the core substance of who I am has not greatly changed. My sense of right and wrong. My perception of what matters and what doesn't. When I first met the woman I eventually married, she did not immediately decide I was the man for her. Indeed, there was much about me that put her off, and it took two and a half years before she decided to marry me. What she slowly discovered during that time was that, despite so many apparent differences between us, my value system, my ethical compass, was in fact very much like hers. I think that basic core of who I am has not changed since I was very young.

JJM. You have taught composition classes. Do you believe that poets can teach students to write poetry?

WDE. No. Good teachers can teach students to appreciate poetry. And if a student is inclined to write poetry, a good teacher can encourage and coach and mentor that student. But the drive has to be internal. The will to be a poet can't be taught. And it is the will that matters far more than any technical aspects of writing. Even the most fervent young poet gives up when he or she discovers that the phone company wants hard cash and won't accept poetry as payment. One can't teach that. And as for poets doing the teaching, some poets are good teachers, but others are not. Poets and teachers are not the same thing.

JJM. Does a poem have to be believable to be a poem?

WDE. No. Just think of Carroll's "Jabberwocky." Or how about my poem "Life in the Neighborhood" in *The Bodies Beneath the Table*. (Not on a par with Carroll, of course, but no less "unbelievable.")

JJM. Do you believe most poets tend to over-write and that part of the editing process is to cut?

WDE. I am hesitant, once again, to try to sum up "most poets," but probably overwriting is more common than underwriting (except in the insurance business).

JJM. Is there a "correct" way to write poetry?

WDE. No.

JJM. Should poets be innovators and risk-takers, even if it makes it difficult for them to "survive" as authors, i.e., to get published?

WDE. Both innovation and risk-taking for their own sakes have no virtue. If the situation calls for innovation or risk-taking, then poets should innovate and take risks. But to do so just for the sake of doing so, no, what's the point of that?

JJM. Can the external world take the passion out of the artist?

WDE. Yes, but so can the internal world (depression, grief, loneliness, boredom, maybe even success). A lot of these questions make me really uncomfortable. As if you think "poets" and "artists" are somehow different from everyone else, special, exalted. Many people are passionate, not just artists. My daughter is passionate about her jewelry-making. My next-door neighbor is clearly passionate about gardening. Many of my colleagues at the Haverford School are passionate about their teaching (as any good teacher must be). I know you are talking about art and poetry here; it is, after all, the focus of the interview, and if I were not an artist, you wouldn't be doing this book. But the older I've gotten, the less I've wanted to talk about art. What I have to say is *in* my art. And when I hear people talking *about* art, I always find myself thinking, "Talk's cheap. What can you *do*?"

JJM. What would you say the state of poetry is in the USA today?

WDE. Poetry has largely been coopted by academia just in the course of my lifetime. Back in the mid-1970s, there were perhaps half a dozen or so schools that offered programs in creative writing. Today, the number of colleges and universities offering BA, MA, MFA, and even PhD degrees in creative writing is mind-boggling. You can actually earn all of those degrees in succession, find yourself as a Doctor of Poetry Writing in your late 20s or early 30s, while never having done anything with your life except be a student. And what often results is highly crafted vacuity cranked out by people who in turn have become tenured professors in creative writing programs that churn out still more certified creative writers. Meanwhile the professor-poets review each other's books, and invite each other to read at their campuses, and sit on committees that give prizes to each other.

I could be wrong, of course. It's happened before, and will probably happen again (I'd take bets on it). Maybe I'm just sour grapes because I don't get considered for the Pulitzer Prize and don't get invited to be interviewed by Bill Moyers and was never offered a tenured university sinecure. It's possible that's the real basis for my skepticism about the relationship between poetry and the academy. Still, I find it all too often a bit incestuous.

On the other hand, there are good poets out there, and some of them are in academia. John Balaban has taught creative writing for years, and is currently in charge of the program at North Carolina State University. And I have heard him give a spirited and persuasive defense of the value of teaching creative writing. Moreover, he's a damned fine poet with something to say. M.L. Liebler teaches at Wayne State in Detroit, and he is indeed now a tenured professor, but he had to fight his way into that position after years and years in the academic trenches. Meanwhile, poets like the late Lou McKee are almost entirely overlooked because they're not hooked into the academic poetry circuit. Gary Metras, a lifetime public high school teacher, has now developed a fine reputation as a letterpress printer, but how many people know what a fine poet he is in his own right?

Now I must admit that I myself earned an MA in creative writing from the University of Illinois at Chicago Circle, matriculating there in 1977–78. But I had already published two books, one as a poet and another as co-editor, and I had already made a serious commitment to the writing life. Moreover, I had already served in the Marines, and worked on an oil tanker and for the Pennsylvania Department of Justice and as a newspaper reporter; I'd driven a forklift, and done heavy construction. For me, that year and a half was a rare opportunity to write poetry at two in the afternoon instead of two at night. My cohort at UICC consisted of nine students. The class that followed me was 22 students. The university was just discovering what a cash cow creative writing could be. Meanwhile, within a few years, most of those newly minted Masters of Creative Writing had vanished entirely from the radarscope. Most were young, just out of undergraduate school, and when they discovered that employers weren't interested in poems and the electric company wouldn't take short stories, they got jobs and stopped writing because they weren't committed enough to write at 2AM. I've encountered published work by two or three of the folks who were at UICC when I was, but that's it.

JJM. Where do you see poetry going? And where should it go?

WDE. I don't see poetry going anywhere. It's been with us for a long, long time. The ancient Egyptians wrote poetry. The Sumerians wrote poetry. The Greeks wrote poetry. And the Romans. And the Chinese. I know that's not what you meant with your question, but it's the answer I'm going to give you. I don't see poetry going anywhere, but if it should go somewhere, I hope it's onto your refrigerator or into your pocket. It should go wherever you go. As I tell my students—it's a boys' school—every chance I get: real men love poetry, and real women (and men) love men who write poetry.

JJM. Should the poet get social or political? Or should he/she stick to the impressionistic and ethereal, to feelings that evaporate off the page?

WDE. I don't know anything about poetry evaporating off the page. What the heck does that mean? You're getting artsy-fartsy on me again. The poet should get whatever the poet feels comfortable getting. The poet ought to be true to himself or herself, and that is going to manifest itself in different ways with different people. Being "social" or "political" merely for their own sakes belongs in the same trash bin as being innovative or taking risks for no good reason.

JJM. Is the poetry community healthy?

WDE. Well, there's no shortage of poets out there writing furiously and vying to get published. I suppose that's a sign of health. A whole lot of what's getting written is junk, or amateurish sincerity, or painfully incompetent, but that's always been true. We remember Keats and Shelley and Byron, but there were others in England who were writing and publishing at the same time, and most of them are forgotten. We remember Edwin Arlington Robinson, but go back and look at the literary journals of his day, and see how many others were writing and publishing what turned out to be ephemeral stuff, transient and fleeting. Meanwhile, amidst the barrage of poetry being hurled into the public domain these days (the Internet is both a blessing and a curse, no?), some of it is very good indeed. So I'd have to say that the "poetry community" is probably no more and no less healthy than it ever was.

JJM. Who would you say these days has a true individualistic voice?

WDE. I honestly don't read contemporary poetry all that widely. As I said, I write poetry, but I'm not a scholar of poetry. I read stuff that comes my way. I just read a wonderful poem by a man named Jeffrey Alfier, who edits *San Pedro River Review*. My headmaster, Joe Cox, is a good poet who happens to have a handful of poems about fathers and sons in the current issue of our school magazine (*Haverford School Today*, Summer 2012). I think Balaban is a terrific poet. I like Dale Ritterbusch, and Dave Connolly. Nathalie Anderson has done some fine work. Lisa Coffman. Who's ever heard of Eileen D'Angelo beyond the Philadelphia area? But I heard her read a sequence of "recovering Catholic" poems a few years ago that was hilarious. And good old M.L. Liebler. And Lou McKee, who died in 2011 and has left behind a large body of work that is practically unknown and sadly will probably remain so. Oh, and Philip Appleman, who has achieved a fair measure of recognition. I'm sure I'm missing lots of my own favorites, but these are some of the people who come to mind right away.

JJM. Do you see the artist as having to cater for a number of factors that have little to do with artistic merit and talent, that he/she then is controlled by others and divided against himself or herself, as Komunyakaa put it?

WDE. Any poet who is willing "to cater for a number of factors that have little to do with artistic merit and talent" doesn't deserve success. But those are the ones who probably most often find it. Or not. In any case, I know what I'm willing to do and not do. What others do is their business.

JJM. Is Vietnam still—at least partly—the background of your writing nowadays?

WDE. Remember, "Vietnam" is not a war; it is a country that exists in the world today, and the majority of its citizens weren't even alive on April 30th, 1975. So are you asking me about the country of Vietnam or about the Vietnam War?

The country of Vietnam has recently been in the foreground of my writing. In 2011, I returned to Vietnam with my Marine Corps comrade Ken Takenaga, and I've written about that in a long piece called "Ken & Bill's Excellent Adventure," which is the final essay in *Dead on a High Hill*.

The war itself is always the background of my writing. Aside from the various factors that shape all of us in the first five or six years of our lives (long before most of us can even identify what those factors are), the Vietnam War was the single most defining experience of my life. It never goes away. Kali Tal got it right in her book *Worlds of Hurt* when she observed that every poem I write is a Vietnam War poem. How could it be otherwise?

JJM. Then, if—in spite of everything—the Vietnam War influences your writing, would you say that when you write a love poem or one related to nature, there are echoes of Southeast Asia, even a faint one?

WDE. Why do you say "in spite of everything"? In spite of what? Anyway, it isn't so much that there are "echoes" as such, but rather that who I am has been so profoundly influenced by my encounter with the Vietnam War and the ongoing consequences of that encounter.

JJM. In the preface of *Dead on a High Hill* you remind the reader that in your first essay collection *In the Shadow of Vietnam*, eighteen pieces out of twenty-three dealt with the war and its aftermath, most of the rest being "at least colored" as you put it by the conflict. And in *The Madness of It All* fourteen out of forty-three essays tackled directly the Vietnam War. In this latest collection of twenty-five articles, you point out that there are again pieces related to the Vietnam War, some of which are long ("They Want Enough Rice," "Ken and Bill's Excellent Adventure"), others are actually short, two or three pages ("The Power to Declare," "Concerning Memorial Day," "One, Two, Many Vietnams?"). However several essays deal with other varied themes. It does indicate that you are not a one-subject man, that your interests reach out to the world, doesn't it?

WDE. Yes. As I've said, the Vietnam War has never been my only subject or concern or interest.

JJM. In this volume you also discuss poetry in four chapters, albeit they have connections to wars, either Vietnam or Korea. In these pieces, isn't it actually verse—which happens to be about wars—which really interests you, rather than the wars themselves? How these authors expressed their visions, their feelings, their hopes?

WDE. I suppose, because of the nature of my own experiences and what I've ended up doing with my own life, the poetry I'm most often attracted to is what others have written about war. Because of my involvement with the various anthologies, I gained exposure to many, many other veteran-writers. I've known Jan Barry since 1971, and first came upon Balaban's poetry in 1974. Dale Ritterbusch and I both knew and were influenced by Daniel Hoffman (Hoffman lived in the town of Swarthmore, but taught at Penn, where Dale was an undergrad when I was at Swarthmore, though we didn't meet until years later). And as I said, while my work with Korean War veteran-poets struck others as "Ehrhart still stuck in that war thing," it was like being on vacation for me. I could have undertaken research on virtually any subject related to American Studies, but at that time I had only an undergraduate degree with an MA in creative writing, so I had to work in a field where I had already established some credibility, which was war poetry. You didn't mention the two essays in the new book that aren't really essays at all, but rather the writings of other veteran-poets. These men's poetry was brought to my attention by others because they knew of my background. Sam Exler's partner, Regina Holmes, gave me Sam's poems after he died. And my colleague at the Haverford School, Gerry Rooney, came into my classroom one day and handed me that material of his grandfather's, who had died in the Great War; he told me his cousin had found the papers in their grandmother's attic, and Gerry thought they might interest me. So one thing has simply led to another over the years, and here I am—as you point out below—a scholar of war poetry. I never set out to become that. It just sort of happened.

Here's another example of the accidental nature of things: A few years ago, a wonderful English teacher named Edward Hallowell, who had taught at the Haverford School for many years, was set to retire. But he was going to teach one last senior semester-long elective for a Swan Song. But then in December of that year, he told the school that his health would not allow him to teach his course after all. So the Department Head came to me right before Christmas break and asked me if I could put together a senior elective for the spring semester, which was due to start in January. I thought about what would be the easiest course for me to slap together at the last minute, and proposed a class on American War Poetry. I still had to figure out how to package the material, but I knew the material itself cold. If I had tried to do a course on Herman Melville or science fiction or anything else, I would have had to do an enormous amount of prep work, and there simply wasn't time for that. So there I was, doing that "war thing" again, but it was the easiest course for me to put together on short notice.

JJM. You were unhappy that the Pentagon had launched a decade-long Vietnam War Commemoration to "thank and honor veterans of the Vietnam

War." So when you write essays, are you trying to shape opinions and influence public policies? Isn't it somehow what you wanted to do with your article "Thank You for Your Service" in the *New Hampshire Gazette* on July 27th, 2012?

WDE. Not "had launched," but rather "has launched." It's supposed to go on until something like 2025. Here's why I wrote that essay: I heard about this commemoration thing back in May 2012, and I thought, "What a bunch of bullshit." What the hell are they going to commemorate? My Lai? Agent Orange? Bach Mai Hospital? It's obvious the whole thing is just another attempt to re-cast the Vietnam War as Reagan's "Noble Cause." I wanted to write something about how I felt. Mostly for me. I long ago gave up imagining that I am going to shape opinions, let alone influence public policies. This is simply my way of saying, "Fuck you, you bastards! You can do this crap, but you can't make me like it." The Vietnam War took away my voice. Writing gave it back to me. As for why I sent that piece to the *New Hampshire Gazette*, well, I figured the editor, Steve Fowle, himself a Vietnam War veteran, would probably publish it. I like to get published. I like to have readers. But that's different than thinking I'm going to influence anyone. The people who read the *New Hampshire Gazette* range from liberal to far left progressive. I'm not going to change their opinions because they mostly already agree with me. But it's nice for all of us, writer and readers, to know we're not alone. I sent the same commentary to the *Philadelphia Inquirer*, but I don't imagine they'll touch it. Can you imagine how the "I Hate Jane Fonda We Shoulda Nuked Hanoi" crowd would react if they read my description of killing, maiming, brutalizing and making miserable a people who had never done me or my country any harm?

JJM. In 1986 in *Passing Time,* you wrote, "The system's got a life of its own, man. You can't kill it, you can't beat it, and you can't change it." Five years later in your essay "Stealing Hubcaps" you also wrote, "Nothing I do will make any difference, but to do nothing requires a kind of amnesia I have yet to discover a means of inducing." However, with your various writing, readings, lectures, teaching, are you not actually trying to change this system?

WDE. Well, it can't hurt to try. Who knows? I might surprise myself, although I'm not taking bets.

JJM. And when in that piece you write, "Frankly, I suspect that this whole Vietnam War Commemoration is less about a grateful nation thanking and honoring us Vietnam War veterans than it is about a frightened and nervous government trying to gloss over the follies and consequences of military adventurism so that the next generation of young Americans remains willing to place their trust in the hands of people who clearly believe that those they send to fight our wars are expendable (rhetoric not withstanding; actions speak louder than words)," are you not voluntarily polemical, to create a response, a debate?

WDE. From time to time over the years, I've heard others describe my writing as "polemical." I'm just writing. I have things to say, and I say them. If others find what I have to say controversial, that's their problem. I suppose it's my problem, too, especially if those who find me controversial—say, the opinion page editor at the *Inquirer*, for instance—choose to deny me access to readers. But I can't help that. I'm just writing what I feel like I need to say.

JJM. In your poem "Visiting My Parents' Grave," you wrote these two lines: "silence to injustice / large or small is simply cowardice." Are you still driven by this idea? Is it partly something which compels you to write essays?

WDE. Yes, I do still feel that way, although I've gotten smarter about how to confront injustice. It isn't really productive to get in somebody's face and tell them they're moral midgets or unfair or bigoted or whatever. I've learned to be more tactful about how and when to challenge what I perceive to be injustice. As for what compels me to write essays, there are a lot of different reasons. Sometimes it's to address an injustice. But there are three essays in the new collection that were actually talks I gave at various senior dinners at my school, and in those I'm simply trying to say something that will entertain the boys, and interest them, and maybe get them thinking a bit. Other essays in the book are what I'd call more academic, exploring a body of work like Korean War poetry or an individual work like *Hell's Music*. So, no, I would not say that what motivates me to write essays is to confront injustice.

JJM. You are a truth-teller. You did not conform to media-generated images of wars. You recreated the authentic voice of your generation, the ones who went to fight. Is it why you did not get contracts from commercial publishing houses?

WDE. Firstly, as the late Paul Lyons makes abundantly clear in his book *Class of '66*, most of my generation didn't go "to fight." Half of my generation was female, for starters, and most of the men managed to avoid fighting by taking college deferments or medical deferments, or joining the National Guard. So I'm not really the voice of my generation. As for why I haven't gotten contracts from commercial houses, you'd have to ask their editors. Bruce Franklin speaks to that point in his introduction to *Busted*, and maybe he's right, but he's only speculating, and if I were to offer an opinion, it would also be mere speculation. The simple answer is that I don't know.

JJM. You say you are not a scholar (referring more specifically to poetry). But with a PhD, twenty books published, including three collections of essays, and numerous articles printed in scores of magazines or journals, you have spent the last thirty years thinking and putting your thoughts down on paper for people to read. Isn't it what a scholar does, or should do?

WDE. Well, actually, yes, by now I guess I am a scholar. But I said I'm not a scholar in the context of questions you were asking me earlier about contemporary American poetry. The stuff you were asking me about, what prompted my response, those things are not my field.

JJM. At the 1993 University of Notre Dame Vietnam Reconciliation Conference, Air Force LtCol. Tom Bowie told you that *Passing Time* was part of the Air Force Academy curriculum. You were surprised. Why was that?

WDE. You've read that book. It is not very flattering of the U.S. military and especially of the U.S. government the military is sworn to obey. I hadn't realized that there were such forward-thinking and open-minded people among the officer ranks. But then, I hadn't had any contact with the military since I got out in 1969. The depth of my knowledge of the modern officer corps extended to watching Stormin' Norman Schwarzkopf puff out his chest and strut around on TV during the First Gulf War. So meeting men like Bowie and Joe Cox and Donald Anderson at that conference at Notre Dame was a real eye-opener. I remember asking Bowie, who was then in the English Department at the Air Force Academy but spent much of his career as a navigator (or maybe it was bombardier) on B-52s, why he was teaching *Passing Time*, and he replied that if these young cadets didn't think about these issues now, they never would until it was too late. And when I said that I didn't mind paying his salary with my tax dollars, he replied, "Don't get me wrong. The Air Force is full of knuckle-dragging, Neanderthal techno-twit cowboys. That's why I teach English literature at the Air Force Academy." Pretty interesting guy, don't you think?

JJM. What were some challenges you had to face when you started teaching at the Haverford School?

WDE. I had no idea, when I first took over in mid-year, January 2001, that the man I was replacing had been very much beloved. And I also came to realize that he had ceased to be a very effective teacher in his last years, assigning almost no homework and asking very little of his students. (I think this had a lot to do with why I was brought in to replace him, though there were medical issues involved.) So many of the boys were very resistant to me, especially the senior boys who were in their second semester and thought they should continue getting a free ride. For at least the first four months, I would get up every morning with a knot in my stomach, absolutely dreading facing rooms full of stubborn uncooperative teenaged boys. But I didn't earn sergeant's stripes in the Marine Corps at the age of 19&½ by being a push-over.

I would be damned before I'd let those boys know they were getting to me. And most of them eventually came around, the juniors faster than the seniors, but almost all of them in the end. And here I am, nearly twelve years later, about to start another year at the Haverford School. But geez, those first four months were tough. If I had known what I was getting into, I never would have taken the job.

JJM. Joe Cox, the headmaster of Haverford School, refers to you as a pied piper of sorts, and says your style of teaching is unique.[4] Do you understand what he means?

WDE. I'm a little uncomfortable with that "pied piper" label. Didn't that guy basically kidnap all the kids in some town, bewitching them with his music? I hope I'm not bewitching my students. I'd like to think many of the boys enjoy having me as a teacher and coach because I'm a straight shooter, I care about them, and I care about teaching. I'm sure that's what Joe really means.

JJM. Joe Cox also says that you despise the Haverford coat and tie dress code, but that you adhere to it, and you demand the same correctness from your students. Isn't it a bit of a contradiction as you also ask people to question many things, people, especially those in power?

WDE. "Despise" is a pretty strong word. Let's just say that I very much dislike having to wear a coat and tie every day. I didn't even own a jacket I could still fit into when I first took the job. I had to go thrift store rummaging with my daughter to pick up a couple of sport jackets. The boys themselves find it puzzling that the old long-haired hippie guy is perhaps the strictest enforcer of the Haverford School's dress code, and I have to remind them that because I have to put that noose around my neck every morning, I'm already in a foul mood before I ever walk out my front door. "And if I gotta do it," I tell my boys, "so do you." As for trying to teach the boys to "question everything," questioning is one thing; flagrantly thumbing your nose at expected and reasonable standards of community behavior just for the sake of thumbing your nose is something else again. Everyone—but especially my students—needs to learn that choices have consequences. You choose to leave your jacket in your locker, you get detention. You choose to drink and drive, you get dead. I see no contradiction at all in teaching boys to question while also teaching them that choices have consequences.

JJM. Are love and truth essential things teachers should give to students? What else should they receive?

WDE. Yes, love and truth. What else? Knowledge. How to find knowledge and the desire to seek knowledge. Tolerance. The ability to imagine life in someone else's shoes. Appreciation. I don't know. Lots of things. But love and truth, yes, that's a pretty good start.

JJM. In teaching history and English to your high school students, are you trying to avoid what happened to you as a young man, as well as to your fellow Marines from Platoon 1005, to make sure that ignorance does not lead their young lives?

WDE. Ideally, yes, I'd like for my students to avoid the kind of disillusion and heartbreak that comes from discovering that what you thought you knew is illusory. Do I succeed? I don't know. Mostly not. On the other hand, because of the way we've dumped the burden of military service onto so tiny a segment of our society, none of my students will ever have to spend a day in uniform, and very, very, very few of them will. (I know of one boy in the last twelve Haverford School graduating classes who eventually ended up as an enlisted Marine after dropping out of college. Most years, we send a boy or two to the service academies. But 99.9 per cent of my students will never join the military.)

Most of our boys, in fact, are very privileged. Even the ones whose families are making huge sacrifices to send their kids to my school, and the kids who are there on scholarship, have a huge leg up on their peers merely by attending and graduating from the Haverford School. These kids will become the leaders in business, finance, the law, politics, civic associations. Ideally, I want them to grasp that they and their families are lucky, that they are not automatically entitled, that the world they inhabit is not the world that most people inhabit, that the oppressed and the downtrodden and the poor do not deserve their lot in life. Maybe a few of the boys I teach will make a better decision somewhere down the road, remembering some seed I planted when they were young. One likes to think so.

In its most naked form, my wish is that no student of mine will ever find himself confronted with some ugly reality, some life-changing disaster only to say to himself, "You bastard, Ehrhart, why didn't you tell me?"

JJM. In November 1994, at the Sixties Generation Conference, Adi Wimmer suggested that your unpopularity stemmed from your insistence on "bearing moral witness" to events the country was trying to forget or even to deny. Would you agree that this was the case then, and maybe still is today?

WDE. I don't know the answer. And I'm not sure what you mean by "unpopular." Some people like my stuff. You, for instance. You think well enough of me to put this book together. I've got very little to complain about. Do you mean by "unpopular" my not being able to get big publishing houses to publish me, and thus not getting reviewed by the *New York Times* or nominated for the National Book Award? As for "bearing moral witness," that is for others to say, not me. As I said, I just write what I write. I get uneasy around the word "moral." I just had a hamburger the other day. Hamburger is made with beef. In India, eating that burger would be immoral. There are folks out there who think it's immoral for two people of the same sex to love each other. Morality is a very dangerous concept. Do I bear moral witness in my writing? Adi Wimmer's entitled to his opinion, but I'm not going to make such a claim.

JJM. In the poem "For a Coming Extinction," published in 1993, you start with "Vietnam. Not a day goes by / without that word on my lips." You told me this too when I visited you in the summer of 1996. What is it like today? Does it still come to your mind that regularly?

WDE. Of course it does. How can it not? I've put hours and hours over many weeks into answering these questions, for instance. Just two days ago, I was on Marty Moss-Coane's *Radio Times* on our local public radio station with Ken Takenaga, my old Marine Corps comrade, talking about our 2011 trip to Japan and Vietnam. At least six different people sent me articles about that Vietnam War Commemoration stuff, especially Obama's mention of it at the Vietnam Veterans memorial back in May. In June 2012, I spent two weeks at the William Joiner Center for the Study of War and Social Consequences in Boston. Just today, someone sent me an e-mail asking if I had a spare copy of *Vietnam–Perkasie* lying around. So in one form or another, often in multiple forms in a single day, "Vietnam" is always present.

JJM. In your memoirs, as well as in your essays, there is regularly self-ironic humor—even some joking (e.g., the episode of the chocolate chip cookies in *Vietnam–Perkasie*). You must be aware of it. Is it something you cultivate as part of your style, or has it a life of its own?

WDE. That section about the chocolate chip cookies is, of course, a bit of an exaggeration, but less so than you might think. We really were deluged with chocolate chip cookies. I couldn't even look at a chocolate chip cookie for years after I came home. But I had fun writing that section of the book. You may not have noticed it, but each successive memoir gets funnier than the preceding one. I think parts of *Busted* are hilarious; at least I hope they are. I certainly meant them to be. And the writer Bill Ehrhart, also, with each successive book, is more able to take Bill Ehrhart the protagonist less seriously. Look at the way those ghosts are constantly poking fun at me and ignoring my dramatics and deflating my angst. I think it's some combination of distance and maturity and perspective that I didn't have when I began *Vietnam–Perkasie* when I was 31 years old, but had begun to develop by the time I was writing *Busted* when I was 44. I've always had a good sense of humor; it just took me a while to begin to put it into my writing.

JJM. When you were a kid you began each school day with the Lord's Prayer and the Pledge of Allegiance. This still exists. At sports games the national anthem is played all over the USA, something which just does not exist in other countries, for example in Europe. How important do you think these symbols are to shape the conscience of the American nation? Should the Pledge of Allegiance, the national anthem remain so powerful in these places?

WDE. Well, nowadays, ever since a Supreme Court ruling in 1963, maybe '62, public schools aren't allowed to make kids say the Lord's Prayer, but I think the Pledge of Allegiance is still a staple in the public schools and many private schools as well (though not mine, thank goodness). As for the Star-Spangled Banana and all those flags and hoopla, you are right, no other country on earth engages in such constant genuflection. As if, if I don't see an American flag at least 27 times a day, I'll forget which country I live in. It's bizarre, but I think it is really designed to make the overwhelming majority of Americans feel like they're a part of greatness while the plutocracy rakes in all the benefits of empire at the expense of the rest of us.

JJM. How much does poetry matter?

WDE. To whom? It matters a lot to me. I've devoted my entire life to it. I'm pretty sure it matters to Dale Ritterbusch and some other folks I know. But I expect it matters not at all to most Americans. Look how many copies any book of poetry sells, and compare that to the number of people who went to see that new Batman movie in the first weekend of its release.

JJM. Do you believe like Dale Ritterbusch that "art is subversive and the artist is the agent of this subversion"?[5]

WDE. I believe art *can* be subversive and the artist *can* be an agent of subversion. But I don't believe art necessarily *has* to be subversive. The City of Philadelphia has a magnificent mural arts program. We've got a couple of thousand huge public murals painted on the sides of buildings. Some of them carry political messages: influential and innovative women, famous civil rights figures. But others are just beautiful to look at, and do much to improve the quality of a neighborhood. Is that subversive? Is my poem "A Scientific Treatise for My Wife" subversive? I don't think so, but it makes my wife happy every time she's in the audience and I read it. On the other hand, I certainly hope that at least some of my writing is subversive. There's a hell of a lot out there that dearly needs to be subverted.

JJM. Has really nothing changed from Vietnam to Iraq, whether it is amongst the American people, or journalists, writers?

WDE. Oh, all sorts of things have changed, and very few of them for the better. Today, instead of a citizen army of draftees, we have a small professional military caste that bears the whole blood burden. In Vietnam, the more ambitious journalists like David Halberstam and Neil Sheehan, and later Gloria Emerson and Arnold Isaacs, could move relatively freely around the country and get real stories; today access to what is actually going on is completely restricted and controlled by the government and the military. And the media themselves, most of the mainstream outlets, are all owned by Corporate America to a degree unimaginable in the 1960s. In Vietnam, we were fighting a largely homogeneous people; in Iraq we're fighting a fragmented nation whose boundaries ignore ethnic, religious, and cultural divisions. And Afghanistan isn't even a country in any meaningful sense. Also, now we can wage war entirely by proxy, using drones operated by people sitting in safety thousands of miles away from the death and destruction, and most folks seem to think this is a great idea. All sorts of things have changed. What hasn't changed is the willingness of so many Americans to be bamboozled and hoodwinked by that small number of people who benefit from an American Empire.

JJM. In 1986 you wrote in *Passing Time,* "Trapped like a cornered rat, I knew at last that nothing I had ever done in Vietnam would ever carry with it anything but shame and disgrace and dishonor; that I would never be able to recall Vietnam with anything but pain and anger and bitterness; that I would never again be able to take pride in being American." This was an extremely strong emotion. Do you feel the same way in the early 2010s?

WDE. Look at it this way: The United States has a higher percentage of its population behind bars than any other country on earth. We have the most expensive, least efficient health care system in the developed world. We kill each other at a higher rate than any other people on earth. We have the worst mal-distribution of wealth in the developed world, and the disparities just keep getting greater with each passing year. We have a poverty-stricken Third World nation imbedded within our own borders. We spend more on our military than the rest of the world combined. Our infrastructure (water, sewer, highways, bridges, etc.) is crumbling around us. Our public education system, except for the prosperous suburbs, is dysfunctional. Am I supposed to be proud of a country with this kind of record?

I was proud of my country, actually, the night that Barack Obama won the presidency. I never thought I'd live to see that. But he fooled me: he's turned out to be just another politician.

JJM. You also write in the same volume, "when I'd gotten back to the States, I discovered that in my absence America had become an alien place in which and to which I no longer seemed to belong." Do you feel as if you belong to America nowadays over thirty-five years later?

WDE. I still struggle with it. Do I "belong to America"? I'm an American citizen. I vote; indeed, I've never missed a single election—general, primary, or special—since I first became eligible (back then the age was 21, not 18). I pay my taxes. I obey the laws. I'm a member of the ACLU, the Southern Poverty Law Center, Vietnam Veterans Against the War, Veterans for Peace, I contribute to Pet Helpers and my local public radio station.

But in many ways, the country of my birth remains an alien land. How can I feel any kinship with the National Rifle Association and the people who belong to it and support it in the face of disaster after disaster? How can I feel connected with politicians who lack the courage to tackle the terrible problems our society is facing? How do I make myself feel as if I belong to a country that is driven by rapacious and insatiable consumerism? Do I belong to a country that sends a few men and women into harm's way over and over again while everyone goes on about their lives as if nothing at all out of the ordinary is going on? Indeed, it has become all-too-ordinary. Do I belong to that? I dearly hope not.

JJM. In 1998 you stated: "my poetry is an ongoing attempt to atone for the unethical, for my loss of a moral compass when I was a young man." Was it still the same when you were writing *The Bodies Beneath the Table* (2010), your last collection of poems?

WDE. Yes, it's still the same. Of course, there are a lot of poems in that new book that don't have anything to do with atonement. But there are also poems like the title poem, and "September 11th," and "Coaching Winter Track in Time of War," and "Kosovo."

JJM. Years later after you were discharged from the U.S. Marine Corps you still have a strong bond with it, don't you? It showed in 1999 with the publication of *Ordinary Lives: Platoon 1005 and the Vietnam War* in which you wrote, "[T]hough I came to hate the American War in Vietnam, I have never hated the Marine Corps." You sometimes go to battalion reunions too. Forty years later what makes this tie so durable?

WDE. Supposedly, Harry Truman once said that the Marine Corps has a propaganda machine that is the equal of Stalin's. Marines took umbrage at that, but the Corps certainly is good at marketing its "brand." And I suppose there's a bit of that propagandizing that never quite got out of my system. On the other hand, I really was very well trained, and I think that training probably kept me alive when I had reached a very low psychological point in the midst of my time in Vietnam. I saw regular army units in combat, and honestly they were something close to a rabble. And this was the vaunted 1st Air Mobile Cavalry Division. The Marine Corps did a lot of stupid stuff, and still does to this day, I'm sure (there are many reasons why we're called Jarheads), but fighting is what they're supposed to do. The Marines don't set policy. That is supposed to be done by the civilian leadership. It's why our Constitution makes the elected president the commander-in-chief and gives the purse strings to Congress.

As for the reunions, I go occasionally (they've been held every other year since 1993; I've been to five of them over the years). It has mostly been at the urging of my old lieutenant from Vietnam, Ron Kincade, who was a wonderful boss and clearly cared about me and the other young enlisted men he was responsible for. He found me in 1995 and asked me to come to that year's reunion, and we've stayed in touch ever since. He and I don't see eye-to-eye politically, but he has practically every book I've ever published. And I think we are able to look beyond our political differences because we shared a difficult time together and we both survived it, at least in part because of each other. That's worth something.

JJM. I certainly am aware that answering my interview questions requires energy from you. I wonder how much energy writing takes out of you, though. And/or if it gives some back to you. The way it happens when we teach. Sometimes in some classes I know very well I have burnt out plenty of calories, but when it's over I feel like I have plenty more!

WDE. This is an interesting question, one I'm not sure I've ever thought about before. The equation between teaching and writing, however, is something I have thought about. So how shall I formulate my answer? Let me begin by saying that, in my experience, concentrated mental effort requires enormous energy and leaves me feeling drained, physically exhausted. The aspect of teaching that I find most exhausting is not teaching *per se*, but rather grading, especially the subjective process of grading essays and papers and offering (what I hope is) clear and constructive feedback. Getting up in front of a class and leading a discussion or dialogue, or giving a lesson or mini-lecture, is fun, exhilarating, energizing. (I seldom actually give lectures as such, but often expound on some point or topic for a few minutes, usually spontaneously when it seems appropriate.) Conducting a class is much like giving a poetry reading: I know my stuff, and I enjoy sharing it with others.

Prep work, on the other hand, is also taxing, though it's also energizing when I end up with what I feel will be a good lesson. But grading, that's the real drain. For me, writing is both taxing and energizing. (Teaching, the pedagogical equivalent of conducting the orchestra, is almost always energizing; grading is never, ever energizing.) Writing takes effort, mental and even physical—sitting here typing for three or four or five hours, as I've done several times with these interview questions, is work! But if I like what I'm writing, and feel good about it as it takes shape on the page, it is more fun than work. I have often said, because it's true, that few things give me as much satisfaction as teaching a good class or writing a good poem or a sharp essay. I write a lot less now than I used to, but I don't feel deprived as a writer because I'm getting almost the same sense of accomplishment and satisfaction from teaching. Both activities can be hard work, but both can be very rewarding.

This interview with W.D. Ehrhart was conducted via email by Jean-Jacques Malo in July and August 2012, while working on editing The Last Time I Dreamed About the War: Essays on the Life and Writing of W.D. Ehrhart, *where the first part of this interview appeared.*

NOTES

 1. Linda Van Devanter and Joan A. Furey, eds., *Visions of War, Dreams of Peace: Writings of Women in the Vietnam War* (New York: Warner Books, 1991), xix.
 2. Jean-Jacques Malo and Tony Williams, *Vietnam War Films* (Jefferson, NC: McFarland, 1994, 2011).
 3. John Baky, curator of the Imaginative Representations of the Vietnam War Collection at La Salle University.
 4. Joe Cox, "W.D. Ehrhart: Transformational Teacher," in Jean-Jacques Malo, ed., *The Last Time I Dreamed About the War* (Jefferson, NC: McFarland, 2014), 219–227.
 5. Dale Ritterbusch, "Poetry and the Art of Resistance: The Literature of W.D. Ehrhart, in Context," in Jean-Jacques Malo, ed., *The Last Time I Dreamed About the War* (Jefferson, NC: McFarland, 2014), 99–108.

Politics, Polemics and Poetry
Meggan McGuire

MMcG. The politics of poetry: What was it like trying to get anti-war (namely anti–Vietnam) poetry published?

WDE. My earliest anti-war poems were published in *Winning Hearts and Minds: War Poems by Vietnam Veterans*, published in 1972 by 1st Casualty Press, an offshoot of Vietnam Veterans Against the War. Obviously, this was a venue that actively sought and supported anti-war writing, and the book was very successful, which kind of hooked me on seeing my name in print. It really was three more years before I began to try to publish regularly, an effort which included but was not limited to anti-war poetry. None of my poetry, anti-war or otherwise, began to appear in anything even vaguely resembling mainstream venues for another decade and more. I was mostly publishing in very small literary magazines and journals. And I mean very small. Very few outlets were interested in my poetry, anti-war or otherwise. Only gradually and over many, many years did I begin to build a reputation among at least some small portion of the literary world—and again, I emphasize the word *small*. I've never had a major publisher, and have never won a major award. I still publish mostly in little magazines and journals. But at this point, almost 43 years after *Winning Hearts and Minds*, I can pretty much get my poems published, regardless of the topic, in one small press publication or another. Occasionally I get into *American Poetry Review*, but never *Poetry* or *The New Yorker* or other big-time venues. For me, at least, the distinction you make between trying to get anti-war poetry published and trying to get any poetry at all published has never existed. Getting poetry published is a struggle, period.

MMcG. How did your experience with publishing your poetry differ from publishing your memoirs like *Vietnam–Perkasie* and *Passing Time*?

WDE. I wrote poetry for fifteen years before I attempted to write prose. In the early 1980s, I did try to interest a small handful of commercial NYC publishers in an early draft of *Vietnam–Perkasie*, but no one showed the slightest interest. I had had some very indirect dealings with McFarland & Company, then a new and small independent press in North Carolina, so I tried them. They took the book and published it in 1983. When I finished the manuscript for *Passing Time*, Robbie Franklin at McFarland said he'd publish it, but he thought I should try for a larger and more commercial publisher because he thought I deserved more than he could do for me. I did land a contract with Avon Books, and they published the book in the spring of 1986—but not without changing the title without consulting me or even asking my permission—and then they took the book out of print in less than a year without ever spending a penny on promoting or marketing. (I had a similar experience with Avon and one of my poetry anthologies, *Carrying the Darkness*.) I decided after those experiences that I'd rather deal with small houses like McFarland (and for my poetry, Adastra) who treated me fairly and personally than with commercial houses that cared about nothing but $$$$. (Prof. Bruce Franklin even managed to get the manuscript for *Busted* into the hands of a hotshot NYC agent, but her only advice to me was to stop writing about the Vietnam War and instead write some other book.)

MMcG. Which community was more receptive to your work—the poets or the prose writers?

WDE. Given my record of sales, reviews, awards, or any other measure you care to use as the standard, I'd say neither "community" has paid much attention to me at all. Nevertheless, over all these years, some people have paid attention. Prof. Franklin has been a staunch supporter and advocate, as have others, mostly people who care about war literature, issues of war and peace, social justice, and other progressive issues. I have managed to build only a small audience for my writing, certainly compared to highly visible contemporaries of mine like Tim O'Brien or Yusef Komunyakaa or Carolyn Forché, but it is a loyal and encouraging audience, and I occasionally get letters and e-mails from new readers who've just discovered me, which is very gratifying. I can't complain about the recognition I have or haven't received. I've even begun to hear from Iraq/Afghanistan veterans who have found that my writing speaks to them and is helping sort out their own feelings. That's cool.

MMcG. Currently speaking, would you say that poets are less willing to publish politically-charged poems? Why or why not?

WDE. I can't speak for any poet except myself.

MMcG. *The New Yorker* has alluded to the idea that the poetry of witness is the new venue for poetic resistance. In a recent article titled "Poetry in Extremis," the author mentions Carolyn Forché, the unofficial founder of this genre. The excerpt below speaks to Forche's hesitation to define the genre as political or ideological:

> "Forché herself shied away from such claims. The poetry that interested her was not political, per se, but was what she called a 'poetry of witness.' This was not the work of partisans but of those who, like Amnesty International, stood in solidarity with 'the party of humanity.' Witness poetry was testimonial rather than polemical."

What are your thoughts on this genre of poetry? Is "witnessing" enough in the age of the endless war?

WDE. Firstly, I've seldom seen a poem in *The New Yorker* that was worth the time it took to read. Once in a very rare while, maybe, but not often.

Secondly, I have no idea what a "poetry of witness" means, nor do I understand the distinction between "testimonial" and "polemical." There is good writing and bad writing. I've often been accused of being polemical. Indeed, every now and then someone says it as a compliment rather than a criticism. I have no idea what any of these people are talking about. I just write. I write about my life. I write about the world around me. I'm just trying to grapple with what I see out there in front of my eyes and what I feel back in here behind my eyes. Some critics have talked about my "political" writing as opposed to my "personal" writing, but it's all the same to me. It's all one story.

Thirdly, is Forche trying to say that Amnesty International isn't partisan? Of course it's partisan. It takes the side of the weak, the helpless, the voiceless; it opposes injustice and tyranny and criminal behavior in the guise of government. That's not partisan?

Finally, is "witnessing" enough in the age of endless war? No, it's not enough. Nothing is enough. One does what one has to do in order to live with oneself and one's conscience, but it's never enough. The bastards have all the guns, all the money, and all the time in the world.

MMcG. In terms of academic publishing and cultural criticism, would you say that it is harder to publish essays that are politically direct and unabashedly candid? Are some things still not fit to print if they are too polemical?

WDE. I have no idea how to put this in terms of "academic publishing and cultural criticism." I don't know what you mean by that. As opposed to what other kind of publishing and what other kind of criticism?

I've written quite a few "politically direct and unabashedly candid" essays over the past 35 years or so. I do notice that I used to have better luck getting them published in newspaper op-eds in the 1990s than I've had in this century. I am not sure how to explain that. Maybe editors are getting more timid. Maybe I'm just running into the wrong editors. The Internet and online publishing have largely offset my diminishing access to print media, but I suspect that anyone reading my essays online already agrees with me, which is why they are visiting the sites on which I've published.

Meggan McGuire was a master's degree candidate at Rutgers University in Newark, New Jersey, enrolled in H. Bruce Franklin's Vietnam & American Culture seminar at the time this interview was conducted on December 7, 2014, for a paper titled "Disinterest and Dissidence: What Happened to the Poetry of Resistance?"

We Shouldn't Have Been There

Adam Gilbert

AG. I think maybe we should start with the most simple question: why did America go to war in Vietnam?

WDE. Oh, simple! Right, okay, sure. I think that it was really a matter of very intelligent people stupidly imagining that communism was this monolithic entity that was being controlled from the Kremlin by Joseph Stalin and that if we didn't stop the commie bastards, I mean, we just had to, it was a struggle between communism and capitalism as to who got control of the world. The thing that's very interesting about this is that the initial decisions that led the United States to any involvement in Vietnam were made with no consideration for what was happening in Vietnam. I started off talking about communism-capitalism, and that's true, but at the end of World War II Europe was in ruins and there was a legal communist party in France, as there was in Italy, and de Gaulle said, "If we can't rebuild the French economy, the communists are going to take power in France and you're going to have a communist country in the heart of Western Europe. Because France itself is in ruins, the only way we're going to be able to revive our economy is by retaking our colonies." French military forces returned to Vietnam in the fall of 1945 aboard United States flagged ships. The French didn't have any ships. We transported their army back to Vietnam. And it was kind of, well, hold our nose and let the French fight this colonial war, not because of what's happening in Vietnam, but because of what's happening in Western Europe and in France. Had Truman at that point said, "No. Go to hell." Had he taken the approach that Roosevelt had, "Hey, you guys have had this country for 80 years and the Vietnamese are worse off than when you started." But Roosevelt died, and Truman didn't have any foreign policy background. And there is this visceral hatred and fear of communism, but it didn't have to do with Asia, it had to do with Europe. It only becomes of particular interest in the

United States after the Chinese Civil War finally ends with Mao in power. Six months later the Korean War starts and that, too, is not anywhere near as simple as it looks. But by June of 1950, the French were able to argue that they're not fighting a colonial war, they're on the forefront of the war against communism. And that's when we start actively supporting France so that, I'm sure as you know, by the end of the French war, we're paying 75 to 80 percent of the bills. And at that point there was nothing the U.S. could do to prevent Ho Chi Minh from taking control of the north, but guys like John Foster Dulles were saying, "We're going to save south Vietnam. We can't let the communists take the whole thing." When Eisenhower talked about the domino theory, they really believed this, these guys believed this. So that by 1954 when France says, "We've had enough," the United States policymakers have already emotionally, mentally committed themselves to war in Vietnam, to preserving a so-called free southern Vietnam. And of course then what they do is they try to find some bizarre third force. It's hard to believe Graham Greene laid this whole thing out in *The Quiet American* in 1955. But that's what Diem's supposed to be, the third force. He's not French, he's not communist, and he's going to rally the forces of freedom. And of course, we spend nine years trying to do that and that doesn't work, and certainly by 1963 we're into this thing. It's like the Tar Baby and the Br'er Rabbit stories. We're stuck, we're suckered. These policymakers aren't going to back out, they're not going to say, "Okay, let the commies have it." They've already been committed for almost, well certainly for 13 years, to a certain outcome in Vietnam, and that outcome involves "we get what we want."

AG. Do you think that they had good reasons?

WDE. No, no, they didn't have good reasons, they were ignorant fools. What happens is, you develop a mind-set, a way of seeing the world, and once you are convinced that's the right way to see the world, everything, all new information gets run through that filter. If the new information matches your belief system, you keep it, and if it doesn't, you get rid of it. From 1945 on there were people telling senior policymakers, "Ho Chi Minh's a communist, but that's irrelevant. He's a nationalist, he wants to keep his country free." Abbot Low Moffat is sent there by the State Department in 1946 to get the goods on Ho, to get the proof that he's taking his orders from Stalin, and Moffat comes back and says, "Guy's not taking orders from anybody. Wants his country to be free of the French." There were others. Archimedes Patti, who was one of the OSS guys. There were guys in the State Department China desk. Basically, anybody who tried to argue, "We really should just send these guys a box of pencils and some aspirin and leave them be," they all got fired. The policymakers did not listen to the guys who knew what was actually going on in Vietnam because what those lower level men were saying did not match this belief that Stalin is out to conquer the world. All you've got to do is look at Eastern Europe, there's your proof. Every country the Red Army occupies is now a Stalinist communist state. Mao Zedong has now won the Chinese Civil War. They simply could not accept the reality in Vietnam because the reality did not match their beliefs.

AG. Do you think the intention was good at least then?

WDE. The road to hell is paved with good intentions, says the Bible. What the hell difference does it make what their intentions were? They killed millions and millions and millions of people. I don't care what their intentions were.

AG. So it's not "a noble cause"?

WDE. No, it wasn't. And all they're trying to do is decide who is going to get to put their fingers in the world pie, us capitalists or those commies. That's all they were finally interested in.

AG. So the war wasn't in any way necessary, do you think?

WDE. Absolutely not. Look at Yugoslavia. Communist country, refused to be part of the Soviet bloc, and we had perfectly normal relations with Yugoslavia all through the Cold War.

AG. So this idea that Ho was the Tito…

WDE. "But Ho is not going to be like Tito; Ho is taking his orders from Stalin. Tito's not, but Ho is." Noble cause? No. It doesn't matter what you imagine their intentions were, it was totally unnecessary, and there were significant people who understood what was happening in Vietnam, who tried to tell senior policymakers, "Don't do this."

AG. What were the alternatives then? Just to back out or never get involved?

WDE. Send Ho Chi Minh a bunch of hospital beds. Maybe some penicillin. Give him diplomatic recognition. Tell him, "Hey, what can we do to help you out with your new country here?" We could have made Ho Chi Minh an ally. Communist? Big deal. Who cares? Well, I tell you who cares, Michelin rubber and various other capitalist businesses. It would not do to have a third world country become independent of Western economic constraints because if one country gets that idea, who knows what's going to happen. And of course as you look at world history between 1945 and 1975 it's just one colonial power after another being kicked out of their colonial possessions, and that terrifies the colonialists. Look at a guy like John Foster Dulles and his brother Allen Dulles. Secretary of State, Director of the CIA. Guatemala elects a socialist president in 1951, guy named Jacobo Árbenz. Are you familiar with this?

AG. Yeah, then they deposed him, right?

WDE. Yeah. One of the first things that Árbenz does is to nationalize the United Fruit Company's holdings. United Fruit owns all the good land in Guatemala, and they're paying Guatemalans 50 cents a week to pick bananas, and Árbenz has this crazy idea that the wealth of Guatemala should actually belong to the Guatemalan people, and he nationalizes United Fruit holdings, and within a year there is a CIA funded military overthrow. Oh, and guess what? The Secretary of State of the United States, at that time, John Foster Dulles, was a board member of United Fruit Company and his brother Allen Dulles was a senior partner in the law firm that represented United Fruit Company. Just a coincidence, I'm sure. But that's what's going on, that's why they don't want a free Vietnam, ultimately.

AG. So it's a mixture of control and money, right?

WDE. Yeah. And of course, John Foster Dulles didn't get up in the morning and look in the mirror and brush his teeth and say, "I'm a greedy son of a bitch and I'm going to do whatever I have to do to foster my interest." He's convinced, "Oh the communists are going to take over everything. Árbenz is a communist, it'll be terrible, the people will be oppressed." They find ways to convince themselves that doing the right thing just happens to correspond with their personal self-interest.

AG. A sort of self-delusion, bad faith.

WDE. Adolf Hitler didn't get up in the morning and say, "I'm the most evil bastard who ever lived." People can convince themselves that anything is right if it suits their purposes.

AG. What about the Cold War context? Could you see any justification for the fear that Vietnam might fall?

WDE. No.

AG. Or the domino theory, any credence?

WDE. The model that we looked at, and that I was taught as a schoolboy, is, "Look what the Russians did to Eastern Europe." Every country the Red Army occupied with the exception of Austria for certain reasons—diplomatic reasons that suited both the U.S. and the Soviet Union—every country ends up with a communist-style government, a Stalinist-style government. And that proves that Stalin is out to conquer the world. Well, that analysis first of all ignores Yugoslavia, which isn't part of that model. It also ignores the fact that the Soviets lost 20 million people. Half the total casualties of the Second World War were Soviet citizens. Half of them. And it's the second time the West had invaded Russia. Stalin was not a nice guy. I would not like him to date my daughter. He certainly killed enough Russians during the '20s and '30s, as many as died in the war, but at least he perceived those people as enemies of the state. He's not a nice guy, but what he's doing is, "Next time the West wants to attack me, they're going to have to kill a lot of other people before they get to my people." That's what he's doing, he's pushing his borders out to the west. We look at the Cuban Missile Crisis as, "How dare those Russians put nuclear missiles 90 miles from the United States." At the very time that they're trying to do that we had missiles in Turkey, we had missiles in Iran, we had missiles in Alaska and Canada. We had the Soviet Union ringed with ICBMs pointed at Soviet cities and yet we're claiming that they're being aggressive by putting a few missiles in Cuba. So the way in which the Cold War was interpreted and the decisions that were made based on that interpretation all had to do with what was to our benefit. Had we taken a different approach to the Soviet Union, at any time between 1945 and 1990, I don't know how things might have gone differently. But I do know that other actions taking place around the world, that we ascribed to and blamed on the Soviet Union, had little or nothing to do with the Soviet Union.

AG. What about China then?

WDE. The rift between Mao and the Soviet government began while Stalin was still alive. We just looked at, "Oh communist, communist, they're buddies," and ignored the reality of that situation. We also—"we," I keep saying, "we." Policymakers, thinkers, guys like Kissinger at Harvard, they're interpreting all of this stuff through that filter that supports the way they want the world to be, which means the United States is the Big Cheese, we're the guys who call the shots. One looks at all these wars of independence that take place in Asia and Africa in the '50s and '60s and into the '70s with Portugal and its African colonies, and, "Oh that's the communists fomenting revolution." Well, I'm sure the Russians, in some cases the Chinese, certainly the Cubans, were perfectly happy to offer support to these folks. But that wasn't the cause of those revolutions. Same thing in Central America with Reagan in the 1980s. What did any of those nations, including Vietnam, ever get from Western capitalist democracies? A boot in the face and a bayonet in the stomach. Ho Chi Minh asked the United States repeatedly for help in freeing Vietnam from France. He did it in 1919, he does it again in 1945 and '46 with a series of letters to Truman. What did he ever get from us? Why wouldn't any of these colonized nations turn to a powerful country that's willing to help them?

AG. Were you aware of any of this geopolitical stuff in the '60s?

WDE. No, absolutely not. I grew up in a world where it was the Cold War, it was the commies against us, we were the good guys, we were the guys who wore white hats. Why the hell do you think I joined the Marine Corps? There were some personal reasons for it, but I absolutely, fundamentally believed when Lyndon Johnson said, "If we do not stop the communists in Vietnam, we will one day have to fight them on the sands of Waikiki." And I believed him. That was the lens I had been given to understand the world I lived in. I thought the Russians were proving their aggression and their murderous intent by putting Russian missiles in Cuba. One morning I woke up, I must have been in seventh grade, maybe, and here's a wall right across Berlin. They literally built this thing overnight. What more proof do you need? People jumping over this wall being shot by East German guards. They'd rather be dead than red. That was my reality. That's why *Passing Time* is the more important book. The guy at the end of *Vietnam–Perkasie* is just one fucked-up confused crazy kid. I don't know what the hell happened to me. My entire world had been destroyed. My intellectual framework had been completely destroyed. I had to construct a world that I could live in. That old filter through which I evaluated everything had been destroyed.

AG. How shocking was it for you to find out these sorts of things were going on?

WDE. Adam, you've read my stuff. You see any anger in the writing that I've done over the years? How shocking was it? It was profound. It's what I say at one point in *Passing Time*, that these murderous bastards, I had given up my honor, my decency, my humanity for these bastards, for guys like Foster Dulles and McNamara and Rusk and Rostow. How shocking was it? I still struggle to deal with it.

AG. A sense of betrayal.

WDE. I will go to my grave ashamed of the country I live in, especially because we haven't learned anything since then. That's the really hard part. The wrong people learned the wrong lessons.

AG. In "The Teacher," you say you emerged carrying "anger like a torch / to keep my heart from freezing, / and a strange new thing called / love / to keep me sane." I think the last time we talked about this, the need to rebuild your entire ethical world after the shock of the war. So sort of like this anger on the one hand, but with a new sense of love or not? Is there something positive in that?

WDE. Oh, I think I have over the years learned to love more appropriate objects of love.

AG. Is that still a good assessment then?

WDE. Probably. I'm often accused of being unpatriotic, I don't love my country. What does it mean to love your country? Am I supposed to love a country that incarcerates more of its citizens than any other country on the face of the earth? Am I supposed to love a country that murders each other at a higher rate than any other country on the face of the earth, including Somalia and Afghanistan? Am I supposed to love a country that has the highest infant mortality rate in the developed world? Am I supposed to love a country that has a Third World poverty stricken nation of 40 to 50 million people embedded within our own borders? Am I supposed to love a country that wants to take away healthcare for women? Am I supposed to love a country where the eight wealthiest people, their wealth increased by $87 billion in the last five years? And meanwhile the Republican Party is trying to kill food stamps. Is that what I'm supposed to be in love with?

AG. What do your fellow Americans think then?
WDE. They probably think I'm a commie creep. I don't really give a fuck what they think.

AG. But what do they think about those issues? Why do they think so differently from you? John Baky and I have been talking a lot about this.[1]
WDE. Because for one thing, most of them haven't had their faces rubbed in the reality of what it means to be an American. Most of them are not aware that, as Americans, the standard of living we have is at the expense of taking what belongs to others on a grand scale. Let's face it, I've learned to live with this, but I wake up every morning angry and ashamed of being an American and I go to bed every night angry and ashamed of being an American. Who the hell wants to live like that? I don't want to live like that. Why do I live like that? Because I can't unlearn what I learned. But most Americans have never learned that in the first place.

AG. Do you think there is a kind of willful ignorance as well?
WDE. Yes, absolutely. That's exactly it, willful ignorance. I used to be more critical of my fellow citizens. The fact is, most Americans are working hard just to pay the mortgage, keep a roof over their heads, keep their family fed and clothed. If they have some time to themselves, what do you want to do, do you want to read about how fucked up your country is or do you want to watch a football game? It's hard to blame them for wanting to just watch a football game. At the same time it is astounding to realize how many ordinary Americans regularly vote for politicians who are quite openly out to screw them. And yet they keep voting for them because, "Well, that guy opposes abortion, I think abortion is a crime, I'll vote for him, who cares what else he's doing." But one of the things that has changed for me over the years, it's taken me a long, long, long time to realize it, I'm a very small man

in a very big world. There isn't much I can do to change things. I write what I write, if people read it, fine, if people think twice because of something I've read, that's great. Don't ask me to explain why my fellow citizens aren't all voting for Bernie Sanders. I don't understand it. I'm voting for Bernie Sanders. I've done something I've never before done in my entire life and I'm 67 years old. I have given money to the Sanders campaign on more than one occasion and will continue to do so as long as he is a viable candidate. I've never done that. Why the rest of my fellow citizens, except for the Koch brothers and a few other rich people, aren't backing Bernie Sanders is a mystery to me.

AG. Because he's a socialist?

WDE. But so is half of Europe, including the Scandinavians and they're the happiest people in the world.

AG. Do Americans want to be Scandinavian though?

WDE. They should. They should want to be. It's also true that the way in which most Americans get information is completely controlled by corporate America, and corporate America is perfectly happy to have things go along the way they've been going. And again, to try to get Joe Blow to sit down at his computer and go look up the latest article in *Mother Jones* or *The Progressive* or *The Washington Spectator*, it ain't going to happen, I wish it would, but it won't. And besides, for the most part, then they learn, "Jesus Christ, this is all fucked up." And what's any one person supposed to do about it?

AG. Going back to the war, and thinking about the American public—we've talked about politicians—do you think the public was in any way responsible for the war?

WDE. Sure. Of course. They're shoveling their kids over, they're as gullible as could be. Support for the war: the only reason why public support for the war began to decline was not because most Americans thought the war was somehow immoral or criminal, that we shouldn't be doing it, but that most Americans, after a period of years, began to be profoundly disturbed by constant images of jet fighter planes dropping napalm on villages, of helicopter gunships shooting up water buffalo in the rice fields, of the most powerful nation on earth pummeling to rubble a third world agricultural country—and with no end in sight, and with no one who could give any good reason for why this was happening. Most Americans finally reached a point where they simply wanted this to stop because it didn't match our own perception of ourselves as the good guys defending freedom against the evil commies or Nazis or whoever the hell we happen to be fighting at any given time. It became harder and harder for Americans to believe what we were doing was okay and they simply wanted this disturbing nightmare to stop. Actually, if you look at public opinion polls, everybody credits this with Walter Cronkite in the middle of the Tet Offensive saying, "We're locked in a stalemate." But, in fact, public opinion begins to shift in the summer of 1967. And it's because American ground forces had been there for over two and a half years. The troop strength keeps increasing with nobody who can say, what does it mean, when do we win, how long is this going to go on.

AG. If it starts declining in '67, how come it takes another five years to extricate?

WDE. There was a great deal of cowardice on the part of public officials. McNamara apparently understood by 1966 that we weren't going to win, but rather than publicly saying, "Here's why I'm resigning," he kept his mouth shut, was a good soldier, was rewarded with the presidency of the World Bank and did not say for another almost 30 years, "We were wrong, terribly wrong." Duh! Thanks pal, nice of you to tell us now. Lyndon Johnson, I don't think he ever understood what happened but he did understand that something had gone wrong and the American people didn't love him anymore. But instead of doing the right thing and extricating the U.S. from the Vietnam War, he abandoned his troops in the field, he wouldn't run for re-election. He slinks off, hands the White House over to Richard Nixon, who wasn't going to be the first American president to lose a war, and who very deftly managed to do some things like using the POW issue as a way of prolonging support for the war. I don't like to say that my fellow citizens are stupid, but they're gullible.

AG. What about apathetic?

WDE. Nixon was able to recast the war. "We're bringing our soldiers home. We're going to get peace with honor. They're going to have to give us back our boys that they have captive." And that's how he actually pulled off a very deft political maneuver. Most Americans didn't understand what was going on. One of the articles of impeachment had to do with the secret bombing of Cambodia. He was bombing Cambodia for three-and-a-half years and the American people never knew it. The American people never paid enough attention, although they should have known because the information was available. As American troops are being withdrawn, the level of the air war against Vietnam, north and south, is increasing exponentially, Vietnamese casualties are increasing exponentially. But what Americans are seeing is, our soldiers are coming home, our casualty figures are dropping, "Look, Nixon really is winding the war down." Then he invades Cambodia, there's a big upheaval over that. Two years later you have the invasion of Laos. Nixon was, unfortunately, very good at deflecting political criticism and maintaining at least enough support so that the war goes on. More people died in Vietnam after Nixon became president than before, and almost as many Americans were killed under the Nixon presidency.

AG. Almost.

WDE. That's only because our troop levels are dropping while Asian casualties are going through the roof.

AG. What about the silent majority? How important do you think they are?

WDE. I don't know. We like these nice terms, "silent majority."

AG. I'm talking about this idea that Nixon calls them the silent majority because he sees them supporting him, but when I spoke to Dave Connolly, he pointed out that it's actually a really good description because it's essentially a description of the American public reaction, the fact that there is this massive war going on and these people are just silent bystanders.[2]

WDE. I would say the silent majority, their silence was apathy not somehow some tacit support of Nixon. As I said, most Americans just wanted this nightmare to go away.

AG. What about the anti-war movement then? Do you think they played an important role in ending the war? Were they successful?

WDE. I don't know if they played a big role, if the anti-war movement made the war any shorter because who knows what would have happened had there not been an anti-war movement. But looking at the tenacity with which Nixon persisted in pursuing the war, in the face of the fact that it was clear that the American people, for whatever reasons, as I said I think it was the wrong reasons, but they really wanted this to stop. And he was able to keep it going. If I look at the absolute obsession of Nixon not to be the guy who loses Vietnam, loses a war, God knows what he and Kissinger and their friends would have done had there not been an anti-war movement. They might well have killed every goddamn person in Vietnam. They wouldn't have used nukes because they were afraid of the Russians. They wouldn't have invaded north Vietnam because they were afraid of the Chinese. But south Vietnam itself, they very well may have depopulated the entire place for all I know. I do know that when the draft ended, to a very large degree that defanged the anti-war movement. It was actually we veterans in Vietnam Veterans Against the War who were the driving force of the anti-war movement from 1970 on. Again, I don't know, do you blame these college kids? As soon as their ass isn't on the line, they go home. I don't know that I would have done anything much different. Certainly self-interest gets your attention. But I do know that if you look at everything going on between the fall of 1970 and the end of the war it's virtually all veterans, stuff that VVAW is doing.

AG. Speaking of the anti-war movement, what did you think of conscientious objectors, before the war and then after the war and now?

WDE. Well, at the time, I can remember the first guy who burned his draft card, a guy named David Miller, it was October of 1965, and he announced he was going to do it, he was a divinity student at Yale or Harvard, Yale I think it was, but he did this on the steps of the New York Public Library. We've just passed the anniversary, the 50th anniversary, earlier this week. It was October 1965, and this was headline news at the time. I remember thinking, "You traitor bastard. They ought to take him out and shoot him." At that point I was a senior in high school. I was 17. While I was in Vietnam, after I'd been there for about nine or ten months, all I knew was this is fucking crazy, this is nuts. I had this long conversation with our battalion chaplain. And Father Lyons says, "You know, if you feel this way there's such a thing as a conscientious objector deferment and I could maybe help you with that." And my response was, "Oh no, you're not hanging that albatross around my neck." To me, at that point, CO was the first two letters of coward. The two years between when I left Vietnam and the killings at Kent State, I'm just mostly trying not to think about anything, drinking heavily, engaged in all kinds of self-destructive behavior. But once I started thinking again, in the late spring of 1970, I very quickly realized these COs, they're right. If the war is wrong, then these guys have the right idea. I knew a guy at Swarthmore who was a senior when I was a freshman. I still have some contact with him. We're the same age because I would have been a senior if I hadn't joined the Marines. He was a CO and he went to prison, he refused to register for the draft, said, "If I register for the draft, they're just going to put some other kid in my place, I can't." And soon after he graduated they put him on trial and put him in prison.

AG. How long did he serve?

WDE. Three years, I think. He got out and became a doctor. I hadn't even known it at the time, but he was one of the guys who was a crewman on that ship, the *Phoenix*, that sailboat that sailed to Hanoi in 1967, I think it was. John was one of the crewmen.

AG. If you had the chance to go back, would you have preferred to have been a CO? Looking back on it as you are now.

WDE. I could have gone to college in 1966. Had my student deferment. I would have been subject to the first draft lottery during my senior year in the fall of 1969, my birthday came up something like number 315 and they never came close to it. I could have avoided the war without even having to do anything. But if I had to do it, I don't know, CO? I'm not a conscientious objector. There was a period of time in the early '70s when I thought I was, but I'm not. If I had been a young man in Vietnam in 1966, I hope I would have had the courage to join the VC and fight the goddamn oppressors. How do you tell black South Africans in the 1960s, you know, "peace, love and brotherhood"? The white government would have blacktopped the highway with them, literally. Pacifism is a luxury of white middle-class Europeans and their American pals.

AG. In what circumstances do you think war can be justified? To resist aggression from the outside?
WDE. Yeah, sure. The Vietnamese certainly had every right to kill us. They didn't come over here. I went halfway around the world to fuck with them.

AG. So you definitely agree that the VC had a right to resist?
WDE. Absolutely.

AG. What about the NVA then?
WDE. Sure. They're all the same. One country. That whole division was totally artificial. The French did it, they divided Vietnam into three territories, tried to claim there is no Vietnam; there's Annam, Tonkin, and Cochinchina. But no, there's one Vietnam.

AG. Do you think the VC and the NVA, then, had more of a right to be fighting than the American soldiers?
WDE. They had every right to fight and we had none. It's not "more of." I had dinner one time in 1985 in Hanoi with these two Vietnamese generals, who had six stars between them, one was a four star, the other was a two star. Between the two of them they had fought for something like 87 years. It turns out that the four star had been the commander of the artillery batteries that were firing on Con Thien when I was stationed at Con Thien in November and December of 67. And I asked this guy, "So what did you think of the American Marines?" And he kind of looks at me and he pauses and then he says, "You were brave." I said, "Come on, seriously, what do you think?" He says, "Well, you know, you guys had all these tanks and jets and helicopters and heavy artillery and you were totally bogged down with all this stuff." And I said, "Would it have made any difference if we had used different tactics?" And he looks at me and he says, "No, not really. History was not on your side. We were fighting for our country. What were you fighting for?" What was I supposed to say? I was fighting because some asshole in Washington told me these guys are my enemy. We had no justification at all for being there. The Vietnamese had every reason. You know, this is something I love to point out to people: I left Vietnam in early March 1968 and from

the moment that airplane left the runway at Da Nang airport, from that moment on, in all these years, no Vietnamese person has ever tried to kill me. Who had the justification to fight? All they wanted was for me to go away and leave them alone.

AG. You talked there for a second about the tactics. Could America ever have won the war?
WDE. No.

AG. No chance?
WDE. We couldn't beat them with a half a million soldiers. How about a million? And what does winning mean? Are they going to turn their AK47s into ploughshares and register Republican and go to the mall? They were prepared to fight forever. The Chinese were there for a thousand years. The French were there for 80 years and there was rebellion after rebellion after rebellion after rebellion. Before the French ever consolidated their control over Vietnam, there was resistance to French domination. How long were we prepared to leave an army of occupation halfway around the world? Half a million didn't do it. A million people we're going to leave on the other side of the world? Oh, and all through that, every day, grenade flipped into the bar in Saigon, three dead Americans, sniper shoots at the truck convoy, dead American. Day in and day out, for how many years? What would winning have meant? It was a meaningless concept because they were home and we weren't, and they were going to fight forever, and history makes that very, very plain. What were they going to do? "Oh, you Americans are right, we'll let these shithead guys that are your puppets run the show and behave ourselves." No. Ten years, fifty years, wouldn't matter how long.

AG. Before you left, you obviously thought it was winnable. How long did it take, when you were in Vietnam, to realize that it was not winnable? Or did you realize? Did anything change your mind?
WDE. It's hard to say because those ideas never crystallized. I certainly understood by early summer of 67 that what was going on was crazy, just crazy. We weren't winning anything. I am sure if somebody had really nailed me down I might have said, "We're never going to win this." I never thought of it in those terms. What I knew was if I'm still alive on March 5th, 1968, I can go home.

AG. Yeah, it's a matter of survival.
WDE. All I need to do is stay alive and I'm out of here, and concepts of winning or losing on a national level cease to be of any relevance. You didn't think about things like that, there was no reason to, no future in thinking

about that. What am I supposed to do if I decide in July of 1967, with another eight, nine months to do in Vietnam, "Oh, we're not going to win." What do I do with that? You don't even ask the question, let alone try to answer it.

AG. How long had you been in country when you went up to Hue for the Tet Offensive? Because you'd been there for a long time.
WDE. That was my last month. I was there for an entire year running around in the frigging countryside looking for somebody to fight, and then all of a sudden, my last month, I'm in an urban setting with every VC in the world trying to kill me. I fought two different wars.

AG. In *Vietnam–Perkasie*, I think there's sort of this sense that you were almost ready to go to Hue.
WDE. Well, I wasn't ready to go. The only reason I went is because I was a teenage kid and how do you say to your buddies, "No, you go, I'll just stay home"?

AG. A sense of solidarity then.
WDE. There was a certain, I don't even know the right word to use, it's not excitement, it's not pleasure, it's not joy, it's not anything except that finally after 12 months of utter frustration, I mean, I saw like eight armed enemy soldiers in the first twelve months I was in Vietnam. You couldn't find them. And now, finally, finally, here they are. We're on this side of the street, they're on that side of the street. "You want these buildings, you American assholes, come get them." We could actually fight, which is what I was trained to do and what I thought I was going to do. It wasn't fun, it was horrifying, it was terrifying, it was frightening, but by damned at least I had an enemy to fight.

AG. It's the lack of ambiguity as well, right?
WDE. Yes. That was, like I said, it's not good, it's not bad, it's not anything except that, at least, this is what I thought I was going to do in Vietnam, fight a war.

AG. Before then, in those first 12 months, could you distinguish between innocent civilians and potentially dangerous combatants?
WDE. No. Not in the least.

AG. Impossible?
WDE. Impossible. And I'm not sure if there are any innocent civilians. Certainly, if there were innocent civilians before the Marines showed up, by the time we left they wouldn't be innocent civilians anymore, they'd either be dead or VC. No, you couldn't tell the difference. And the guy who's out

there plowing his rice field in the afternoon is the guy who's planting the mine that night that your guys are going to step on the next day.

AG. I suppose that's the nature of guerrilla war.
WDE. That's guerrilla warfare.

AG. How did you respond to the "in-between" categories of people? Because it's really obvious when someone is a combatant like the people you're fighting in Hue, and then you've got these farmers who appear innocent. Did you ever come across people who were hiding food or guns and were they considered as bad as VC?
WDE. We never found anybody hiding guns, we did find what we thought were food caches.

AG. Yeah, that's what I was thinking of.
WDE. Of course, you're a young professional now, I don't know how big your refrigerator is, but if you walk into any American house, look in the fridge, you're going to find it's full of food, you're going to find a pantry full of food. Are they hoarding food for the enemy? No, it's just their food. But we go into these Vietnamese houses in these villages and find food and say, "Ah ha! You're going to give this to the VC," and we take their food and beat them up and blow up their house. That's what I mean, if they weren't VC when we got there, they sure as hell were by the time we left.

AG. So you treated them like VC anyway almost?
WDE. Yes. If you found anything that looked like more food than they should have. But what's more food than you should have? We didn't know.

AG. I suppose, as well, not only is that a difficult question, but you're in a country where the food is different, right? So you don't know how much rice a family needs for a year or whatever.
WDE. That's right. Who knows? Certainly anybody who's hiding weapons has got to be a VC, but what's a VC in a guerrilla war? Somebody who takes a 40 pound bag of rice and carries it to the mountains to give to the guerrilla fighters, is that a VC? The longer the Americans stayed the fewer neutrals there were. If you've got to choose between guys that look like you and talk like you and understand your world, and guys who are foreigners with guns who treat you like turds, who are you going to pick? So we were their best recruiters. I was taught, when I was in junior high and high school and we'd read in *Life* magazine and stuff, we were taught that the VC terrorized the civilian population and forced them to turn over their rice and stuff. They didn't need to do that. All they had to do was wait for an American

patrol to come through a village, wreck the place, and then they'd come in that night and say, "There's the Americans for you. Whose side do you want to be on?"

AG. So the tactics, not only do they make the distinction harder in practice but they're actually just pushing people over the line.
WDE. Absolutely.

AG. So America didn't win the hearts and minds of the Vietnamese people then?
WDE. Not even close. No, we didn't. I'd suggest that we're probably losing that same struggle in Afghanistan and in Iraq and in, well, wherever.

AG. For me it's depressing reading about Iraq and Afghanistan because I work on this stuff, and I read it and it's exactly the same, but for you it must be unbelievable.
WDE. It's where you learn to accept the fact that there's nothing I can do. I write what I write and I say what I say. The talk I gave at the University of Tokyo is called, "The American War in Vietnam: Lessons Learned and Not Learned," and it's all about what's going on now. I'm going to vote for Bernie as long as I can. My guess is that if he actually were to win the White House, he wouldn't be able to get much done anyway—as Carter proved—if the bureaucracy ain't on your side. We think our presidents have far more power than they really do. The Imperial Courts are run by the courtiers and bureaucrats and the king gets to do what he wants only if they think that's a good idea. But yes, it's heart-breaking, and especially so because the worst thing that the worst people learned from the Vietnam War is that if you remove the American people from any responsibility for foreign policy, then you can make your foreign policy be anything you want it to be. So that you can wage war in Afghanistan for 14 years and there's no anti-war movement. But that's because the burden, the entire blood burden, is being borne by a tiny proportion of the population, and by and large that portion of the population with the least amount of political clout, and nobody else cares because the rest of us, we're not at war.

AG. If there was a draft, do you think it would be different?
WDE. Absolutely. But there's not going to be.

AG. So that's one of the bad lessons learned?
WDE. Yes.

AG. Presumably control of the media as well?
WDE. Yes.

AG. The other thing which John Baky and I were talking about in the car this morning actually is this prevalent idea of "support the troops," which is a backlash against this memory of the Vietnam War.

WDE. Which is a false memory. We were supported. We used to get giant boxes of cookies and all sorts of stuff every damn week in the mail. We'd get letters from Girl Scout troops. I've still got them. "We try harder" button that's camouflage black and green, a whole big box of them sent to us by Avis rental car. "We try harder," that was their slogan. Bicycle Playing Card Company used to send cases of decks of cards, all of which were aces of spades. Fifty-two aces of spades in a deck because the rumor, it turns out it's totally bullshit, but we imagined that the ace of spades somehow was this bad luck charm in Buddhism and so you'd kill somebody and leave the ace of spades on the body and that was supposed to spook everybody. And the Bicycle Playing Card Company got wind of this and they would send entire cases with thirty or forty decks of cards all in their wrapping in cellophane and every single card is the ace of spades. We were certainly supported.

AG. But do you think there's less questioning of war now than there was back then?

WDE. Sure, because the people coming home in boxes are for the most part from that segment of society that has no political clout at all anyway. Moreover, now we don't even have to send troops. Now you can literally kill them with the push of a button. We're killing hundreds of people a year with drone weaponry. Some of them are "bad guys," most of them aren't. Hell, we just blew up a Doctors Without Borders hospital last week. "Gee, what a mistake, sorry." I bet the people that were killed have a lot of relatives who if they ever had any sympathy at all for what these Americans are trying to do over there, that's gone. You can build all the roads you want and all the hospitals you want and all schools you want, you do one thing like that and it wipes it all out, doesn't matter.

AG. How do you see this thing playing out then, Afghanistan and Iraq? Is it going to end? It's been a long time now.

WDE. Eventually. What I know is that eventually the United States in one form or another will no longer be involved in either of those parts of the world and those parts of the world will continue being what they are and what they have been for centuries. We can stay in Afghanistan another five years, another fifty years, sooner or later we're going to leave and Afghanistan is still going to be there and it's going to be what it always has been, which is a collection of tribes. Most people in Afghanistan have no sense of being Afghan. Afghanistan is a cartographer's wet dream. It exists on a map and that's it; it doesn't exist for most of the people living there. And as far as Iraq goes, God only knows what's going to happen over there, but who the hell is ISIS? You know who those guys are? They're Saddam Hussein's army, which the United States completely disbanded immediately upon taking control in Iraq in 2003. We disarmed all these guys and sent them home. Oops, all of a sudden, thousands of people had no job. And then they become…

AG. "Radicalized"?
WDE. Yes. We almost had a civil war between Sunnis and Shiites, especially up around Fallujah and the only way we managed to stop that, you know how we stopped that? We paid them to stop killing us. That was Petraeus' strategy. Buy them off. Pay them to stop killing us. And that worked as long as we paid them but eventually we stopped paying them. Most of the people involved in ISIS are former soldiers in Saddam Hussein's army.

AG. Which reminds me, at the time there was lots of, "There's nothing worse than Saddam Hussein," as the justification for Iraq, and, "What could possibly be worse than Saddam Hussein?" But now we have the answer, right? We found out.
WDE. ISIS is the direct result of the American invasion of Iraq and the removal of Saddam Hussein.

AG. I think a lot of the public, at least in Europe, recognize that link.
WDE. Europeans are much smarter than Americans. Europeans are willing to look at America and recognize that we're a bunch of dumb shits.

AG. So was Britain though, we were there with you, we're a bunch of dumb shits too.
WDE. Well, yeah, and I think that most people realize that. It's one of the reasons Tony Blair is not the prime minister anymore.

AG. And probably one of the most reviled people in Britain.
WDE. And as far as the rest of Europe goes, well, for one thing they get real news.

AG. Do you think the media has a role here then?
WDE. A lot of it. You know enough about it, you've seen American news.

AG. Unfortunately.
WDE. It's all about America. Most American news isn't even news. You turn on network news and you get maybe a five minute story, and you get the heart-warming story of the one-armed kid on the Ferris wheel and all

this bizarre stuff. It's not news, it's entertainment, it's pabulum. If you want news you've really got to go digging for it. It's there. Probably the most readily available source is BBC but even that you've got to go looking for. Al-Jazeera USA is a terrific source of news but most people either don't know where it is or go, "Oh those Arab guys, that's Al-Qaeda."

AG. Back to previous depressing questions. Do you think American soldiers on the ground in Vietnam used more force than was necessary?
WDE. No.

AG. No?
WDE. What do you mean? You know what, let me take that back. Your question is meaningless.

AG. Could you expand?
WDE. What is more force than necessary? What force was necessary? The force we applied didn't cause the enemy to stop fighting us so what is more force than necessary? That very question says we should have been there, we just did it wrong. No, we shouldn't have been there. More force than necessary? You get sniped at from a village and you drop napalm on them, that's probably an overreaction. But what are we doing there in the first place? Individual American soldiers, I suspect, most of them, it was certainly true of me, were trying to do the best we could do. You get put into this impossible situation and it's not like most Americans went around trying to kill anybody they could get their hands on. It was simply an impossible situation. More force than necessary was any force at all.

AG. What about the aerial bombing, did that help militarily?
WDE. Oh, Jesus Christ, that was a disaster. That was a real war crime. Aerial warfare never succeeds at anything. They certainly knew this at the end of the Second World War when they did the Strategic Bombing Survey of Germany and it turns out that German war production was higher in April 1945 than it had been in April 1942. They actually were able to continue to produce war materials in spite of being bombed to rubble. What does the bombing do? What did German bombing of Britain do in 1940? What did it achieve? You know what it achieved?

AG. Strengthened the resolve of the people.
WDE. It pissed off a bunch of Brits who said, "You can't do that to us." Guess what bombing of Germany did? Pissed off a bunch of Germans who said, "You can't do that to us." Japan was ready to keep fighting in spite of the bombing. You know why Hiroshima was picked as a target? It was one of the

few cities in Japan that hadn't already been totally destroyed by fire bombing. We wanted to have a target that actually showed them what this thing did. Bombing in Korea did not in any way stop the Korean War and we bombed North Korea extensively. Aerial bombardment simply doesn't work. Why do we keep bombing people? Somebody is making a lot of money building airplanes, building bombs, building all the things that airplanes need. But they're not effective.

AG. I think we've already answered this question, but it's more directly related to your experiences: do you think any of the violence you participated in personally was justified?

WDE. No. Simply because if I had not been there they would not have been trying to kill me. And again, you're looking at this as, the individual, here I am in Vietnam, boots on the ground. Am I using too much violence? You know, the very act of being there basically negates much of the logic of your questions.

AG. Personally, I agree. I have to ask these questions.

WDE. I know you do.

AG. We talked about this idea, when you came in, of morality in war as completely ridiculous. Tom Cossentino sent me this video of this black American veteran, he was talking about this idea of rules of fighting and then he said this quote which I find really interesting, he said, "That's ridiculous. How are you going to have rules to fight a war where you're killing people?"[3] Is that something you agree with?

WDE. Yes.

AG. But then does that mean that anything you can do in a war zone is fair or should there be restrictions on anything?

WDE. As I said, there are valid reasons for engaging in violence even on a national level. If you are being attacked, if your choice is destruction or violent resistance. The Poles were justified in fighting the Germans when Germany invaded in 1939, the Germans were not justified in invading Poland. If I were a VC, if I had been a young Vietnamese, I hope I would have joined the Vietcong. Then I could have fought a war and felt good about what I did.

AG. Let's assume that a war could be justified, which I think you believe because you're not a pacifist.

WDE. That would be the only way. One side in any war is usually in the wrong.

AG. Then the correct side, can they use any means possible?

WDE. If you buy the idea of a correct side; if one side really is justified to fight at all.

AG. So the ends justify the means?

WDE. It's not ends justify the means; it's just once you start killing people, you're going to try to tell me you're allowed to kill this one but not that one? You're not supposed to kill women and children, you're not supposed to target civilians. Wait a minute, what were we doing in the Second World War bombing the hell out of Germany and Japan? "Oh, well, that's okay for us to do that, it's not okay for Al-Qaeda to run airplanes into our buildings, they're innocent civilians." These distinctions are intellectual nonsense. The idea of some sense of rules of war, of morality in war, is quaintly bizarre, don't you think? Especially now, we're not talking about medieval knights out there on the battlefield. The way in which we are now capable of waging war is, I don't know how to answer this. The idea that it's okay, so long as you follow certain rules, to kill other people is laughable.

AG. What about banning certain weapons?

WDE. How do you ban certain weapons? Fifty caliber machine guns are supposed to be illegal. Napalm is supposed to be illegal. We're not supposed to engage in chemical warfare. What the hell do you think CS gas is that we throw into their tunnel systems? "It's okay to fight a war with this, but not with that." I think that all of this stuff you're talking about, banning certain weapons, "That weapon's not okay, you shouldn't be using it, but you can use this other weapon. You can kill this person but you can't kill this person," that's the kind of intellectual nonsense which allows people who think it's okay to fight wars to go ahead and think they're somehow doing this in some moral fashion.

AG. Like some sort of rules of the game which make the game itself acceptable?

WDE. When in fact, there's very seldom any good reason for wars. Ultimately, you look at the history of war, it's, "You've got something I want and I'm going to take it from you by force." And I think there's something really sick about saying that I'm allowed to do this, but not allowed to do that. If I have a weapon and you don't, and I shoot you, I've murdered you. But if I come over with a drone hellfire missile and fire that at John Baky and it happens to kill you too, that's just collateral damage, that's okay. Well, not where I come from.

AG. Do you think it's intellectually dishonest?

WDE. Yes.

AG. But it helps these people who wage war.

WDE. Well it does, it helps them justify what they're doing. I actually said, "You hold the infantry men responsible for shooting someone but not the guy who flies over at 10,000 feet and drops bombs." I said that at the Air Force Academy one time in 1998.

AG. How did they react?

WDE. Oh I had a bunch of officers up in the audience apoplectic over this. I didn't say, "Fuck you," but I said something along those lines, "You're just kidding yourselves, you're just as much a bunch of murderers as I ever was."

AG. I think one of the reasons I like Horace Coleman's work so much is he wasn't on the ground killing people but he really claimed responsibility for those deaths, because he's like, "I'm directing these planes and I'm as responsible as anybody for killing." And that's probably one of the reasons I like *In the Grass* so much because I think he really takes ownership of that in a way that those guys probably would never do, right? One question about the treatment of Vietnamese prisoners of war: did you ever take any Vietnamese prisoners of war? Because you couldn't hardly find these guys.

WDE. The only people I ever was directly connected with were what we called "detainees," who were civilians detained for questioning. They were not in any way caught as combatants.

AG. Not technically POWs, yep, okay.

WDE. And what we would do with them is, generally, you might beat them up, might have our interrogators work them over, and then we'd turn them over to the national police, the "Vietnamese white mice" we used to call them. We'd turn them over to the national police down in Hoi An, and God only knows what they did with them, killed them, made them pay bribes to get out of jail, who knows, they were about as corrupt as you could get.

AG. Did you ever extract any useful information?

WDE. No, no. And I was not directly involved in that, but I remember one particularly vivid incident soon after I got there, I describe it in *Vietnam–Perkasie*, the "county fair" that we went on. We were supposed to be winning hearts and minds. And our guy, who was from the interrogation team, which was at the regimental level but they send them down to operate with you, and this guy, some old man, we had the old style M16, which had a three prong flash suppressor, and they stuck it right into the top of this old man's foot and split his big toe away from the rest of his foot, the skin-muscle part. That was an interrogation technique. I practically threw up. After a while, I walked out of the tent, I couldn't stand there and watch this. I don't know what the guy knew. I mean, probably all these guys were VC, probably their nephews and their kids and I don't know. But, why not? Why wouldn't they be? And certainly, that day, if the people in that ville weren't Viet Cong when we got there that morning they sure as hell were when we left. The only prisoners I ever saw, actual prisoners, I think they must've been NVA because they were captured in Hue, and they were put in a little holding compound barbed wire area, a shed in the MACV compound that caught fire. I watched these guys burn to death, four or five of them. They were tied, they couldn't move, by the time that we were aware that there was a fire they were on fire. That was the night that we killed a fucking ARVN and wounded another one. They were stealing our food and I think it was the ARVN guys that set the fire in order to distract us so they could steal food from us, C-rations. The guys we shot each had a case of C-rations over their shoulder running away. I don't have any qualms about that one. Probably should because they were just poor shmoos who probably got drafted into their army. But at the time I'm thinking, "We're fighting your fucking war and you're stealing our food." Those were the only prisoners I ever saw and I watched them burn to death. Michael Herr refers to that in his book *Dispatches*. I didn't know it at the time but he witnessed the same thing. And he talks about how the Vietnamese stood around watching, "Death enthralled as all Vietnamese are."

AG. Did he really say that?

WDE. Herr actually writes that in his book. We stood around watching too! It's pretty amazing watching people burn to death. It gets your attention. And yet Herr makes this stupid statement. Totally off the wall.

AG. I read your review of *Dispatches*. I think you say in the review, the problem with the book is it's so well written.

WDE. Beautifully written. It's sort of like Tim O'Brien's *The Things They Carried*. Brilliant writing, but you don't learn much about the Vietnam War from it.

AG. So in '73 the war ends, essentially, for America.

WDE. No. No, it ends in '75.

AG. So you don't think that Kissinger and Nixon managed to bring "peace with honor"?

WDE. Of course not. They put a fig leaf over the statue of David to cover his private parts, but the war doesn't end. For one thing, some thousands of Americans simply took off their uniforms and they were portrayed as civilian advisers.

AG. Almost like a return to the beginning of the war.

WDE. By that time the south Vietnamese had the third largest air force in the world, somebody had to take care of that sophisticated technology. We had all sorts of people there. What really happens is that they so-called retire or resign from the military and then two years later they're back in the military with no loss of seniority, no loss of rank, no nothing, and you can find this happened in multiple instances. So the idea that somehow all the Americans came home in March of 1973 is nonsense.

AG. Okay. Do you think anyone should have been punished for what happened in Vietnam?

WDE. Yes.

AG. Who?

WDE. Henry Kissinger is a war criminal, he should have been put in prison forever. All those guys.

AG. All of them? Like Rostow? He's like a proto–Kissinger.

WDE. Rostow, Rusk, McNamara, the Bundy brothers, they're all criminals.

AG. Do you think they should have all been tried?

WDE. Yes. The lot of them.

AG. A lot of these guys end up going back into university life, which always astounds me. Do you think they should have been tried for war crimes or something different?

WDE. Can you try people for stupidity?

AG. But these guys aren't stupid, are they? Kissinger's not stupid, McNamara's not stupid.

WDE. Well, they're not exactly stupid, but they're ignorant as hell.

AG. There's a difference, right?

WDE. Well, yes, I think war crimes. And actually, not just those guys at the top. I just got done reading Dan Ellsberg's memoir *Secrets*. And over and over and over again, all these people at the level below the big shots, the Deputy Secretary of State, the Undersecretary of State, the Deputy Undersecretary of State, they all know the war is unwinnable. But not one of them has the courage to say to the guys above them, "This is nuts, we shouldn't be doing this." Because they'd rather have a job and rather have that inside power to be a player in the Pentagon or in the White House, they'd rather have that than tell the truth.

AG. What about the average American guy on the ground?

WDE. No, they don't know shit, but these are guys who have inside knowledge, who know we're losing, who come back from Vietnam and say, "We don't have a snowball's chance in hell of winning," and then do a press conference saying, "We're making real progress here." McNamara did that. Maxwell Taylor did that. All these guys, they all know. That's criminal. Millions of people died because these guys didn't have the courage to tell the truth. Put their own self-interest in front of the lives of not just thousands of Americans, millions of Asians. There's something criminally wrong with that. And Kissinger, those guys knew. Good God. Just such a despicable person.

AG. I just remember what D.F. Brown says in that symposium you did back in 1998, where he says he was annoyed when Nixon died because he wanted him to die painfully.[4]

WDE. About four days after Nixon died, I was up at Phillips Exeter Academy, which is this rich private school that all the Bushes went to. I was speaking there with anti-war activist Dave Dellinger, and we're talking about the war and the anti-war movement and this whole junior class, a couple hundred kids are there, and in the middle of this I say, "No, you don't actually understand. You're looking at this white-haired guy and this middle-aged guy," which I was then, I was in my late 40s. "And we're sitting here talking about this as though we're talking about a tea party or something. You know that son of a bitch that just died a couple of days ago?" And of course they all knew I'm talking about Nixon. "When I got the news he'd died, my heart soared up to heaven on the wings of a dove." This whole auditorium, they're all fucking Republican right-wing, I suppose. Dead silence. I said, "That's what I'm talking about, that's the level of passion we're talking about, that's the 60s!" Well, I had an office hour session the next morning, supposed to be two hours, in the history department office. Not a single kid came in. Not a single adult. And they never invited me back. But I was glad when Nixon died. And I'll be happy when Kissinger dies. It bothers me that he's still out there and all those people he's responsible for are dead. Millions of them.

AG. Cambodia as well, right?

WDE. Cambodians, Laotians, Vietnamese.

AG. Do you think America should have paid compensation to Vietnam after the war then?

WDE. Yes.

AG. What about now? Do you think, even now, they should still pay compensation?

WDE. Sure, we ought to. Of course, now we're putting up Nike factories and they're making sneakers and electronics. You should see modern Vietnam now, it's totally transformed, it's all this western stuff.

AG. So do you ever feel like, in a way, America won in the end?

WDE. Well, no. The Vietnamese won in the end. That's who won. But we could have had this outcome in 1945. We could have had it in 1955. We could have it in 1963. When the French threw in the towel, if we had just sent Hoi Chi Minh some Elvis records and blue jeans, this all could have been avoided.

AG. Have you ever felt the need, for yourself, to apologize to the Vietnamese people? I know you've written about this in your poetry.

WDE. I've actually done so on a number of occasions, quite directly. I've been back three times. Have you seen that "Ken and Bill's Excellent Adventure"?

AG. Yeah, I read that.

WDE. That was the third trip back. But in '85 and '90 I was doing things in some sort of official capacity. And I took hundreds of copies of "Making the Children Behave," in Vietnamese. A guy I knew who was on the staff at the UN translated it into Vietnamese for me and then I'd photocopy an entire ream of paper each time, 500 pages. And I was handing these things out everywhere I went. And I even have a poem about this old lady I met in Cu Chi where I literally say, "I'm sorry," it's the only thing I could think of to say.

AG. Do you think America should issue a formal apology?

WDE. What's the point?

AG. Just as a symbolic act of contrition. Because maybe it would be important for the American people to realize that something went wrong.

WDE. I guess that'd be nice. I hadn't really thought about it much because it seems to me, I don't know if the Vietnamese would feel better. They don't really care anymore. "Just send us your jobs, send us tourists, send us stuff we can make and make money." I don't think most people in Vietnam could give a rat's ass one way or another if we apologized. Most of them, hell, like 60 percent or 70 percent of them, maybe even more, weren't even alive on April 30th, 1975. It's ancient history. They want jobs, they want a house to live in, they want to fall in love, they want motor scooters, they want to live their lives, they don't care about the war.

AG. But maybe it would be an important act for Americans because then, perhaps, if you apologize for a war it makes future wars…

WDE. To apologize for the war in Vietnam and continue to do what we're doing in Afghanistan and Iraq and other places is ridiculous.

AG. I get that would be hypocritical.

WDE. Rather than apologize for a war we fought 50 years ago, let's stop fighting wars. Fat chance that's going to happen. No, I don't see any value at all in some symbolic apology.

AG. Do you think the violence of the war is still unfolding? I was just with Dave Connolly, and he's had an operation, what like 10 weeks ago, to remove shrapnel. Do you feel like the war is in some ways still going on? Or is it over? Is it ever going to be over?

WDE. I don't know. I'm far more concerned with the continuing repercussions of the war in and on Vietnam. Whatever happens to us Americans, as cruel as it sounds, we deserve it. But there are still people, apparently a couple of hundred a year, who are dying from unexploded ordnance. Farmers, kids playing with stuff that blows up. There are still huge areas that are poisoned with Agent Orange, there are still kids being born, there are still living people suffering from the effects of dioxin poisoning. That stuff is all still going on. As for Americans, my friend David Willson, who wrote that wonderful essay in *The Last Time I Dreamed About the War*, he's dying of multiple myeloma, which the VA attributes to Agent Orange.[5] He's dying at 70 or 71. I'd rather have David alive for a while longer, a sentiment I'm sure he shares, but when something is killing you that long after the fact, is it the Vietnam War or is it just the way life works? My dad was dead at 69, died of cancer, wasn't ever in the military, let alone in a war. My mother died at 70, cancer, she was never in a war. Two different kinds of cancer. I think that the long-term repercussions of the war have far more to do with what the Vietnamese are still having to deal with. It was their country that we destroyed. It's their country that has tens of thousands, probably hundreds of thousands, of explosive devices simply lying around waiting for somebody to stumble on them and die.

AG. I think Laos has the highest concentration of unexploded ordnance in the world.

WDE. It very well may. In 2011, I still was not able to go up to Con Thien because they had not yet demined the area around it. I was there in November and December of 1967. In 2011, it's still too dangerous to go there because of the mines we planted.

AG. It's almost like the land remembers.

WDE. So in that way the war is still going on. For Americans what's going on is not of any real significance compared to what the Vietnamese have had to deal with. But of course that's the American way of looking at things. The war was all about us. Our Vietnam Veterans War Memorial in Washington is all about us. Our books are all about us. As though somehow the Vietnam War was something that happened to us instead of something we perpetrated against another people.

AG. Okay. Final question. I think it's really obvious, the answer by now. Was the American war in Vietnam immoral?
   WDE. Yes. And it was stupid and counterproductive. That's even more important.

Adam Gilbert was a Leverhulme Early Career Fellow at the University of Sussex, Brighton, England, at the time this interview was conducted on October 17, 2015.[6] Previously, he contributed to The Last Time I Dreamed About the War: Essays on the Life and Writing of W.D. Ehrhart, *Jean-Jacques Malo, ed., McFarland, 2014.*

NOTES

1. John Baky is the Director of Libraries and Curator of Special Collections at La Salle University, where this interview was conducted and which holds Ehrhart's archives.
2. Like Ehrhart, David Connolly is an American veteran of the war in Vietnam and a poet.
3. Tom Cossentino is a doctoral candidate at Rutgers University whose dissertation focuses on American veterans of the war in Vietnam. The video mentioned is of Akinsanya Kambon.
4. "War, Poetry, & Ethics: A Symposium": "I wasn't glad when Nixon died. I wanted him to suffer for a long, long time with phlebitis and throw little clots off to his brain."
5. David A. Willson, "W.D. Ehrhart, Essayist: Musings of a Librarian and Friend," in Jean-Jacques Malo, ed., *The Last Time I Dreamed About the War: Essays on the Life and Writing of W.D. Ehrhart* (Jefferson, NC: McFarland, 2014), 31–48.
6. This interview was funded by the Leverhulme Trust as part of Gilbert's research project "A Moral History of the American War in Vietnam."

Going Back and Coming Back

Mia Martin Hobbs

MMH. In *Passing Time: Memoir of a Vietnam Veteran Against the War*, you describe requesting a transfer back to Vietnam during the war. The reason that you give for this is that in Vietnam "it at least made sense to be lonely" and that "America had become an alien place in which and to which I no longer belonged." In *Going Back: A Poet Who Was Once a Marine*, you say that you returned because you wanted a great catharsis, a personal healing that would finally allow you to put demons to bed and get on with your life. That even though, as you say, you had come to your own conclusions and been able to live with them, you wanted to see the Vietnamese getting on with their lives and the war gone, then you would also be able to let go. Is there any connection between these two desires to return? If so, what is it?

WDE. There is no connection between my desire to return to Vietnam in 1968 and my desire to return in the 1980s. In 1968, I was a broken 19-year-old in a lot of pain and no idea how to cope with my situation. I volunteered to return to Vietnam because I knew that if I stayed in North Carolina for my last 15 months in the Corps, I would end up in the brig (military prison) or dead (from drunk driving and/or other self-abusive behavior). I figured that, as an E5 sergeant, I could probably save about $5,000 during another tour in Vietnam, and if I got killed instead, my problems would be solved and the pain would end.

By 1981, I had learned to cope with the situation I found myself in—not always in the healthiest or best ways, but I was managing to get by. I was married, had begun publishing my writing, and at that time had a job teaching. My desire to return to Vietnam was a search for emotional catharsis, not a veiled suicide wish.

MMH. You returned to Vietnam for the first time in 1985, but had been interested in returning since 1981—trying to return since 1981. Why at this time did you actively start trying to return? How long had you been thinking about returning before you started trying?

WDE. Actually, I have only the vaguest recollection of my thoughts in 1981. I think a mutual friend had put the Canadian journalist Don North in touch with me about a possible trip back, but nothing came of it. However, in 1983, when I saw Episode 5 of *Vietnam: A Television History*, I was stunned to hear another veteran describe Vietnam as the most beautiful place he'd ever seen with colors so vivid they vibrated. As I sat there watching and listening, I could not recall ever thinking or feeling during my time there that Vietnam was beautiful. Indeed, I realized to my shock that all my memories, when I played the "movie" of the war in my head, were in black-&-white. I realized that during my 13 months in Vietnam, I had not seen Vietnam at all. I'd seen a war. I determined right then that I wanted to see the country of Vietnam.

MMH. Had you been thinking about visiting again before you were invited to return with the writers' group in 1990? What about in 2011, with Ken Takenaga?

WDE. My trip in 1985 was the one I needed to take. I call it my trip-of-the-heart. I had no intention of returning a second time. But when the Joiner Center invited me to join a delegation of writers in 1990, and the entire trip was paid for, *and* I arranged to earn $2,000 writing articles about the trip for *The Virginia Quarterly Review* and *Gallery*, of course I agreed to go back.

As for the trip in 2011, again the entire trip was paid for by someone else (Japan National Tourism Bureau and Kumamoto Prefecture Tourism Bureau), and arranged by Ken so that I didn't have to do a thing except, once again, write about the trip. And this time I could travel with my old Marine buddy, and take my wife along with me, again a no-brainer.

MMH. In "Ken and Bill's Excellent Adventure," you say you went back in 2011 to see a country, not a war, and that you succeeded. When you visited in 1985 and again in 1990, had Vietnam still felt like a war to you?

WDE. What I wrote in 2011 was largely predicated on the assumption that few people would have read my earlier writings about return trips. (I'm not exactly a bestselling author who's read by millions or even thousands.) But it is also true that in 1985, evidence of the war was everywhere, and even in 1990 the war was still very present (heck, our hosts were all VC and NVA veterans). By 2011, little remained of the physical evidence of the war.

MMH. In *Passing Time*, you describe feeling like "a freak in a carnival show." Did that feeling subside with time—did you become accustomed to feeling like a curiosity, or did the people around you become accustomed to being around Vietnam veterans?

WDE. Most of my peers at Swarthmore College never got much beyond the fact of my being a veteran of the war. Here's an example: the day before graduation, a classmate I'd known for four years wanted to introduce me to his parents. By that time, I'd been a varsity swimmer for four years and captain of the team my senior year, I'd done water ballet for four years (the only man ever to receive a four-year award from the women's PE dept.), I'd written for the school newspaper and published in the school's literary magazine. But Rick introduced me by saying, "This is Bill Ehrhart; he was a Marine in Vietnam."

I did have some friends who could have cared less about that. I liked to drink beer and smoke weed, and among these friends I could forget that I was a veteran. They became lifelong friends. And though several of them have died in recent years (we're getting to that age), I'm still in touch with others. I just got a long e-mail from one of them a couple of days ago.

MMH. In the preface to *The Madness of It All*, you say that the "focus on war in your life is not entirely my doing. Once people begin to think of you in a certain way, that tends to have a self-reinforcing effect." How far do you feel that your identity as a Vietnam War poet and veteran was shaped by others in your country?

WDE. I've always considered myself a poet who fought in Vietnam, not a Vietnam War poet. Certainly, however, the only real recognition I've ever received as a poet and writer has been in my capacity as a veteran of the war. It's irritating, but I've learned to accept the fact that if I were not identified as a Vietnam War poet, I probably would be receiving no recognition at all. I can't change other people's perceptions. And it is important to remember that 99.9 percent of "others in [my] country" have never heard of me at all.

MMH. Did you find any preconceptions or stereotyping about your identity as a Vietnam veteran from the Vietnamese, on any of your return journeys? If so, how was it similar/different to how you were thought of in the U.S.?

WDE. I have no idea how most Vietnamese I met during my three visits perceived me. During my first two visits, I was interacting almost exclusively with other veterans (albeit from the other side), and they seemed to accept me as a kind of comrade or brother. In 2011, I don't suppose most of the Vietnamese I interacted with even knew I was a war veteran. The country has moved on, and the population is young.

MMH. What about in Japan—specifically when you and Ken spoke to the congregants of a Buddhist temple about the Vietnam War. What were the preconceptions you felt from the Japanese Buddhists about Vietnam veterans, if there were any—and how were they similar/different to Vietnamese and American preconceptions?

WDE. I was surprised that so many Japanese were even interested in hearing about the Vietnam War. I have no idea what their preconceptions or stereotypes were, or if I managed to dispel them or reinforce them by what I said. I have since learned that a great many Japanese my age were involved to one degree or another in the anti–Vietnam War movement in the 1960s and early 1970s. This received little or no press coverage in the U.S. at the time, but was apparently extensive (as were anti-war movements in Europe at the same time, also under-reported). Last year, my book *Passing Time* was translated and published in Japan,[1] and when I gave a talk at Japan Women's University on a Saturday afternoon in June, 150 people showed up, many of them roughly my age.

MMH. In your poem "The Teacher," you describe the promise you made to teach others and the search for a way to communicate with those you want to teach. Do you feel like you ever found the voice you were searching for? Do you think your students understood what you were trying to teach them?

WDE. I think I did manage to find my voice simply by being me. I have had a sporadic career as a teacher until the last 15 years, but I have always connected with young people. Many of my peers in this profession seem to forget what it is like to be a teenager; I have not. I don't suppose I manage to change many minds in the course of my fleeting contact with these kids, but who knows what might stick, or what might come back in later years? I certainly manage to challenge my students on an almost daily basis, making at least some of them think and re-think what they believe and why they believe it. This past Veterans' Day, November 2015, I put this sign up on my classroom door:

Veterans' Day

I went halfway around the world
to kill, maim, and make miserable
a people who had never done me or my country any harm,
nor ever would or could.
Are you really going to thank me for that?
Dr. E

(My students call me "Dr. E," or "Doc E," or just "Doc.")

MMH. In "Letter to the Survivors," you try to explain how the world felt leading up to a nuclear war. You are describing events like the Cuban Missile Crisis. Do you find it difficult to explain to younger generations the anxiety that was so widespread in the 1960s? Is this something that your students found it hard to understand?

WDE. Yes, it is hard to explain. They are all wrapped up in the fear of "terrorism," which the U.S. government is happy to exploit and the media happy to accommodate. They think they live in a scary world, but al Qaeda killed thousands and ISIS has yet to kill even a dozen Americans. I grew up in a world where total annihilation was a very real possibility. How does one explain that? But also, what would be the point if my students did "get it"? Should they feel sorry for me? Count their lucky stars? Whose fear is worse? Fear isn't a contest. My frustration is not in failing to make them understand what I feared growing up, but rather with trying to get them to understand that they have more to fear from their own government and their fellow citizens than they do from terrorists foreign or domestic.

MMH. You say in *Passing Time* that when you returned to the U.S., "you considered yourself lucky to get out of the airport without being assaulted by bands of rabid hippies." Was this a potential reality? Was there, to your knowledge, harassment of veterans by anti-war protestors, spitting on, being called baby-killer?

WDE. I had a subscription to *Time* magazine and also occasionally read the daily military newspaper *Stars and Stripes*, so I had some awareness of the anti-war movement, but no real understanding of what was going on. My worries were entirely unfounded. I was never harassed or abused by anyone in the anti-war movement during my time in the Marines. We now know that this sort of behavior by the anti-war movement was entirely fabricated postwar. If you want me to explain, I can, but there is an entire book debunking this mythology and explaining how it came into being: Jerry Lembcke's *The Spitting Image: Myth, Memory, and the Legacy of Vietnam*.

MMH. In *Passing Time*, you say of anti-war protestors, "what the hell did these kids know about what was important? These children of the rich and powerful." Could you elaborate on class and status in the U.S., specifically on how you saw class and status affect the war and the anti-war movement?

WDE. What I was feeling in the fall of 1969 was still enormous emotional pain and confusion and hurt. I still had no idea how to explain to myself or anyone else what had happened in the previous three years. My resentment of my fellow students was a kind of whiny sour-grapes. But I also realized, in attempting to write a poem actually, that those students' right to protest and speak out, their freedom of speech, had nothing whatever to do with what I had done in Vietnam. I was not fighting to defend either my country, or our constitution, or the rights we enjoy as Americans (which, incidentally, are being steadily stripped away under the guise of protecting us from the terrorists). The sentiment you are asking me about did not survive in me for very long. As for class and status, I didn't think about it in those terms at that time. I wasn't thinking in terms that broad. Christ, I was trying to figure out—with little success—my own situation. At the time, I really had no "class consciousness." Besides, I was certainly from the privileged middle class and could have legally avoided the Vietnam War if I hadn't voluntarily joined the Marines.

MMH. In Australia, the anti-war movement was prominently anti-conscription. Over the years, this aspect has been forgotten and many veterans felt and still feel agitated by the anti-war movement as they felt it targeted their actions, rather than being opposition to the draft. Did your experience in the anti-war movement reflect this? Was it as much about the draft as it was about being in Vietnam?

WDE. Certainly the possibility that one might be drafted to fight in the Vietnam War, or one's brother or son or friend, provided a major incentive to oppose the war. When the draft ended, much of the steam was taken out of the anti-war movement. By the early 1970s, the major driving force of the anti-war movement was no longer students but the soldiers and former soldiers who had fought the war. But I think many anti-war participants were also genuinely aghast that the country we had grown up believing was always right and good and just could be engaged in this endless, senseless war pitting the most powerful industrial power on earth against a bunch of rice farmers who ploughed their fields with water buffalo.

MMH. Do you think the anti-war movement was a success?

WDE. It didn't end the war as quickly as we would have liked. Indeed, resistance within the active duty military itself by 1971 may have had more to do with ending the war than the anti-war movement (see Col. Robert Heinl's "The Collapse of the Armed Forces"[2] or the documentary *Sir! No, Sir!*[3]) But the anti-war movement convinced LBJ that something had gone terribly wrong (though he never understood what), and just imagine what King Richard the Milhous and Henry the K would have done to Vietnam if there had been no domestic opposition. So, yes, I think the movement was a success. (Unfortunately, the wrong people learned the wrong lessons, and have since managed to remove foreign policy from any domestic consequences, largely by removing 99 percent of Americans from bearing the burden of foreign adventurism.

MMH. In *Passing Time* you explain very clearly how you became anti-war. It seemed to be the Kent State shooting that really forced a change. You say that "the war was a horrible mistake, and my beloved country was dying because of it. I did not want my country to die. I had to do something. It was time to stop the war." This seems to indicate that your anti-war beliefs stemmed from patriotism. Is this an accurate summation?

WDE. Yes, patriotism. I loved my country. I was convinced that the war was a terrible mistake, that U.S. intentions were good and noble, but that somehow we had gone off on a tangent, been misled or got side-tracked or something. Because of my upbringing, I could not believe that my government would willfully perpetrate such a travesty as what was happening in Vietnam. A year later, however, when I read *The Pentagon Papers*, I had to come to terms with the fact that the war really was deliberate and evil, and it had been perpetrated by a government that had consistently lied to the American people for 25 years. That was a hard and bitter pill to swallow.

MMH. You imply later in *Passing Time* that the whole of American mythology was fraudulent. This comes up a few times: when you describe going to Washington for your first street protest, when you read the *Pentagon Papers*, and speaking to Roger about the war and the military industrial complex. Did you still feel at all patriotic and protective toward America as you did at the time of the Kent State shooting, when you decided to act? What about now?

WDE. I would still very much like my country to live up to the ideals I was taught it stood for, but after a lifetime of experience, I have little hope that it ever will. No hope might be more accurate. Do I love my country? Am I supposed to love a country that incarcerates more of its citizens than any other nation on earth? Am I supposed to love a country that spends trillions on weapons systems but can't afford decent education for most of its citizens? Am I supposed to love a country that contains within its borders a 3rd world impoverished nation of 40 to 50 million souls? Where guns outnumber citizens, where armed citizens slaughter each other at a rate higher than any other country on earth? Where far fewer than half the eligible voters can be bothered to vote? A country that has the highest infant mortality rate in the developed world? The most expensive and least efficient health care system? What, exactly, am I supposed to love? What does it mean to be a patriot? As Samuel Johnson said, "Patriotism is the last refuge of a scoundrel." I love my wife and daughter. I love my friends. I love my students. I love a good cup of coffee in the morning. I love my cat. But when you ask me if I love my country, just exactly what are you asking me to love?

MMH. It is possible to feel protective towards something without being proud of it. Do you still feel that you can never again take pride in being an American? If so, does this still produce, as you say in *Passing Time*, overwhelming rage and sorrow?

WDE. When Barack Obama was first elected president, I actually found myself proud to be an American. Even if Obama isn't really "a black man" (only 50 percent African, not at all "African-American," but rather half African and half American, and definitely raised in a white environment), I never thought I'd live to see the day when someone of his background could get elected president. Trouble is, I forgot that whatever else he might be, he's still a politician. His presidency has been mostly a profound disappointment (silly me; even after all these years, I was hoping). And should I take pride in a country that arms the world, that closes its doors to the very refugees we're responsible for creating, that can actually present a Donald Trump as a serious candidate for president?! I'm supposed to be proud that we have military forces stationed in over 150 countries? That we fire Hellfire missiles at the rate of 1,000 a year and a cost of $71,000 per missile, but a private charity called Wounded Warriors has to ask Americans for money to take care of our wounded veterans because the government can't or won't live up to its promises and obligations? Seriously. How much time do you have? How much do you want from me? What am I supposed to be proud of? That I have running water and electricity? I bet you've got that in Australia, and you don't have 12 aircraft carrier battle groups, 70+ nuclear submarines, 9,000+ Abrams main battle tanks, and a minimum wage that can't support one person for a year, let alone a family of four.

MMH. Have you ever figured out what it was that made you join the street protest in April 1971?

WDE. Yes. When I saw the veterans hurling their medals over the fence onto the steps of Congress, I realized I should have been down there with them. So a week later, when the larger May Day demonstrations took place, I was trying to make up for having stayed home during Dewey Canyon III.[4] As for going to the Justice Department, I was far away from the stage at the main demonstration, and felt detached and kind of useless, and I don't like large crowds anyway, so when someone announced an action over at the Justice Department, I just figured I'd go check it out.

MMH. Your first experience at an anti-war meeting seems like a moment of catharsis. You say that you thought it might be similar to going to confession. You later joined VVAW, which became well-known for the use of rap groups. Did you ever join a rap group, and did you find those meetings cathartic in the same way as speaking in front of the anti-war students was? Do you find that writing has a similar cathartic or confessional effect?

WDE. I was never part of a "rap group." I do think—no, I'm certain that my writing served a similar purpose, especially in the years I was in college and simultaneously trying to understand what I'd been through. The writing helped me sort out my thoughts and discover how and what I felt, and why.

I don't like to think of writing as "therapy" because I've spent a lifetime honing my art, but if I'm honest with myself, I suppose it was therapeutic.

MMH. You said to Mike in *Passing Time* that "they're going to keep on killing until they've turned all of Southeast Asia into a parking lot for Disneyland." Does this statement apply to U.S. foreign policy since Vietnam as well? If so, would you agree that "colonization" is an appropriate word to describe U.S. foreign policy?

WDE. It took until the Reagan Wars in Central America for the foreign policy establishment to implement the real lessons of the Vietnam War (as long as Americans aren't dying, Americans don't really care what is being done in their names and with their tax dollars). The U.S. has since engaged in three open wars of aggression and multiple "mini-wars" (Grenada, El Salvador, Nicaragua, Somalia, Libya, drone warfare in Yemen, Pakistan, Syria, and who knows how many other countries we're not even told about?). Colonization? I'd call it economic colonization. In the 19th and early 20th centuries, colonial powers sent in troops, claimed sovereignty, set up governments, and ruled foreign countries. The U.S., beginning in the early 20th century, realized it is cheaper, more efficient, and carries less negative public onus to simply colonize through economic domination. Now and then, one has to send in the Marines to remind the natives who's in charge, but mostly the U.S. can rule through proxies such as Batista, the Somozas, Armas, the Shah, and other pisspot dictators like Noriega (he was our pal until he got uppity), and Saddam (he, too, was our pal until he got uppity), while exerting economic control. This is all far more complicated than I have time or space to explain here, but books like *Endless Enemies* by Jonathan Kwitny or the more recent writings of Andrew Basevich can explain far better than me what I'm trying to get at here.

MMH. You say in the essay "Learning the Hard Way" that you "still believe that all of us owe something to our country."[5] You make it clear that the obligation of the government to the people has not been met, but what is the obligation of the people to the country?

WDE. I wrote "Learning the Hard Way" in about 1981. That was 35 years ago. What I believe the American people owe their country I will never see fulfilled: an informed citizenry that demands of its government fairness and equity, responsible foreign and domestic policies, government for the benefit of the people rather than for the oligarchs, repeal of the 2nd Amendment, dismantling of the surveillance state, restoration of the Bill of Rights, et cetera, et cetera. That is what citizens owe their country: intelligent involvement in governance for the benefit of the whole American people and the betterment of the world. Think that obligation is ever going to be fulfilled? I don't.

MMH. From your experience in other countries—Vietnam in peacetime, but also the Philippines, Japan—is the failure of government to fulfill its obligations to the people a particular problem for America, or do you see it equally everywhere?

WDE. I see similar failures in other countries, but I also see many countries where governments do a much better job of serving the people than ours does—indeed, that put the United States of America to shame. Most of Europe provides decent health care for its citizens, free or affordable education through university level, adequate pay and benefits for its workers, efficient and cheap public transportation. Japan, too, largely fits this model.

MMH. Did your experience in the Vietnam War change your political views? If so, when and how did they change?

WDE. In 1964, when I was a high school 10th grader, I campaigned for Barry Goldwater. I thought Lyndon Johnson was too soft on communism. In 1972, the first time I was eligible to vote in a presidential election, I voted for George McGovern. Need I say more?

MMH. In the poem "Old Myths," you say that "you've lived the myth and know what lies are made of. Yet even now, sometimes you find traces of an older pride."[6] And in *Passing Time*, you describe your decision to do active duty while on reserve: "what bizarre comic-book mentality had locked onto my soul in the murky depths of my childhood and refused, absolutely refused in the face of all reason to let go?"[7] Do you still have that lingering allegiance and pride in military service?

WDE. No.

MMH. In *Passing Time*, you say that you knew at last that nothing you "had ever done in Vietnam would ever carry anything with it but shame and disgrace and dishonor," that you would "never be able to recall Vietnam with anything but pain and anger and bitterness." Did returning to Vietnam, either in 1985, 1990 or 2011, have any effect on these feelings?

WDE. No. I am still ashamed, disgraced, and dishonored by what I did in Vietnam, and by what my country did in Vietnam. And the U.S. failure to amend its behavior in the world—indeed, it has gotten worse, as I tried to explain above: now we can kill others with a literal touch of a finger—has certainly done nothing to alleviate the pain, anger, and bitterness.

MMH. You say in *Going Back* that when you began to meet people in Vietnam, you "began to get interested," despite yourself. Can you elaborate on this?

WDE. I'm sorry, but I have absolutely no recollection of what you are referring to here. Unless maybe I was talking about how, when I first realized I would not be able to visit the old I Corps areas during the 1985 trip, I was initially angry and disappointed, but after awhile I began to realize that meeting people was as good as and better than just seeing "old haunts." Maybe that's what I meant? I'm not sure. I don't recall writing that I "began to get interested."

MMH. It's very clear that your experiences in the Vietnam War and in postwar America changed your attitude toward America. How about the return trips? Did they change your attitude to or your opinion of your home country?
WDE. No.

MMH. How has discourse around the Vietnam War changed over the years? How has the way the war is discussed affected you?
WDE. How has it changed? Well, through much of the 1970s, no one wanted to discuss it at all. Then in the 1980s, the myth of the spat-upon and unappreciated Vietnam War veteran arose, along with the "analysis" that we lost the war only because the meddling politicians would not let the military fight to win, the liberal press turned the nation against the war, and the traitorous hippies destroyed the morale of the troops (all three arguments were and are bogus). In the 1990s, the mantra became "Support Our Troops" (in contrast to the shabby treatment Vietnam War veterans had received; again, nonsensical propaganda and factually untrue). And in the past decade, well, not much discussion at all of any kind. How has this changing discussion affected me? How do I answer that? With a big question mark, I guess. I've yet to hear, in any serious public setting or forum, any sensible discussion of the war. Sure, in settings like Haverford College's 2014 forum "The Vietnam War in Poetry" or the conference in Washington, D.C., in May 2015 called "The Power of Protest," but these are "niche" discussions taking place among people and audiences that are far out of the mainstream.

MMH. Your essay "On Michael Herr's *Dispatches*" critiques the obsession with the warrior-myth. You call it "just another paean to men-at-war, a glorious-grisly-romantic tribute to the ultimate insanity."[8] In "Soldier-Poets of the Vietnam War," you note that the initial rejection of Vietnam veterans has given way only to Rambo, Chuck Norris, and "the sorry spectacle of America's Vietnam veterans driven to build monuments to themselves and throw parades in their own honor."[9] Do you find that Herr's characterization of the war and the Rambo spectacle have become representative of how the Vietnam War is discussed in America?
WDE. Again, you are dealing with two essays I wrote in 1977 and 1985 respectively. A lot of time has passed. A lot of things have changed. To a very

large extent, the Vietnam War simply isn't discussed anymore. When it is, it is usually in the context of the false contention that Americans didn't "support the troops," but we'll never make that mistake again. Now we support the troops with yellow ribbon magnets stuck to our cars, and military fly-overs at NASCAR auto races, and giant American flags covering the entire field at the start of NFL football games, and presentation of the colors at the start of NHL hockey games, and *ad infinitum*. The Vietnam War is nowhere to be seen or heard. Meanwhile, Americans "honor" their soldiers with these empty displays while 99 percent of Americans live their lives as if the U.S. is not waging war all over the globe. You have to understand that the attacks on 9/11/2001 all-but-obliterated the history of the U.S. between 1945 and 2000. The students I teach now were either in diapers when 9/11 happened, or they were not even born. This year's college graduates were born in 1994 and 1995. The Vietnam War might as well be the Punic Wars. Heck, the parents of my current students were toddlers and kindergarteners when the Vietnam War ended. It just doesn't matter to most Americans. It isn't discussed. My students don't even know who Rambo is.

MMH. You say in "The Invasion of Grenada" that what you wanted was a simple recognition of the limits of our power as a nation to inflict our will on others, that you wanted an understanding that the world is neither black-and-white, nor ours.[10] Do you think that there has been a shift in how America as a global power is perceived by Americans since you wrote this poem?

WDE. No. Most Americans blindly accept the government's arguments that U.S. security is constantly at risk, that we must have more and more and more military spending to keep us safe from (name your demon; the current one is ISIS, which has displaced al Qaeda as the agent of our imminent demise). And of course, all these external enemies hate us because merely they are evil; the U.S. has done nothing to provoke their hatred. So the reasoning goes, and most Americans buy it. Why not? Between August 2014 and the end of November 2015, four Americans died at the hands of ISIS. If you throw in the San Bernardino killings, and call those two crackpot killers part of ISIS, the number rises to 17. Meanwhile, in the first 11 months of 2015, 9,940 Americans died at the hands of other Americans with guns. But Americans are terrified of ISIS while accepting the cold fact that murder-by-gun is simply part of daily American life. How fucked-up is that, eh? Why? Look at how the government and the media play up ISIS beheadings and the Paris attacks. Or the San Bernardino killings. But what about when a group of armed white men seize control of a U.S. government building and refuse to leave? How is that playing in the news? Can you imagine how it would be played if those men were armed Muslims?

MMH. Also in "The Invasion of Grenada," you say that what you wanted was an end to monuments.[11] Have there been changes in how you feel about war commemoration since the Vietnam War?

WDE. Yes, now if I had my way, I'd dynamite every war memorial in the United States of America. I would replace them with memorials to Rosa Parks and Eugene Debs, Joe Hill and Jane Addams, Viola Liuzzo and Harriet Tubman and Chief Joseph and Carl Sandburg, with memorials to the Homestead Steel Strikers and the victims of Wounded Knee and the Triangle Shirtwaist Fire. We ought to memorialize people and events worthy of memorialization.

MMH. What about monuments or commemorations in Vietnam? Do you feel the same way about them as you do in the U.S.?

WDE. The Vietnamese have good reason to memorialize their war dead. Those men and women died fighting for their country's freedom.

MMH. In the essay "Who's Responsible?," you go into great detail comparing veterans of Vietnam to veterans of other wars and show their suffering to be context specific, but similar. You say that "Pity the poor Vietnam veteran ... is a largely displaced sentiment." What effect do you think this sentiment has had?

WDE. "Pity the poor Vietnam veteran" has been used, ever since the Reagan years, to rehabilitate the public image of military service and relegitimize military intervention as an instrument of U.S. foreign policy. If you criticize the government's policies, you are by extension criticizing those who carry out those policies, or at least that's how it has been successfully pitched. We were no more neglected or abused on our return than were veterans of any other U.S. war. The only group that got any kind of decent break at all were the World War II vets who got an amazingly generous GI Bill that for the first time offered home ownership and higher education to millions of Americans, but those gains were eroded and lost by the mid–1970s. And no other generation of American veterans has ever been treated so generously.

MMH. In the preface of *In the Shadow of Vietnam*, you say that "for better or worse, virtually everything you see, do and think is filtered through that seminal experience" of the Vietnam War. You also say that "Vietnam is of interest to me now ... only in so much as it informs the world I live in now." Has returning to Vietnam in peacetime affected your memories of that "seminal experience" in war? Have your memories of wartime experience changed since you have returned to Vietnam?

WDE. No.

MMH. If so, then because, as you say, all your experiences are filtered through the war experience—have your returns to Vietnam altered the way you consider all past events, and your opinions and attitudes on them?

WDE. No.

MMH. What do you feel being in Vietnam has accomplished?

WDE. I had some wonderful experiences and have some wonderful memories to go along with my unhappy memories of the war. I got to experience a Vietnam that is not at war and really internalize that reality instead of merely understanding it intellectually from a distance. I have been able to experience Vietnam at various times and therefore have gotten to see it emerge from the destruction of war into the light of modern life. Vietnam was a damaged and suffering country when I was there in 1985. In 2011, I saw a vibrant, thriving, pulsating society full of drive and ambition and life and hope for the future.

As to whether or not my visits accomplished anything for Vietnam and the Vietnamese, I have no idea. Put a tiny amount of $$$ into their economy? Got them a minuscule amount of good PR from the various articles and essays I wrote as a result of my trips?

MMH. You say when you returned in 1985 that you began to feel "a bit ashamed of myself—after all, here was a poor nation struggling against enormous odds—and I had been pouting because I couldn't play out my private little fantasy." But when you went back in 1990, you were able to do more of that fantasy—returning to Hue City. From "Hue City Revisited," it seems that that return really did provide you with the cathartic moment you had been looking for the first time around: you didn't think about the violence you had experienced and participated in there, except in an abstract way, you say, and instead you have a dreamlike feeling, euphoric, elated, "light as a feather." How did returning to Hue affect you long term? Did it impact you psychologically in a permanent way?

WDE. My return to Hue in 1990 didn't change my life in any dramatic way. It confirmed, or perhaps re-confirmed is more accurate, the realization that the Vietnamese were not and had never been my enemy, that I had been sent to make war on a people who did not deserve what I and my country did to them, that my enemies lurk much closer to home.

MMH. In "Ken and Bill's Excellent Adventure," you say that evidence of the huge Marine base at Phu Bai was all gone, and that generally evidence of the war is hard to find. It seems that you were partly looking for evidence of the war—finding your old battalion command post, for example—but were also very pleased to find villages, people, houses and roads rather than old bunkers.

There is a common tension in many returning veterans' narratives, which is that when they return to the place they fought and they are both sad to find no remnants or evidence of their time there, and also happy, perhaps relieved, to find no evidence. Did you feel a tension between wanting to find and wanting not to find evidence of your time in the war?

 WDE. Not any tension strong enough to spend time thinking or fretting about it. Do you have access to my poem "Finding My Old Battalion Command Post"? It touches, I think, on what you are asking about. It's in *Beautiful Wreckage*, but here it is:

> What we came here to find
> was never ours. After the miles
> we've traveled, after the years
> we've dreamed if only we could touch
> the wound again, we could be whole,
> no small wonder to discover
> only a lethal past between us,
> what we thought a brotherhood
> only a mutual recollection of fear.
>
> Something was lost, but it wasn't ours,
> and if not here, we'd only have lost it
> somewhere else. The young always do.
> That is why we remember the young
> who die too soon to lose
> anything but their lives.
> That is why we envy them.
> They will always believe the world
> is simple, and they only die once.
>
> This is not what I intended,
> but it won't stay down: nobody
> wants a fool for a lover, a fool
> for a father, a foolish friend.
> Nobody wants excuses. Still,
> there are stars that burn with no light;
> there are things too evil for words,
> too evil for silence.
> Even a fool needs a friend.
>
> But only the dead are permanent,
> so we've come to this place to find—
> what? Lost innocence? Our true selves?
> What we think we were before we learned
> to recognize incoming enemy mortars
> in our sleep? What you've found is just
> how frail I am. Now you think I can't
> be trusted to my buttons. Grunt to grunt,
> you say, it's all that matters.

> Nevermind particulars. This is just
> between the two of us: "Heave ho,
> into the lake you go with all
> the other alewife scuz and foamy
> harbor scum. But isn't it a pity."
> Yes, a pity, though I've long since learned
> that losses are the way things are.
> And look, I've found a village where I once
> thought nothing green would ever grow.

MMH. You say the most amazing experience of your trip with Ken was finding the building you had been wounded in, and that finding the building, combined with lighting candles on the river, made that evening "magical," "profoundly satisfying." Can you go into why these experiences were so particularly profound—what kind of things were you feeling and thinking?

WDE. I feel like you're asking me to explain the obvious. When we were 19-year-old kids, we were caught up in the midst of the biggest battle of the Vietnam War. People were trying to kill us—with good reason, to be sure, but when you're 19 and in the middle of it, you don't say to yourself, "Well, heck, these people certainly have good reason to be trying to kill us." You just fight from day to day and hour to hour and hope you survive. We saw friends die. We were both wounded and both came within a rice shoot's thickness of dying. I didn't even see or have contact with Kenny again for over 32 years. And now here we were, in this same place that had been nothing but destruction and death, alive and together on a quiet river on a peaceful night surrounded by the people we had come there so long ago to kill. And you want me to explain why that evening was profound? Really?

MMH. When you talk about saying goodbye to General Kinh Chi in 1985, who has become your friend, you say "perhaps a day will come when you do not have to feel the need to defend your affection for the man who was once your adversary." Do you still feel the need to defend this feeling of friendship?

WDE. No. Tran Kinh Chi was a gracious host and a solicitous companion. When I learned that he had died (of old age), I wished him a fair journey to wherever his soul was off to next.

MMH. You seemed initially reluctant to accept the title of Vietnam Veteran writer, and yet when you returned in 1990 you found, as you say, that "everybody over the age of 35 is a 'Vietnam writer,' and for once I could feel like just one of the gang." Did returning with the Veteran Writers Delegation change your perception of the title you had been given?

WDE. No, except that it was an easier title to carry in Vietnam than it is in the U.S. In Vietnam, as I said, at least at that time, just about everyone was a "Vietnam writer," a veteran of the American War as they call it. I fit right in. Here in the U.S., being identified as a "Vietnam writer" is to be pigeonholed, identified, labeled, and quite often subsequently dismissed. I'm included in the *New Oxford Book of War Poetry*, but not in the *Norton Anthology of American Poetry*, the Columbia anthology *American War Poetry*, but not in U of Illinois's *Modern American Poetry*. Well, better some recognition than none at all, as I said, but my experience in Vietnam in 1990 didn't change a thing back here in the U.S.

MMH. How have people reacted to your participation with the Vietnamese-American Veteran Writers Association?

WDE. The only people who had any reaction at all were people who were involved in Vietnam War literature and largely sympathetic to the antiwar perspective. For the most part, there wasn't any reaction. Again, remember, this took place 26 years ago. It is long-forgotten, even by those who might have cared in 1990.

MMH. Does this group of writers make it easier to explain the friendship you found with General Kinh Chi?

WDE. No. Again, you are raising issues that have long since vanished from relevance to anyone but you and me.

MMH. You seemed very relieved in 1990 that every trace of your wartime presence has been grown over. You don't like monuments. But you are a part of the legacy and ongoing remembrance practices of the war. You are also dedicated to teaching younger generations about the war. You say that you see this as a duty and an obligation, a way of turning disaster into hope. But it also seems to me that, in addition to functions of reconciliation and political education apparent in your commemorative activities (education potentially preventing future generations from making the same mistakes), there is an organic element to your commemorative activities: soldier's stories and what is often called "history from below." And it seems to me that these commemorative activities are in defiance or even conflict with the nostalgic and often propagandist functions of commemorative activities such as memorials, monuments and preserved ruins. What are your thoughts on this?

WDE. Once again, the long passage of time has changed what I wrote, or made it largely irrelevant. My whole adult life has been a slow, painful process of adjusting my expectations downward, of coming to terms with the cold fact that I am a very little man in a very big world. There is very little I can change. I certainly can't save my country from itself or my fellow citizens from their ignorance and complacency and fear. I do everything I can to make my students think, to challenge their assumptions, to throw sand in the gears of their brains. But I have no illusions about the impact I'm likely to have. I am one small voice in the midst of a cacophony of voices that are filling these kids' heads with a message far different from mine. I continue to do what I do because what else am I supposed to do? Sell life insurance? Become a stockbroker? I know what I know and I can't un-know it. I do what I do because I have to live with myself, not because I think it'll make any difference. And who knows? Maybe I'll surprise myself and actually make some small difference in the world or at least in a few lives. Awhile back, I got this e-mail:

> Mr Ehrhart,
> I want to let you know what your books have done for me. I served in 2/6 wpns co from 2004–2008 and did two combat deployments to Iraq. I felt I was never able to relate or connect to anyone once leaving the Marine Corps, whether it be civilians (because of having no comprehension of war) or even some of my fellow Marines (some still very strong that America is and was doing the right thing in Iraq) but your books have given me the validation to know my feelings are real and true. When I joined I believe the war was just and right but now after 2 deployments and 5 years of being out, it breaks my heart more then ever that Marines are dying in these wars. Your books have shown me that love for others and knowing right from wrong are the most patriotic things you can do.
> Thank you
Cody N

Is that cool or what? I get e-mails and letters like that every now and then. It certainly makes me feel like I haven't totally wasted my life.

MMH. Do you feel your presence in Vietnam is beneficial to the country?

WDE. Which country, Vietnam or the U.S.? I guess it doesn't matter. I wouldn't know how to assess the benefits of my presence in either country.

MMH. How do your actions in Vietnam affect the legacy of the war there?

WDE. Another ambiguous question, alas. Do you mean my actions in 1967–68, 1985–86, 1990, or 2011? And again, in any case, I have no way of gauging that. You'd have to ask the Vietnamese. Really. I'm not being smart-ass.

MMH. You say that "it did my heart good" to see thriving villages, to meet war survivors from the other side, to walk around without gunfire going on around you. Do you think that you being there in a peaceful capacity might have had the same positive impact on veterans from North Vietnam? What about veterans of the ARVN, and civilians?

WDE. I'd like to think the Vietnamese—North, South, soldier, civilian—

got to see that I am capable of kindness, remorse, decency, gratitude, sorrow, joy, and friendship, that I am not just a foreigner with a gun intent upon sowing destruction and misery.

MMH. Could you talk a bit about when Mrs. Na told you that "you did this" to her? How did you feel when she held you seemingly personally responsible for the deaths of her sons?

WDE. Did I not describe that in detail in *Going Back*? I felt nauseous, lightheaded, physically woozy, sad and guilty for what I and my country had done to her and her family. It was the most difficult moment of all three of my trips back to post-war Vietnam.

MMH. How do you think Vietnam has changed since the war?

WDE. Well, no one is dropping bombs on them or herding them into refugee camps or turning their daughters into whores and their sons into shoeshine boys. That's a big improvement. There is poverty in places. The socialist equality Ho and others hoped for has gone the way of all human dreams. But most Vietnamese are far better off than they were when the nation was at war. It is a young, educated, ambitious, and vibrant population with a future.

MMH. In the essay "On US Policy toward Postwar Vietnam" you say that despite all the efforts of the U.S. government to punish the Vietnamese for winning through the embargo, "Vietnam and its people have made remarkable progress in the past five years."[12] This was in 1990, five years after your first visit, four years after Doi Moi. Were the changes you saw mostly positive?

WDE. Yes, almost uniformly positive.

MMH. What about in 2011? You saw that the Majestic Hotel in Saigon had been transformed into a five-star hotel and casino. How do you feel about developments like these?

WDE. Realizing that western consumer culture has come to Vietnam in spades took some getting used to. The old revolutionaries must be turning over in their graves. I doubt that modern Vietnam is what they had hoped for with its Louis Vuitton stores and condos for sale on the fairway of the Greg Norman Golf Course at China Beach. But it's their country, not mine. It's none of my business what they do with it. It never was.

MMH. What do you think the war did to Vietnam and to the Vietnamese people?

WDE. The war left Vietnam impoverished and broken. It left millions of bomb craters and hundreds of thousands of unexploded mines and bombs and artillery shells. It destroyed thousands of acres of farmland and forests and mangroves. It killed countless animals both wild and domestic. And it killed, maimed, or made miserable millions of human beings. The damage done by the war will take generations to overcome.

MMH. In the essay "The War That Won't Go Away," you say that you "often see brilliant conspiracies where there is only arrogance, hubris and stupidity."[13] Was the Vietnam War a conspiracy, or a consequence of arrogance, hubris and stupidity—or both?

WDE. The war was created and perpetuated by arrogant, hubristic, ignorant (not stupid, but ignorant) men who didn't have a clue what was actually taking place in Southeast Asia or what to do about it. The conspiracy was all in the lies policymakers, diplomats, politicians, and generals told to hide the truth of what was happening as a result of their arrogance, hubris, and ignorance.

Mia Martin Hobbs was a Ph.D. candidate in the School of Historical and Philosophical Studies at the University of Melbourne, Australia, researching veterans' postwar returns to Vietnam, when this interview was conducted on January 10, 2016.

NOTES

    1. W.D. Ehrhart, *Memoir of an Anti-Vietnam War Veteran* (original English: *Passing Time: Memoir of a Vietnam Veteran Against the War*), Yoko Shirai, trans. (Tokyo, Japan: Tosui Shobo Publishers, 2015).
    2. Col. Robert D. Heinl, Jr., *Armed Forces Journal*, June 7, 1971.
    3. In 2005 David Zeiger wrote, produced and directed the documentary *Sir! No Sir!* about the anti-war movement within the ranks of the United States Armed Forces during the Vietnam War.
    4. "Operation Dewey Canyon III" took place in Washington, D.C, April 19–23, 1971.
    5. W.D. Ehrhart, "Learning the Hard Way," *In the Shadow of Vietnam: Essays, 1977–1991* (Jefferson, NC: McFarland, 1991), 51.
    6. W.D. Ehrhart, *To Those Who Have Gone Home Tired* (New York: Thunder's Mouth Press, 1984), 17.
    7. W.D. Ehrhart, *Passing Time: Memoir of a Vietnam Veteran Against the War* (Jefferson, NC: McFarland, 1989), 210.
    8. W.D. Ehrhart, *In the Shadow of Vietnam: Essays, 1977–1991* (Jefferson, NC: McFarland, 1991), 7.
    9. Ehrhart, *In the Shadow of Vietnam*, 98.
    10. Ehrhart, *To Those Who Have Gone Home Tired*, 71.
    11. *Ibid.*
    12. Ehrhart, *In the Shadow of Vietnam*, 149–50.
    13. W.D. Ehrhart, *The Madness of It All: Essays on War, Literature, and American Life* (Jefferson, NC: McFarland, 2002), 77.

Three Unusual Questions

Miriam Sagan

MS. What is your personal/aesthetic relationship to the poetic line? That is, how do you understand it, use it, etc.

WDE: Wow, when you asked me if I'd be interested in being interviewed, I had expected something—I don't know—more traditional? When did you start writing? What poets influenced you? At least a few warm-up questions before we got to the more esoteric questions. But what the heck; I opened the door, so now I can't very well say, "Forget it, go away."

The only thing is: I don't really know how to respond to the first two questions. Let's take #1, which is the more difficult of the two, for me at least. I suppose I must have some kind of relationship to the poetic line. I write poetic lines all the time, or try to, so there must be some kind of relationship. But I've never really thought much about it, certainly not in these terms. I do think about line lengths, and as I've gotten older, I notice that my line lengths—generally speaking—tend to be longer than they were 40 years ago (I've been writing a long time: 52 years); I think more in syllabics now, and often end up writing in rough tetrameter or pentameter lines. But I can't explain why that transition occurred. I have always tried to shape lines that work, that do what I want, that say what I want. As you can probably tell, I don't really know what I'm saying. So much of what I do—I suspect this is true of many other poets, though I can't speak for them—I do intuitively, by "feel," by some kind of instinct. One might call it dumb luck or guesswork, though I think there is something more deliberate about it. But what that is I can't explain, have never tried to explain that I can recall, and as you can gather from this rambling response, we're all probably better off if I don't try to explain. What matters to me is: does my poem work for you? Does it speak to you? Is it any good? The older I get, the less I care to talk about poetry. What I do is in my poems. What I think is in my poems. It's there for you to see, to read, to make sense of, to come to your own conclusions about what my personal/aesthetic relationship to the poetic line might be.

MS. Do you find a relationship between words and writing and the human body? Or between your writing and your body?

WDE: Another question I don't think I've ever given any thought to, and find myself wondering: of all the things one might ask me, why this? The only part of my body that I have given any conscious thought to is that I have always composed poems by hand, hand-writing drafts until the poem is well along. I can't compose poetry on a keyboard. There is something about connecting my brain to the paper by way of my arm and hand and pen that doesn't translate to a keyboard, whether typewriter or computer. Increasingly, as I've gotten older, when I'm writing prose, I tend to move back and forth between pen/paper and keyboard, more a function of laziness and hands that get tired quicker than they used to. But poetry I still draft longhand until the poem is well along to completion, at least of a first draft.

MS. Is there anything you dislike about being a poet?

WDE: Well, yeah, I don't make any money writing poetry. I wish more people would read poetry and actually buy poetry. I wish I could fill Madison Square Garden with 20,000 paying fans screaming to hear my poetry. I'm still working fulltime at the age of 68. Being a poet has not put me in a position to buy a seaside home in Bermuda and enjoy the sunsets.

Other than that, though, I don't really have any complaints. I like being a poet. I get a good feeling when I write a poem that I like. I get an even better feeling when I write a poem somebody else likes. One could do a whole lot worse in this world, and a lot of people do.

Miriam Sagan, poet and teacher at Santa Fe Community College, New Mexico, conducted this interview on September 21, 2016, for her website Miriam's Well: Poetry, Land Art, and Beyond.

Military History of W. D. Ehrhart

W. D. Ehrhart enlisted in the United States Marine Corps on April 11, 1966, while still in high school, beginning active duty on June 17. He graduated from basic recruit training at the Marine Corps Recruit Depot, Parris Island, South Carolina, on August 12, receiving a meritorious promotion to private first class, and completed basic infantry training at Camp Lejeune, North Carolina, on September 12, 1966. (While at Parris Island, he qualified as a rifle sharpshooter on July 18, 1966, subsequently qualifying as a rifle expert on April 11, 1968, and as pistol sharpshooter on April 24, 1969.)

Assigned to the field of combat intelligence, Ehrhart spent October 10 to December 15, 1966, with Marine Air Group 26, a helicopter unit based at New River Marine Corps Air Facility, North Carolina, meanwhile completing a clerk typist course at Camp Lejeune in November 1966 and graduating first in his class from the Enlisted Basic Amphibious Intelligence School at Little Creek Amphibious Base, Norfolk, Virginia, in December 1966. He also completed a Marine Corps Institute combat intelligence correspondence course in December while at New River.

Before leaving for Vietnam on February 9, 1967, Ehrhart received additional combat training with the 3rd Replacement Company, Staging Battalion, Camp Pendleton, California, in January and February. Upon arrival in Vietnam, he was assigned to the 1st Battalion, 1st Marine Regiment, first as an intelligence assistant, later as assistant intelligence chief. In March 1967, he was temporarily assigned to the Sukiran Army Education Center, Okinawa, where he graduated first in his class from a course in basic Vietnamese terminology before returning to permanent assignment.

While in Vietnam, Ehrhart participated in the following combat operations: Stone, Lafayette, Early, Canyon, Calhoun, Pike, Medina, Lancaster, Kentucky I, Kentucky II, Kentucky III, Con Thien, Newton, Osceola II, and

Hue City. He was promoted to lance corporal on April 1, 1967, and meritoriously promoted to corporal on July 1, 1967.

Ehrhart was awarded the Purple Heart Medal for wounds received in action in Hue City during the Tet Offensive, a commendation from Major General Donn J. Robertson commanding the 1st Marine Division, two Presidential Unit Citations, the Navy Combat Action Ribbon, the Vietnam Service Medal with three stars, the Vietnamese Campaign Medal, a Cross of Gallantry Meritorious Unit Citation, and a Civil Action Meritorious Unit Citation.

Ehrhart was next assigned to the 2nd Marine Air Wing Headquarters Group at Cherry Point Marine Corps Air Station, North Carolina, from March 30 to June 10, 1968, where he was promoted to sergeant on April 1. After a brief assignment with the Headquarters Squadron of Marine Air Group 15 based at Iwakuni Marine Corps Air Station, Japan, he was then reassigned to Marine Aerial Refueler Transport Squadron 152, Futema Marine Corps Air Facility, Okinawa, from July 20 to October 30, 1968, where he received a commanding officer's Meritorious Mast.

Ehrhart completed his active duty with Marine Fighter Attack Squadron 122, based alternately at Iwakuni and Cubi Point Naval Air Station, Philippines, from October 31, 1968 to May 30, 1969. While in the Philippines, he completed a field course on jungle environmental survival in February 1969.

On June 10, 1969, Ehrhart was separated from active duty, receiving the Good Conduct Medal. While on inactive reserve, he was promoted to staff sergeant on July 1, 1971. He received an honorable discharge on April 10, 1972.

An Ehrhart Bibliography

Books

Poetry

Beautiful Wreckage: New & Selected Poems (Easthampton, MA: Adastra Press, 1999).
The Bodies Beneath the Table (Easthampton, MA: Adastra Press, 2010).
The Distance We Travel (Easthampton, MA: Adastra Press, 1993).
From the Bark of the Daphne Tree (Easthampton, MA: Adastra Press, 2013).
A Generation of Peace (New York: New Voices Publishing Company, 1975).
Just for Laughs (Silver Spring, MD: Viet Nam Generation & Burning Cities Press, 1990).
The Outer Banks & Other Poems (Easthampton, MA: Adastra Press, 1984).
The Samisdat Poems (Richford: VT, Samisdat, 1980).
To Those Who Have Gone Home Tired (New York: Thunder's Mouth Press, 1984).

Prose

Busted: A Vietnam Veteran in Nixon's America (Amherst: University of Massachusetts Press, 1995).
Dead on a High Hill: Essays on War, Literature and Living, 2002–2012 (Jefferson, NC: McFarland, 2012).
Going Back: An Ex-Marine Returns to Vietnam (Jefferson, NC: McFarland, 1987).
In the Shadow of Vietnam: Essays, 1977–1991 (Jefferson, NC: McFarland, 1991).
The Madness of It All: Essays on War, Literature and American Life (Jefferson, NC: McFarland, 2002).
Ordinary Lives: Platoon 1005 and the Vietnam War (Philadelphia, PA: Temple University Press, 1999).
Passing Time: Memoir of a Vietnam Veteran Against the War (Jefferson, NC: McFarland, 1989).
Vietnam–Perkasie: A Combat Marine Memoir (Jefferson, NC: McFarland, 1983).

Translations

Memoir of an Anti-Vietnam War Veteran (original English: *Passing Time: Memoir of a Vietnam Veteran Against the War*), Yoko Shirai, trans. (Tokyo, Japan: Tosui Shobo Publishers, 2015).

Editor

Carrying the Darkness: Poetry of the Vietnam War (Lubbock: Texas Tech University Press, 1989).
Unaccustomed Mercy: Soldier-Poets of the Vietnam War (Lubbock: Texas Tech Univ. Press, 1989).

Coeditor

Demilitarized Zones: Veterans After Vietnam (Perkasie, PA: East River Anthology, 1976), with Jan Barry.
Retrieving Bones: Stories & Poems of the Korean War (New Brunswick, NJ: Rutgers University Press, 1999), with Philip K. Jason.

Chapbooks

Poetry

Channel Fever (Port Jefferson, NY: Backstreet Editions, 1982).
Empire (Richford: VT, Samisdat, 1978).
A Generation of Peace (Revised) (Richford: VT, Samisdat, 1977).
Greatest Hits: 1970-2000 (Johnstown, OH: Puddinghouse Press, 2001).
Matters of the Heart (Easthampton, MA: Adastra Press, 1981).
Mostly Nothing Happens (Easthampton, MA: Adastra Press,1996).
Praying at the Altar (Easthampton, MA: Adastra Press, 2017).
Rootless (Richford: VT, Samisdat, 1977).
Sleeping with the Dead (Easthampton, MA: Adastra Press, 2006).
A Sort of Peace: Echoes and Images of the Vietnam War (Canandaigua, NY: Fox Photo Arts, 2005), with photographer Don Fox.
Winter Bells (Easthampton, MA: Adastra Press, 1988).

Booklet

Going Back: A Poet Who Was Once a Marine Returns to Vietnam (Wallingford, PA: Pendle Hill Publications, 1987).

Selected Works About W.D. Ehrhart

Anderson, Donald, and Thomas G. Bowie, Jr., interviewers. "A Conversation with W.D. Ehrhart." *War, Literature & the Arts: an International Journal of the Humanities*, 8:2 (Fall/Winter 1996), 149–157.
Boughman, Ronald, ed. *The Dictionary of Literary Biography Documentary Series*, vol. 9 (Farmington Hills, MI: Cengage Gale Research, 1991), 63–82.
Bova, Annalisa. *Every Day I'm Always on Patrol: testimonianza a trauma di W.D. Ehrhart*, dissertation: A.A. 2002–2003; Università degli studi di Bergamo, Facoltà di lingue e letterature straniere, Italy, 2003.
Casale, Frank D. "W.D. Ehrhart and the Extremes of Foreign Policy, Ideology, and American Hegemony." *Entertext 6.2: War & Society*, 6:2 (Winter 2006–2007), http://people.brunel.ac.uk/~acsrrrm/entertext/issue_6_2.htm.
Chattarji, Subarno. *Memories of a Lost War: American Poetic Responses to the Vietnam War* (Oxford: Oxford University Press, 2001).
Goldensohn, Lorrie. *Dismantling Glory: 20th Century Soldier Poetry* (New York: Columbia University Press, 2004).
Gollner, Nicole. *Writing the War: The Works of William Daniel Ehrhart; From Patriot to Poet to Pacifist*. Master's Thesis, Am Institut für Amerikanistik, Karl Franzens-Universität Graz, Graz, Austria, 2005.
Gotera, Vince. *Radical Visions: Poetry by Vietnam Veterans* (Athens: University of Georgia Press, 1994).
Jason, Philip K., ed. *Critical Survey of Poetry*, 2nd rev. ed. (Ipswich, MA: Salem Press, 2002).
Jason, Philip K., and Mark A. Graves, eds. *Encyclopedia of American War Literature* (Westport, CT: Greenwood Press, 2001).
Malo, Jean-Jacques. *The Last Time I Dreamed About the War: Essays on the Life and Writing of W.D. Ehrhart* (Jefferson, NC: McFarland, 2014).
Rosso, Stefano. "Conversazione con William D. Ehrhart e John S. Baky, Philadelphia, ottobre 1997." *Ácoma* (no. 19, Primavera-Estate, 2000, anno VII), 40–47. Republished in Stefano Rosso, *Musi gialli e Berretti Verdi: Narrazioni Usa sulla Guerra del Vietnam* (Bergamo: Bergamo University Press, 2003), 233–249.
Sagan, Miriam. "Miriam's Well." https://miriamswell.wordpress.com/, posted September 21, 2016.
Slabey, Robert M., ed. *The United States and Viet Nam from War to Peace* (Jefferson, NC: McFarland, 1996).
Tal, Kali. "Chapter 4: The Farmer of Dreams: The Writings of W.D. Ehrhart." *Worlds of Hurt: Reading the Literature of Trauma* (Cambridge: Cambridge University Press, 1996). 77–114.
Waring, Brett. "The Individual in War Literature: A Case Study of W.D. Ehrhart and Modern War Narratives." Master's Thesis, California State University at Dominguez Hills, 2011.

Index

ace of spades 184
Adastra Press 113, 165
Addams, Jane 208
aerial bombing 186, 187
Afghanistan War 62, 65, 88, 108, 136, 142, 144, 160, 183, 184, 194
Agent Orange 88, 95–96, 121, 153, 194
Alfier, Jeffrey 115, 150
Ali, Muhammad 64, 136
Along the Way 134
al Qaeda 200, 207
al-Sadr, Muqtada 108
"America Takes Charge" 127
American Poetry Review 52, 115, 164
"The American War in Vietnam: Lessons Learned and Not Learned" 183
American War Poetry 119, 212
Anderson, Donald 1, 155
Anderson, Doug 121
Anderson, Nathalie 150
Anisfield, Nancy 121
anti-war movement 8, 15, 35, 55, 75, 102, 103, 104, 106, 120, 177, 192, 199, 200
anti-war poetry 164
Apocalypse Now 78, 100, 136
Appleman, Philip 119, 150
April 30th, 1975 49, 151, 193
Árbenz, Jacobo 170–171
ARVN 190
"Asian Peace Offers Rejected Without Publication" 46
Avon Books 118, 165

baby-killers 103, 200
Baky, John S. 3, 4n13, 135, 174, 184, 188
Balaban, John 17, 47, 50, 64, 65, 119, 127, 148, 150, 152
Barry, Jan 9, 117, 120, 121, 152
Basevich, Andrew 204
Baughman, Ronald 46
Beautiful Wreckage 68, 70, 71, 89, 113, 141, 210
Beck, Glenn 129
"The Beech Tree" 23

Beidler, Philip 9
Bettelheim, Bruno 11
"Bicentennial" 38
Billy Budd 134
Black Mountain School of Poetry 8
Black Panthers 56
Blackford, Staige 115
Blair, Tony 185
Blake, William 119
"The Blue Hotel" 134
Bly, Robert 8, 23, 46
The Bodies Beneath the Table 147, 161
Bowie, Tom 155
"Briana" 12, 23
"The Bride Comes to Yellow Sky" 134
broken-hearted love poems 68, 82, 99, 145
Brown, D.F. 64, 192
Bryan, C.D.B. 7
Bulletin of Concerned Asian Scholars 5
Bundy brothers 103, 191
Burns, Ken 1
Bursk, Christopher 70
Bush, Duncan 134
Bush, George W., Jr. 141
Bush, George W., Sr. 18, 42, 48, 76, 92, 116, 141
Busted 1, 32, 79–80, 126, 154, 158, 165
Butler, Robert Olen 47
Butler, Smedley Darlington 134
Byron, George Gordon 150

Cambodia, secret bombing of 176
Camus, Albert 135, 140
Candide 135
Caputo, Philip 53, 128
Carroll, Lewis 147
Carruth, Hayden 65
Carrying the Darkness 5, 8, 46, 54, 64, 118–121, 122, 165
Carter, Jimmy 141, 183
Castro, Fidel 137
Catcher in the Rye 140
Cather, Willa 140

225

226 Index

Central America 10, 20, 41, 62, 88, 172, 204
Césaire, Aimé 146
Channel Fever 113
Chattarji, Subarno 2
Cherryh, C.J. 133
Cheyney, Dick 76
Chief Joseph 208
Child, Lydia Maria 28
"The Children of Hanoi" 116, 128
Chomsky, Noam 56
Class of '66 154
Clinton, Bill 141
"Coaching Winter Track in Time of War" 83, 161
Coffman, Lisa 150
Coker, George 42
Cold War 170, 171
Coleman, Horace 119, 189
"The Collapse of the Armed Forces" 200
Collected Poems 98
"Coming Home" 54
Coming Home 78, 100
Common Sense 29
Con Thien 179
"Concerning Memorial Day" 151
A Coney Island of the Mind 135
"A Confirmation" 16, 25
Connolly, David V. 64, 85, 121, 150, 177, 194
Conrad, Joseph 79, 135
Cossentino, Tom 187
Cox, Joe 54, 72, 150, 155, 156
Cragg, Dan 133
Crane, Hart 13
Crane, Stephen 8, 61, 66, 119, 134, 135
Cronkite, Walter 176
Cu Chi 33
Cuban Missile Crisis 172, 199

D'Angelo, Eileen 150
Dark Seasons of the Mind 38
Dead on a High Hill. Essays on War, Literature and Living, 2002–2012 129–132, 143, 151
Debs, Eugene 208
The Deer Hunter 10, 78, 100, 124, 135, 136
de Gaulle, Charles 168
Dellinger, Dave 192
Demilitarized Zones 9, 117–119, 121, 122
DePalma, Brian 6
Desert Shield 141
Desert Storm 141
Dewey Canyon III 203
Dickinson, Emily 61, 119, 120, 146
Diehl, John B. 140
Diem, Ngo Dinh 35, 169
Dispatches 56, 190, 206
The Distance We Travel 43, 71
DMZ see *Demilitarized Zones*
Domino Theory 137, 169, 171
Dostoyevsky, Fiodor 73, 135
Douglas, John 120
"The Dream" 45, 80n2

Dreiser, Theodore 11
Dulles, Allen 170, 171
Dulles, John Foster 169, 170, 171, 173
Dulles brothers 103

East River Anthology 9, 117
Eisenhower, Dwight 57, 82, 99, 103, 137, 145, 169
El Salvador 24
Eliot, T.S. 63
Ellsberg, Dan 191
Emerson, Gloria 160
Empire 113, 138
"Empire" 12
Endless Enemies 204
The Epic of Gilgamesh 62
Estevez, Emilio 134
"The Ex-Officer, Navy" 65
Exler, Sam 152

"The Farmer" 49, 50
Ferlinghetti, Lawrence 135
Fifty Contemporary Poets: The Creative Process 9
"Finding My Old Battalion Command Post" 210
1st Casualty Press 9, 114, 117, 164
Fitzgerald, F. Scott 82, 140
Fonda, Jane 36, 103
"For a Coming Extinction" 158
Forché, Carolyn 165, 166
Ford, Gerald 141
Fourteen Landing Zones: Approaches to Vietnam War Literature 60n11
Fowle, Steve 153
Franklin, H. Bruce 1, 26, 42, 58, 91, 121, 154, 165
Franklin, Robert (Robbie) 124, 126, 127, 165
Free Fire Zones 117
Friendly Fire 7
Frost, Robert 61, 140
Furey, Joan A. 122
Furst, Alan 134
Fussell, Paul 54–55, 143

Gallery 128, 197
geese in the autumn 68, 82, 99
A Generation of Peace 112, 113
"A Generation of Peace" 47
The Genre of Silence 134
Gibran, Kahlil 61, 66, 135, 136
Gibson, William 17
Gilbert, Adam 2, 3
Ginsberg, Allen 8, 35, 46
"Glimpse" 39
Go Tell the Spartans 136
Going Back: A Poet Who Was Once a Marine 196, 205
Going Back: An Ex-Marine Returns to Vietnam 127–128, 214
Goldensohn, Lorrie 119, 121

Index

Golding, William 134
Goldwater, Barry 205
The Good Earth 134
The Good Soldier Svejk 140
Gray, Patrick Worth 120
Green Grass Grace 79, 133
Greene, Graham 134, 169
Grenada 62
Gruening, Ernest 136
Gruner, Elliott 42
Guatemala 170
"Guerrilla War" 32, 54, 85
Gulf War 18, 27, 51, 53, 62, 116, 141, 142, 143, 155
"Guns" 63, 116, 141
Guy de Maupassant, Henri René Albert 140

Haines, Harry W. 26
Halberstam, David 160
Hallowell, Edward 152
Hamilton, Alfred Starr 48
Hardy, Thomas 61, 99, 135
Harassment & Interdiction artillery fire 75
Hasek, Jaroslav 140
Hasford, Gus 52
Hawthorne, Nathaniel 140
Hearts and Minds 42
Hedin, Robert 119
Heinemann, Larry 128
Heinl, Col. Robert 201
Hell's Music 154
Hemingway, Ernest 110
Henry, O. 140
Here, Bullet 143
Herr, Michael 56, 190, 206
Higginson, Thomas Wentworth 119, 120
Hill, Joe 208
Hiroshima 11, 186
Hitler, Adolf 171
Ho Chi Minh 14, 48, 91, 136, 169, 170, 172, 193
Hoffman, Daniel 71, 152
Hollenbach, Robert F. 139, 140
Hollywood 6, 37–38, 78, 99, 124, 135, 136
Holmes, Regina 152
"Holy War" 116, 141
How I Live 44
"How I Live" 71
Huddle, David 64
Hugo, Richard 8, 61, 66, 135
The Hurt Locker 136
Hussein, Saddam 18, 84, 185

"I have a rendezvous with Death" 140
The Idiot 73
The Iliad 62
Imaginative Representations of the Vietnam War Collection 3, 4n13
In Country 47
In Retrospect 31
In the Grass 189

In the Shadow of Vietnam: Essays 1977–1991 56, 131, 151, 208
The Inheritors 134
"The Invasion of Grenada" 25, 26, 207, 208
invasion of North Vietnam 77
Iran 12, 108
Iraq War 62, 65, 76, 83–84, 88, 100, 108, 136, 142, 144, 160, 183, 184, 185, 194
Irish, Jane 100
Isaacs, Arnold 160
ISIS 185, 200, 207

"Jabberwocky" 147
Japan Women's University 199
Jarhead 143
Jason, Philip K. 60n11, 118, 121
Jeffers, Robinson 61, 82, 140
Johnson, Lyndon 57, 91, 103, 137, 173, 176, 201, 205
Johnson, Samuel 76, 202
Jones, James 9
Just for Laughs 44, 54, 141

Kalkstein, Ben 137
Kambon, Akinsanya 195n3
Keats, John 20, 82, 99, 150
Keeling, Judith 120
"Ken & Bill's Excellent Adventure" 130, 151, 193, 197, 209
Kennedy, Bobby 15
Kennedy, John F. 50, 57, 103, 110
Kent State 15, 75, 103, 105–106, 111, 178, 201, 202
Kincade, Ron 162
King, Martin Luther, Jr. 15, 65
Kissinger, Henry 26, 31, 91, 103, 113, 172, 177, 190, 191, 192, 201
Komunyakaa, Yusef 64, 128, 146, 150, 165
"Kosovo" 161
Kwitny, Jonathan 204

Lang, Steve 133
Laos, invasion of 176
"Last of the Hard-hearted Ladies" 10
The Last Time I Dreamed About the War: Essays on the Life and Writing of W.D. Ehrhart 2, 3, 194
Le Duc Tho 91
"Learning the Hard Way" 204
Lembcke, Jerry 200
Lessons Learned 120
"Letter" 36, 48, 130, 138
"Letter to the Survivors" 12, 199
Levertov, Denise 8, 35
The Lewd Librarian 135
Lewis, Sinclair 11
The Lice 135
Liebler, M.L. 148, 150
"Life in the Neighborhood" 147
Limbaugh, Rush 129
Lincoln, Abraham 110
Liuzzo, Viola 208

"The Living Christ" 39–40
Lomperis, Timothy 18, 22
The Long Road Home 124
"Long Road" poems 39
Lowell, Robert 13
Lumumba, Patrice 137
Lyons, Paul 154

MacDonald, Walter 64
The Madness of It All 141, 151, 198
Mahoney, Philip 121
"Making the Children Behave" 47, 85, 193
Making Time 126–127
Mandelstam, Osip 140
March 5th, 1968 15, 33, 125, 180
The Marine Corps Times 143
Mason, Bobbie Ann 47
Matterhorn 123
"Matters of the Heart" 10, 20
Matters of the Heart 113
McAuliffe, John 127
McBride, Shawn 79, 133
McCain, John 92, 93–94
McCarthy, Gerald 64, 119
McCarthy, Jerry 52
McDonald, Walt 118
McFarland & Co. 32, 124, 126, 127, 130, 131, 132, 165
McGovern, George 205
McGrath, Thomas 100, 131
McKee, Lou 148, 150
McNamara, Robert 26, 31, 92, 103, 173, 175, 191, 192
McPhee, John 79, 133
Melville, Herman 8, 119, 134, 152
Merritt, Clifton 7–8, 113, 115, 124
Merwin, W.S. 8, 61, 66, 135
Metras, Gary 113, 149
M.I.A., or Mythmaking in America 91
MIAs 91
Millay, Edna St. Vincent 79, 140
Miller, David 178
Miss Saigon 136
Moby Dick 134
Modern American Poetry 212
Moffat, Abbot Low 169
"Money in the Bank" 48, 52
Moore, Madeline 51
"A Moral History of the American War in Vietnam" 195n6
morality in war 187
"Morality, Soldier-Poetry, and the American War in Vietnam" 3
Morse, Wayne 136
"Mostly Nothing Happens" 64
Mother Jones 175
Moyers, Bill 148
Muller, Bobby 128
My Lai 11, 34, 153

napalm 175, 188
The Nation 1
National Public Radio 116
Neary, Lynn 116
Negroponte, John 92
Nemerov, Howard 65
Netherlands American Studies Association 101
The New Hampshire Gazette 153
New Letters 52
New Oxford Book of War Poetry 212
The New York Times 7, 9, 51, 140, 157
The New Yorker 116, 164, 166
Newman, John 123
Nicaragua 10, 57, 127
Nixon, Richard 31, 48, 58, 91, 103, 176, 177, 190, 192, 201
Norris, Chuck 206
North, Don 197
Norton Anthology of American Poetry 212
"Nothing Profound" 71

Obama, Barack 141, 144, 160, 202–203
O'Brien, Tim 30, 53, 165, 190
Old Glory 119
"Old Myths" 205
"On a Certain Engagement South of Seoul" 62, 65
"On US Policy toward Postwar Vietnam" 214
"One, Two, Many Vietnams?" 151
"The Open Boat" 134
Ordinary Lives: Platoon 1005 and the Vietnam War 161
Orr, Gregory 115
Orwell, George 23
Owen, Wilfred 6, 8, 39, 61, 67, 98, 135

Paine, Tom 29
Palin, Sarah 100
Panama 62
Paquet, Basil 120
"Parade" 41, 141
Pargeter, Edith 133
Parks, Rosa 208
Passing Time 7, 14, 15, 23, 30, 31, 32, 40, 41, 75, 76, 85, 99, 118, 126, 128, 155, 160, 164–165, 172, 196, 197, 199, 200, 201, 202, 203, 205
patriotism 28, 29, 76, 202
Patti, Archimedes 169
peace with honor 190
"The Peaceable Kingdom" 46
The Pentagon Papers 30–31, 202
The Perfect War: Technowar in Vietnam 17
Peters, Ellis 133
Petraeus' strategy 185
The Philadelphia Inquirer 127, 134, 153
Phillips Exeter Academy 192
Piercy, Marge 46
Pine Ridge 11
Platoon 136
Poe, Edgar Allan 61, 82
"Poetry in Extremis" 166

Index   229

Poetry magazine 8, 116, 164
Postmortem 9
Pound, Ezra 63
"POW/MIA" 41
"The Power to Declare" 151
POWs 91, 176, 189–190
Pratt, John Clark 117
Prisoners of Culture 42
The Progressive 175
The Prophet 66
PTSD 99, 107–108, 142

The Quiet American 169

Rabbit, Run 135
Rabe, David 136
Rambo, 206 207
Rambo: First Blood, Part II 136
Rawlings, Marjorie Kinnan 140
Reading the Wind 18
Reagan, Nancy 126
Reagan, Ronald 11, 12, 42, 141, 153, 204
"The Reason Why" 12
"Redeployment" 65
"A Relative Thing" 18, 20, 42, 85, 111, 113
"Renascence" 140
"Rendezvous" *see* "I have a rendezvous with Death"
"Re-Runs" 65
"Responsibility" 10, 20, 23, 45
Retrieving Bones: Stories and Poems of the Korean War 118–119, 121
revision process 72
Ridenhour, Ron 136
Ritterbusch, Dale 50, 64, 85, 120–121, 150, 152, 159
Robinson, Edwin Arlington 61, 140, 150
Rolvaag, Ole 140
Rooney, Gerry 152
Roosevelt, Franklin Delano 168
Rootless 113
Ross, Bobby 75
Rosso, Stefano 3
Rostow, Walt Whitman 173, 191
Rottmann, Larry 120
Rowe, Bobby 75
A Rumor of War 53
Rumsfeld, Donald 76
Rusk, Dean 46, 57, 103, 173, 191
Russell, Norman 134

Sagan, Miriam 2
Saint Joan 133
Saki 140
Salinger, J.D. 135
Samisdat 7, 8, 115
The Samisdat Poems 113
San Francisco poets 8
San Pedro River Review 150
Sandburg, Carl 10, 11, 208
Sanders, Bernie 175

Saner, Reg 65, 119, 121
Santayana, George 23
Sassoon, Siegfried 67
Schoendoerffer, Pierre 136
Schwarzkopf, Norman 155
"A Scientific Treatise for My Wife" 23, 84, 159
"Second Thoughts" 89
Secrets 191
Seeger, Alan 140
self-abusive behavior 196
self-destructive behavior 105, 177
"September 11th" 161
Sewanee Review 116
Sexton, Anne 13
Shakespeare, William 20, 99, 136
Shaw, G.B. 133
Shea, Dick 52
Sheehan, Neil 160
Sheen, Martin 134
Shelley, Percy Bysshe 61, 82, 150
Sherman, David 133
Shields, Bill 121
"Shoulders" 120
"Sins of the Fathers" 72
Sir! No, Sir! 200
Slabey, Robert 19
Slavery by Another Name 134
Slaves in the Family 134
"A Small Romance" 71, 84
Smith, Lorrie 23, 50, 52, 115
Soft Spots: A Marine's Memoir of Combat and Post-Traumatic Stress Disorder 80n3, 100, 143
"Soldier-Poets of the Vietnam War" 50, 54, 206
"Soldier's Home" 110
"The Soldier's Return" 40
"Some Other World" 43
"Song for Leela, Bobby, and Me" 23
"Song of Napalm" 65
"Speaking the Language of Pain" 55
The Spitting Image: Myth, Memory, and the Legacy of Vietnam 200
Stalin, Joseph 140, 161, 168, 169, 170, 171, 172
Stars and Stripes 200
"Starting Over" 44
"Stealing Hubcaps" 22, 153
Stevens, Wallace 63
Stickney, Trumbull 119
Sticks & Bones 136
Stone, Oliver 6
Suicide Charlie: A Vietnam War Story 134
Swarthmore College 105, 177, 198
Swofford, Anthony 143

Takenaga, Ken 106, 128–129, 130, 132, 151, 158, 197, 211
Tal, Kali 22, 55, 151
Taylor, Maxwell 192
"The Teacher" 17, 18, 173, 199
Terkel, Studs 1

Tet Offensive 176, 181
Thanh Nien Daily 3
"Thank You for Your Service" 153
"They Want Enough Rice" 151
The Things They Carried 190
Thompson, Hugh 136
The 317th Platoon 136
Tito, Josip 170
"To Maynard on the Long Road Home" 37
"To My Mother" 39
To Those Who Have Gone Home Tired 2, 5, 11, 22, 25, 48, 50, 112, 113, 138
Tracers 136
Tran Kinh Chi, General 127, 211, 212
Truman, Harry 57, 103, 161, 168, 172
Trump, Donald 203
Tubman, Harriet 208
Turner, Alberta T. 9
Turner, Brian 143
"Twice Betrayed" 43

Uhl, Michael 52
Unaccustomed Mercy: Soldier-Poets of the Vietnam War 118–121
unexploded ordnance 88, 192
United Fruit Company 171
United States and Vietnam: From War to Peace 19
Updike, John 135

Van Devanter, Linda 122
Van Winkle, Clint 80n3, 100, 143
The Veteran 116
Veteran Writers Delegation 211
Viet Journal 9
Vietnam: A Television History 127, 197
Vietnam-Perkasie 1, 14, 32, 53, 75, 77, 78, 79, 85, 100, 106, 123, 126, 128, 132, 158, 164, 172, 181, 189
Vietnam Simply 52
Vietnam Veterans Against the War 5, 7, 19, 56, 111, 113, 114, 116, 117, 120, 122, 161, 164, 177, 203
Vietnam Veterans Memorial 26, 27, 36, 195
The Vietnam War in American Stories, Songs, and Poems 26
Vietnamese white mice 189
The Virginia Quarterly Review 49, 52, 115, 128, 197
"The Vision" 12
Visions of War, Dreams of Peace: Writings of Women in the Vietnam War 122–123

"Visiting My Parents' Grave" 154
VVAW *see* Vietnam Veterans Against the War

The Wages of War 142
"Waiting for Word from Alaska" 40
Walsh, Jeffrey 9
"The War and the Academy" 19
"War & War's Aftermath" 101
War Crimes Commission 127
War Crimes Museum, Saigon 43
War, Literature & the Arts 1, 23
"The War That Won't Go Away" 141, 215
Warrior Writers Project 143
The Washington Post 116, 143
The Washington Spectator 175
Watergate 24
"The Way Light Bends" 71
"W.D. Ehrhart, Essayist" 3n2
Webb, Jack 137
Weigl, Bruce 50, 64, 65, 115, 119, 127
Westmoreland, William C. 57
WHAM *see Winning Hearts and Minds*
"What Makes a Man" 116
What Thou Lovest Well, Remains American 135
"What's the Point of Poetry?" 132
Whitman, Walt 8, 61, 66, 82, 119, 135, 140
"Who's Responsible" 208
William Joiner Center for the Study of War and Social Consequences 13, 128, 158
Williams, Jonathan 48
Willson, David A. 1, 3n2, 194
Wilson, George 116
Wilson, Keith 65
Wimmer, Adi 3, 50, 157–158
Winning Hearts and Minds: War Poems by Vietnam Veterans 7, 8, 9, 51, 52, 106, 114, 117–118, 120, 122, 164
"Winter Bells" 40
Winter Bells 40, 46
"Words for My Daughter" 65
Wordsworth, William 61, 79, 82
"The World Is Watching" 132
Worlds of Hurt 151
Wounded Warriors 203

Yeats, W.B. 8, 23, 61
Yugoslavia 170, 171

Zedong, Mao 169, 170, 172

www.ingramcontent.com/pod-product-compliance
Lightning Source LLC
Chambersburg PA
CBHW032050300426
44116CB00007B/674